ABOUT THE AUTHOR

Linda Joyce has been a life coach and astrological counsellor for nearly twenty years. She lectures, teaches workshops and gives private consultations all over the world and is a frequent guest on radio and television shows. She was *Good Housekeeping's* first astrologer in 100 years of publishing and was consultant on *The Simian Line*, a movie starring Lynn Redgrave, William Hurt and Cindy Crawford. Also, *Red* magazine hired her to do their first ever workshop, as did *Here's Health* magazine. She divides her time between New York, London and Hong Kong.

THE
STAR
WITHIN

*A Radical New Approach
to Self-Mastery*

LINDA JOYCE

RIDER
LONDON • SYDNEY • AUCKLAND • JOHANNESBURG

1 3 5 7 9 10 8 6 4 2

Copyright © 2003 Linda Joyce

Linda Joyce has asserted her right to be identified as the author of this work in accordance with the Copyright, Designs and Patents Act, 1988.

Published in 2003 by Rider,
an imprint of Ebury Press, Random House,
20 Vauxhall Bridge Road, London SW1V 2SA
www.randomhouse.co.uk

Random House Australia (Pty) Limited
20 Alfred Street, Milsons Point, Sydney,
New South Wales 2061, Australia

Random House New Zealand Limited
18 Poland Road, Glenfied,
Auckland 10, New Zealand

Random House South Africa (Pty) Limited
Endulini, 5A Jubilee Road,
Parktown 2193, South Africa

The Random House Group Limited Reg. No. 954009

Papers used by Rider are natural, recyclable products made from wood grown in sustainable forests

Printed and bound in Great Britain by
Mackays of Chatham Plc, Chatham, Kent

A CIP catalogue record for this book
is available from the British Library

ISBN 1844130339

This book is dedicated to everyone with an unfulfilled dream.

CONTENTS

ACKNOWLEDGMENTS

No book or life achievement is ever accomplished alone. I have been fortunate in my life to have many teachers and helpers along the way. First, I would like to thank my agent and dear friend in England, Esther Fieldgrass. Together, we have tested our concepts of faith and manifested some amazing things. Our first meeting was serendipitous, and since that moment we have been magically intertwined. She has opened doors for me, but more important, she is never afraid to take a risk for anything either she or I believe in. That, to me, is the most admirable of qualities.

I would like to thank my parents, both of whom are deceased in life, but are certainly not gone from my heart. They had their problems, but they gave me the best gifts that life has to offer—imagination, inspiration, and faith. My father, Edward Schmitt, never wanted for a newer or greater idea. In that way, he was never defeated. Camille, my mother, had a more practical strength, and she expressed it by meeting head-on every challenge that life ever tossed her. I have yet to meet her equal. She taught me more than anyone else that if you believe in what you are doing, nothing and no one can or will stand in your way. I saw the impossible happen over and over again, and because of her, no one had to teach me how to endure or overcome. What I didn't have was a voice of my own and the strength to manifest my own dreams. That I had to learn the hard way, the way that teaches you so that you will never forget. The person who helped me every step of the way was my sister, Paula Wesselmann. She, too, was struggling for her independence and truth, and our journeys have been blessed by a generous exchange of love, support, and new ideas that make even the most difficult situations memorable moments filled with happiness and laughter. Don't take your journey alone. Yes, there is a part of it that can never be shared with anyone, but the part that you can will make up for all the rest.

I'd also like to thank my grandparents and the Ferrara family, who came over from Italy as immigrants and struggled to survive through the Depression and the incredible change that life in the twentieth century took on as it evolved faster than anyone had ever dared to imagine. Josephine was known for her great beauty, and Joseph for his strength and his desire to change the world into a better place. Their offspring, seven of them, were all unique individuals with great power and conviction: Mary, Don, Sam, Camille, Helen, Josephine, and Joe. The three sons became doctors, and the women, each of them, struggled to find their voices in a world that was just learning how to listen to women with dreams. Each of their journeys has inspired me.

My friends, the tried and true ones, are always there to tell me I can do whatever I want, and their support means everything to me. I would like to mention Maureen, Elvira, Helen, Shelley, Judy, Alan, Marti, Eve, and all my friends in Alex Murray's spirit class (Kathy, Patti, Karen, Bob, Nancy, and Evelyn, to name just a few). I would like to extend special thanks to Lou Romita for his faith, and to Linda Yellen and Stephen Silverman for both their friendship and their professional support. They each had their own unique way of helping me, both practically and personally, and for that I am eternally grateful.

My children deserve to be acknowledged, for my work has definitely taken time away from them, and yet it has given me the understanding to help them on their own paths. Michael and Jordana are amazing souls with great heart and passion. I am delighted to announce that they have both found their own dreams and are at this moment pursuing them.

Last, but not least, I would like to acknowledge my editors, Elaine Will Sparber and Judith Kendra, for their faith, support, and insight into this book. It was not an easy project, and I thank the universe every day that they were sent to help me make *The Star Within* a dream come true for me.

Introduction

Have you ever taken a leap of faith—that is, followed a path that defied logic, intelligence, and good advice? If you haven't, your life is probably ridden with anxiety, fear, and a sense of isolation. Contrary to common belief, our need for security is not met by resisting change or protecting and holding on to what we have. Life is paradoxical, and our goal of certainty can be attained only by taking risks, by experiencing ourselves in strange, new, and demanding situations.

The twentieth century, with its revolution in technology, gave people more possessions, money, and opportunity than ever before. What it didn't provide was faith and the skills to cope with this new world. If you're caught in the frenzy to achieve, then you're on a fast track competing for more money and success, but totally unprepared to deal with the emotional and spiritual challenges you meet along the way. To do the latter, you cling desperately to the defense mechanisms that helped you survive as a child, and although these responses may cause you pain as an adult and prevent your further growth, you hold on because of fear and the knowledge that they "used" to work. The old is known; the new requires you to test yourself in unfamiliar territory.

On September 11, 2001, terrorists attacked the United States and left thousands of people paralyzed by fear. Fear is a retractile emotion; it pulls you in, limits your thoughts and actions, and forces you to focus on the immediate moment. To stay in your psyche, fear must connect to fear—old fear. If you have unresolved emotions related to terror, death, rejection, sorrow, pain, or issues of abandonment, the new fear will join forces with the unresolved fear and push aside love and the courage it gives you to meet the challenges of the day.

The good news is that your general level of fear can be radically reduced by identifying each individual fear instead of letting them unite and take over your peace of mind. Most fears are empty voices from the past created at a time when you were dependent and helpless. If you can find the courage to look at these fears as an adult, the chances are you will see them for the imposters they are. The twelve questions in this book will help you rid your life of empty fears and see what skills you need to keep new ones at bay. When you can protect yourself from the desires and expectations of others, you are ready to hear your own voice. This is the beginning of personal power, purpose, and passion.

By answering the twelve questions provided in this book, you can magically transport yourself back to the emotions of the past that helped to shape you. From this position, you can choose which emotions to keep, which to change, and which to ignore. The greatest cause of helplessness, the fertile ground for fear, is the inability to say no. When you must please others—when the fear of disappointing, of not fulfilling expectations, of being selfish directs your life—you have no life. Instead, you're living for others. A shift to self must occur before self-esteem can develop. You must learn to be "selfish"—that is, to take care of your truth and your needs. This is your job; don't delegate.

The reason you feel others are more important than you goes back to the time when approval meant survival. You depended on your parents to protect and nurture you, and you feared that if you didn't please them, they might abandon you. You accepted this because you had no choice, and the fears you had were as potent as they were because they were interlaced with the fears of abandonment and death. Experience is one way to develop new ideas and change your past beliefs. The secret of power is not in what actually happens to you, but in how you interpret and integrate the experience. *Genius lies in your ability to choose an attitude and position that encompasses all of your life; one that allows you to take everything you have experienced and felt, and make it serve you.*

The twelve questions presented in this book will help you become your own Life Coach. They will introduce you to a teacher that knows you better than anyone else, a guide that will never abandon you: your Star Within. Only from this sacred inner space will you be able to hear the universe, God, and your higher self speak to you and give you the messages necessary to stay safe and on your path.

Hundreds of people survived the collapse of the Twin Towers of the World Trade Center in New York City because they listened to this inner voice. The chef and owner of Windows on the World, the famous restaurant that overlooked the city from the top floor of Tower One, decided on the spur of the moment to get a new pair of eyeglasses before continuing on to work on the morning of September 11. He was already standing at the elevator in the lobby of Tower One, but he followed his instincts and turned away, a decision that definitely saved his life.

When life doesn't happen the way you think it should, you may judge your life, feelings, choices, and emotions as wrong or inadequate. If you don't judge them, others will, and if you accept their criticisms as truths, you give them the power to shape your psyche and your life.

Your inner voice is nothing more than your instincts finely tuned. A connection to your inner voice is frightening because your voice doesn't value social morals, ideals, or ideas that limit or bind. Instead, it responds to the universal laws of respect for self and others, and the desire in every soul to be a creator of life. To follow it means your personal truth will clash with social taboos and ideas of right and wrong. To survive in the competitive world, however, you must take these ideals within, not demand them from without. The competitive world has its own rules, and they have little to do with your childhood values. Intuition is the only sure way to recognize illusion and deception with confidence. Without an intuitive eye, you will believe what others tell you. You will fall prey to people whose values are less than yours, whose hearts are capable of cruelty and rejection, whose spirits inspire while hiding their true intention to deceive. The goodness in you will not trust that truth and love can conquer hate, greed, and evil. Once you make this assumption, you will seal your fate by separating from love. You will dismiss the dreams of your childhood as foolish whims of fantasy, and your need for security will greatly increase along with your fear.

I'm here to tell you that you can have as much of the world as you wish. If you follow the steps described in this book, you will become your own Life Coach. You will have to face fears, climb mountains, take risks, and test your faith, but with a map and a vision of what lies ahead, with the needed skills developed, with awareness and an emphasis on personal satisfaction rather than results, you can turn the nightmare of living into a challenge and your life into a ladder leading toward your goals.

There are twelve steps presented in *The Star Within* and they come from the divine harmony of the zodiac. Astrology has always been one of the tools

I use to help people see their destiny and their lives with new clarity. Unfortunately, most people prefer to use this science as a source of entertainment rather than as a path to self-realization. The twelve questions in this book are just the twelve sun signs turned into questions. Your answers re-create the emotional environment of your childhood, which shaped your beliefs and fears. When you can see the problem, you can overcome it.

The twelve questions concern twelve gifts that you should have received from your parents. Each gift is a power point essential in the act of creation. When one of the gifts is either missing or damaged, you are lacking one of the skills or attitudes necessary for a good foundation. When you can claim all twelve gifts, you are ready to become a master creator—that is, you are ready to go out in life and manifest a dream, change the world, change your world, change the world of others. Peace and happiness become by-products of your actions and choices, not things you directly seek. The more honed these power points are—that is, the more you can separate them from the people and experiences that gave them to you—the more useful and versatile they are. *Pure power involves attitudes not bonded to judgments.* The attitudes are free to be used wherever you need them.

Everyone has a power talent, a "thing" developed to survive childhood. I call this talent the *super-self*. The super-self was forged, like a diamond, under great pressure. The situations that nearly killed you made you strong. If you can remove this super-self from the fear-based environment that forged it, you will have a talent that will never let you down. For example, Walt Disney's super-self talent was his imagination. Constantly moved from place to place, he was never in one town long enough to make friends and feel like he belonged. He learned how to live in magical worlds of his own creation, and he re-created those magical kingdoms as an adult and called them Walt Disney World and Disneyland. I have a client whose mother paid attention to her only when she told outrageous stories. She's a successful writer today.

The twelve questions, as I have already mentioned, reveal the twelve gifts you were meant to receive from your parents. Six relate to your mother, six to your father. When you have defined and taken these twelve positions yourself, you're ready for life. Your parents' ideals and values (questions six and seven) are the wings and anchor of your Star Within; when you are grounded by beliefs that work you are free to be inspired so that you can rise above your problems and fears. Love and nurturing (questions four and five) are there to protect and sustain you, so that you can reach out and bond with others without fear. Your strength and the ability to separate (questions eight and nine) come from the faith and wisdom you received from your parents. It takes belief in yourself and in your destiny to say no to temptations, expectations, and love ridden with guilt. Judgment and desire (questions eleven and two) are your starting blocks: You need both an immovable force to provide the rigidity to resist and rebel and a motivation powerful enough to provide the strength necessary to make the choice for truth instead of safety. Risk (question three), is very important because, with the courage to try something new, you can break through the fears and limitations (question ten) that keep you from exploring the world and creating your dreams. And finally, *the two greatest gifts you can receive from your parents are the empowering interpretations of their own lives*. From your father, you need a great attitude (question one), an attitude that will help you experience to the fullest both the joys and the sorrows you will inevitably face. From your mother, look for a dream (question twelve), her vision of a perfect world. Her dream is meant to keep you warm and feeling loved when she's not there. These are your parents' gifts. If you didn't receive them, don't worry; you can give them to yourself.

The questions in *The Star Within* work in pairs; they represent your parents as both opposing and unifying forces. How they bridged or didn't bridge their differences is the source of your problems. If they didn't resolve their differences, there is a gap that you don't know how to cross unless you've learned something new through your own life experience or by observing another role model. The power of *The Star Within* is not in its individual answers, but in the relationships of the answers to each other and in the emotional images they create. To meet the challenges presented in this book, you must be ready to give up the child in you who doesn't want to grow up, the piece of yourself that still desires to be taken care of, the self that refuses to accept anything less than unconditional love. Until you are willing to be responsible for yourself, you can't change your life. Until you see unconditional love as the prison it is for anyone over ten years of age, you will not be ready to implement or own the skills needed to become a master creator. Know that the human heart cannot maintain the intensity of uninterrupted love without enlightenment. What it can maintain is beliefs. Believe in yourself, and you're ready to become a creator.

Freedom is usually associated with physical independence, but being able to support yourself and live alone is only a first step. True freedom comes from *emotional independence*, the ability to make a selfish choice—that is, to choose what's right for you and your dreams. When you gain this ability, it will lead you to the next level and the ability to seek a greater truth, one that will unite the division of opposites presented through choices that separate and paralyse you from action. You may have to disappoint someone to do this, but until you can stop protecting others from your truth, you can never bring your uniqueness into the world. Without emotional independence, you will never leave home, your past, or your memories, even if you move thousands of miles away.

To grow, you must stop listening to others and focus on what feels right for you. Your family and friends may mean well, but if they're preaching fear rather than faith, you're taking advice from people who have failed, from people who have never felt their own passion or freedom, who have never lived on faith or creative joy. People who have been stopped by fear are afraid you may succeed where they didn't, for if you do, they can't continue to believe that destiny, fate, illness, circumstances, lack of money, lack of opportunity, or social prejudice is what prevented them from living their dreams. *The truth is that your friends and family will seldom support your quest for freedom and creativity.* It is too threatening. You must learn to support yourself and make it happen. *You* must believe in *you*.

To love yourself requires an ego and the ability to be selfish when necessary. What no one tells you is that the only way to true love, generosity, and compassion is through selfishness. If you follow the path of *The Star Within*, you will be guided through the confusion and rejection, the obstacles and expectations, that stop even the most courageous of souls when they don't understand the process. The creative process has steps; *The Star Within* will teach them to you.

A Prayer for the Journey

Dear Lord, please give me the heart and faith to meet the challenges you have placed on my path, so that I may discover my strength and uniqueness and use them to create something wonderful in the world. Help me choose joy and happiness over sorrow and sadness, so that love is what I express and share as I go forth on my journey. Help me seek the surprise, the greater idea, and the primal heartbeat that is heard when one lives close to instinct and on the thin line between the past and the future. And help me accept and understand that whatever comes forth from the unknown is a gift from God. Amen.

PART ONE

Preparing to Find the Star Within

"All that a man achieves or fails to achieve is the direct result of his own thoughts."

—James Lane Allen, American author (1849–1925)

The Star Test

Y OU came into this life with an open heart, ready to give and receive love, and a curious mind, strong and restless in its desire to understand its new environment. Your spirit did not know defeat or feelings of hopelessness; all it had were faith and total loyalty to you and your destiny. You were meant to play in God's dream, His creation. And if you have forgotten who you are, it's time to go back and find the missing pieces.

The most important things you receive in life are not bought, nor can they be grasped in your hand. The gifts that empower you and keep on giving are the attitudes and perceptions that allow you to meet life with faith and confidence in yourself and in the world's abundance. Parents give these gifts. The presence or absence of your parents' love and guidance helped to shape your perceptions of yourself and the world in which you live. The child has no choice; it sees the world through the eyes of those it loves and the people it depends upon. If you didn't like that world, you probably opposed it, but chances are you never took the next step and formed a position of your own. Learning to choose a response versus automatically responding is the first step toward changing your life. The more of your beliefs you can free from negative childhood associations, the more opportunity and possibilities you will create around yourself. If you feel limited or isolated, your parents probably did, too. You can keep your parents' limitations or you can learn how to transcend them. *The Star Within* will help you go back and identify the negative associations you made when you were a dependent and powerless child.

The next step is to break down your old perceptions by separating the event or parent that shaped them from the issues of today. If your mother was always angry, you may see love and anger as a unit and choose a partner to love who is always angry. If you look for a partner with no anger (the opposite polarity), you may find a person who is disconnected from anger, which attracts it. The power to change comes from an open mind. To open your mind, you must challenge your beliefs and why they developed the way they did. You must realize that the world the way you see it was created by your inner world and by how much love you felt for yourself and others. All the steps in this book are meant to give you confidence in the unknown and to help you create from uncertainty, rather than from set rules or boundaries that give you the feeling of security but at a sacrifice to faith and opportunity. To create something new, you must see the world as offering you something new. This means you cannot remain set in your ways and rely on the past for all your knowledge. The more you add faith to your choices and reach out to the unknown, the more powerful and successful you will be. You've got to be able to free yourself from the negative associations that keep bringing about the same negative results. You cannot escape from your beliefs until you identify, confront, and change them.

The Star Within divides the journey into two legs. In the first leg, you will identify your problems and your missing pieces by answering twelve questions about your parents and then about yourself. In the second leg, you will take the twelve issues or attitudes that are necessary for success and happiness and break them down into twelve steps.

To take back your power, you first need to recognize what is depleting it. At the root of all problems are attitudes that don't work, beliefs that keep you small and limited, emotions that can't be expressed or contained. If you repeat your parents' choices, you'll just re-create their lives, and if you oppose their lives, you will still get the same results. All you do is flip the same coin; you don't create one of your own. However, if you can use what your parents gave you (no matter what it is), if you can see what's missing and add your own creative ideas, your own yearnings and desires, your own inspirations and dreams, you'll have your own life, one that you make with your own voice and talents. This is what you were meant to do. Thus, your first challenge is to identify the patterns that shaped you and to challenge them. Are they working for you? Are they helping you to grow, create, and love? This is what the twelve questions help you discover.

It's not a bad idea to ask yourself the twelve questions at different times. Once you begin to probe your past, it begins to re-emerge in your psyche, and things you have long ago forgotten begin to pop up. Do not worry if you can't answer a question; leave the space blank. Don't worry if you didn't have parents; use whoever raised you along with the fantasies you created concerning your missing parents. If only one parent raised you, use that one for all twelve questions. If you were raised by multiple people, write down answers for each of them. There is no right or wrong way to do this.

The twelve questions are derived from the twelve signs of the Zodiac. Six of the questions pertain to your mother, six to your father. You may find it amazing how little you know about the two most important people in your life, and it may stun you that their *inner worlds*—their dreams, desires, hopes, and fears—shaped you, not how much money they had or what they looked like. Whatever you can't answer indicates a problem area, a gift you never received from your parents, a void that you may have been trying to fill through a relationship or compensate with wrong choices.

Since life begins prior to birth, I begin this book and the questions with the sign of Aquarius, the eleventh sign, rather than Aries, the first sign. By beginning with Aquarius, you can see how your vision of the world was created, and this helps you to change it.

The first step is to answer the twelve questions as best as you can. When you're finished, turn to "Your Answers to the Twelve Questions" on page 29 for help in analyzing your answers. Once you have identified the issues of your past, you'll be ready for the second leg. Go to the chapter on your sun sign and take the twelve-step journey that will challenge the way you look at yourself and the world.

When you have read your sun-sign chapter, you might also find it helpful to read the chapters on the gifts you never received from your parents. For example, if your father had nothing in his life that inspired him, read the chapter on Libra to learn how important it is to have something that lifts your spirit and takes you above the pettiness and worries that surround you. If your mother never protected you, read the chapter on Cancer to learn how too much or too little protection can keep you from persevering and from discovering the greater idea that is always waiting beyond fear. Each sun-sign chapter has its own twelve steps. Follow the steps in each missing-gift chapter and you will begin to understand how things unfold. If something doesn't make sense, don't panic. Just keep the thought that is confusing close to you and seek the answer around you in your everyday experiences. I guarantee that the right information will come to you. If you are ready for change, it will happen quickly. If you are still too afraid, you will plant the seeds for change now and will be challenged when you are finally ready to let go. Commit to change and it will be yours. Don't be in a hurry. This is a book that works at many levels. As you begin to understand more, it gives you more. There is something for everyone.

The First Leg of the Journey: The Twelve Questions

To begin to create your life your way, you must first separate yourself from the past and from the beliefs and emotions that shaped you as a child. *The Star Within* and its twelve questions is the quickest and most painless way of returning to both the joys and the horrors of your childhood so that you can decide what you want to keep and what has to go. Some of your attachments may have brought you a sense of safety when you were a child, but you're not a child anymore and it's time to grow up and choose the beliefs and attitudes that will help you be independent, successful, and happy.

The first set of twelve questions deals with your parents, or the people who raised you; the second set asks you the same questions but reworded so that you can answer them in terms of where you are now. It's important to see what you've changed and what you've kept the same. What really happened is less important than what you believed at the time was happening. If there are gaps or a mystery surrounding your answers, you may be attracted to others who are also unclear about themselves or, worse, you may desire certainty and control (desires that are always fear-generated). The more you understand your past and see how it is reflected in your present choices, the more opportunity you have because you will be able to create something new instead of repeating an old pattern.

The Twelve Questions About Your Parents

The following twelve questions are about your parents. Six pertain to your mother and six to your father. These are the gifts that your parents should have given you. Pay attention to what is missing because you will have had to overcompensate for its lack and, if you couldn't, you will have felt lost and disconnected from the world, believing that something was missing in you. Whatever is missing can be added! Go to the chapter that represents the issue or question, and study it. There are steps you can take and skills you can learn that will help you develop this area of your life. Please do not try to protect your parents from your answers. You can love them and still see their flaws. Chances are they did their best with what they were given by their parents. The more knowledge you have, the more you can go beyond their limitations and fears, and become a creator—someone capable of living life from the heart.

Put your answers to the questions on the lines provided below the questions and again in abbreviated form on the lines provided in Figure 1.1. The questions begin with numbers eleven and twelve because these are the questions that show you the results of living a life of love or fear. The rest of the questions will reveal to you why your parents gave up on being unique or living their dreams. It is the balance between love and fear that propels one forward safely. Too much faith and no fear creates danger and increases your chances of failing. Not enough faith or love creates paralysis, or the inability to act and choose. By beginning with the results of your parents' lives, you are in a better position to understand how their choices created those results. Don't worry about "right" answers; there are no such things. What you have is what you were given to play with. If you don't like the colors of your palette, you can change them. But first you must identify the issues by answering the twelve questions of *The Star Within*.

Question Eleven: Aquarius: Father: How much freedom and uniqueness did your father choose to experience in life? What were the judgments that limited his self-expression and experiences? _____

_____

_____

Question Twelve: Pisces: Mother: What was your mother's dream? Did she fulfill it? If not, what stopped her? _____

_____

_____

Question One: Aries: Father: What was your father's vision of life? What attitude supported this vision? Was he positive; did he believe that life was worth living? Or, was he negative and depressed because he gave up on his dreams? _____

_____

_____

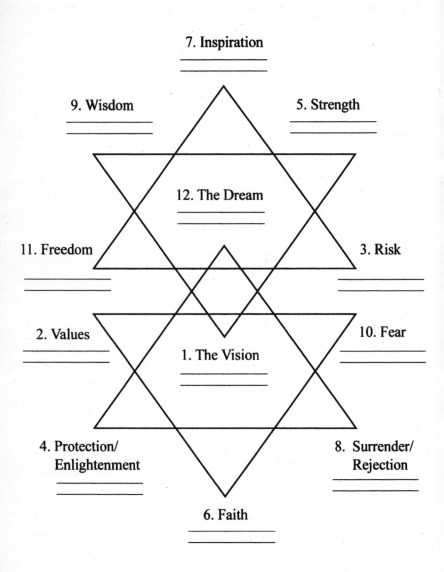

Figure 1.1. The Star Within

Question Two: Taurus: Mother: What were your mother's values? Did she live with love and joy, and follow her desires? Or, did she live with fear, which drove her to choose security and live with sorrow? _____

_____

_____

Question Three: Gemini: Father: Did your father have enough faith to take risks in life? Did his risks pay off? _____

_____

_____

Question Four: Cancer: Mother: How did your mother express her love and prepare you for the world? Did she make you feel protected? Did she know the secrets of your heart? _____

_____

_____

Question Five: Leo: Father: What were your father's strengths and talents? Did you see him as successful? _____

_____

_____

Question Six: Virgo: Mother: In what did your mother have faith? What did she believe would give her strength or a feeling of importance? _____

_____

_____

Question Seven: Libra: Father: What inspired your father in life? _____

_____

_____

Question Eight: Scorpio: Mother: Was your mother able to express anger and separate emotionally from you when you misbehaved or stood up to her rules? _____

_____

_____

Question Nine: Sagittarius: Father: How much did your father rely on his inner wisdom and personal experience? Did he change what he could and accept what he couldn't? Or, did he follow the rules and try to escape through idealism, rationalization, anger, drugs, or drink? _____

_____

_____

Question Ten: Capricorn: Mother: What rewards did your mother expect from life? Did she achieve her goals? What did she fear? _____

_____

_____

To help you understand how the Star works, I will use Tony Blair, the prime minister of England, as an example.*

Question Eleven: Aquarius: Father: How much freedom and uniqueness did your father choose to experience in life? What were the judgments that limited his self-expression and experiences? *Tony Blair's father, Leo Blair, was very unique, charming, and ambitious. He felt that freedom was independence and that the way to independence was through success in your career. He desired recognition and power because he didn't have them as a child. Therefore, he chose politics as the vehicle to accomplish his dreams. Raised by foster parents, Leo felt abandoned by his real mother and smothered by his foster mother. His ambition and work ethics didn't allow him the time to be free and the faith to go beyond his desire for success so that he could discover what lay in his heart. In fact, his inability to rest and reflect gave him a stroke, which ended his career.*

Question Twelve: Pisces: Mother: What was your mother's dream? Did she fulfill it? If not, what stopped her? *Tony's mother, Hazel, was a strong, spiritual woman whose dream reflected her environment and the times: she wanted her family safe and healthy. Her father had died of appendicitis six months after she was born, so she had her own issues of abandonment. In Tony's case, the dream came from his father and his father's desire to be prime minister. When his father had his stroke, all his ambition was transferred to Tony. Children often fulfill their parents' dreams instead of following their own.*

---

*The book I used to answer the twelve questions about Tony Blair and his parents is *Tony Blair: Prime Minister*, by John Rentoul (New York: Warner Books, 2001).

Question One: Aries: Father: What was your father's vision of life? What attitude supported this vision? Was he positive; did he believe that life was worth living? Or, was he negative and depressed because he gave up on his dreams? *Leo Blair had a very powerful and positive vision of life. He believed that if you work hard, you succeed at whatever you believe in. This is a very useful philosophy because it is based on belief and what inspires you. It gave Tony the courage to, at first, pursue his love of music rather than just follow in his father's footsteps.*

Question Two: Taurus: Mother: What were your mother's values? Did she live with love and joy, and follow her desires? Or, did she live with fear, which drove her to choose security and live with sorrow? *Hazel Blair was a very spiritual woman. She taught her children how to pray and how to endure without complaining. She was honest, loyal, reliable, and loving. Tony describes her as a rock. Hazel's spirituality worked in her life; it wasn't fake. When Leo had his stroke, she nursed him back to health. When Tony's younger sister Sarah became ill with Still's disease, a juvenile form of rheumatoid arthritis, she coped with that, too. She never showed fear, only faith. However, Hazel didn't have too many personal desires. She wanted to make her family safe and happy.*

Question Three: Gemini: Father: Did your father have enough faith to take risks in life? Did his risks pay off? *Leo Blair took risks for his career. He had confidence in his personal charisma and in his ability to commit to hard work. He studied by night for a law degree at Edinburgh University, then took a job as a lecturer in administrative law at the University of Adelaide in Australia. Although he knew no one in Australia, he never hesitated moving his family to this new country for three years. The abilities to take a risk and to accept change are essential to success.*

Question Four: Cancer: Mother: How did your mother express her love and prepare you for the world? Did she make you feel protected? Did she know the secrets of your heart? *Tony Blair most likely felt very protected by his mother because she was so down-to-earth and stable. She was a constant in his life through good times and bad. This type of behavior gives a child something on which to hold. What Hazel Blair didn't do was probe into the inner world of her soul or share her feelings and dreams; those she kept locked inside herself. This creates in the child both the ability to contain oneself and the desire to break free and express oneself. Tony was a rebel.*

Question Five: Leo: Father: What were your father's strengths and talents? Did you see him as successful? *Tony saw his father as both strong and powerful before the stroke. The stroke caused him to realize how easily success and power could be lost in the hands of fate. It made him see that a power stronger than man exists, and that there is something more to which we must pay attention than just worldly needs. Leo did not bring Tony into his world until after his stroke, when he needed him. From disaster good things can come. His father's success paved a path of confidence that Tony could follow. Being vulnerable brought Tony good things: his father's loss of worldly power improved their personal relationship.*

Question Six: Virgo: Mother: In what did your mother have faith? What did she believe would give her strength or a feeling of importance? *Hazel Blair had a great deal of faith. It gave her strength during the tough times. When she had cancer later in life, she tried to hide its severity from her children. She had faith, but she overprotected everyone from her feelings. So she passed on fear, too. This fear came from her lack of ego and inability to inconvience others for herself. Tony has an ego. He rebelled against protection and authority early in his life, but his mother's faith was always with him.*

Question Seven: Libra: Father: What inspired your father in life? *Leo Blair was inspired by politics, recognition, success, and the opportunity to help others. These are certainly qualities he passed on to his son.*

Question Eight: Scorpio: Mother: Was your mother able to express anger and separate emotionally from you when you misbehaved or stood up to her rules? *Hazel Blair was described as a "rock" by John Rentoul in* Tony Blair: Prime Minister *(New York: Warner Books, 2001), so it is very likely that she was always there for her children. This is both good and not good because children need to learn how to separate emotionally. If they don't learn this at home, they may hold on to unhealthy situations and friendships for too long. Hazel never expressed her own needs; she felt they were secondary. Tony exhibits the symptoms of a steadfast mother. He often supports others more than he should. Loyalty is almost too important to him.*

Question Nine: Sagittarius: Father: How much did your father rely on his inner wisdom and personal experience? Did he change what he could and accept what he couldn't? Or, did he follow the rules and try to escape through idealism, rationalization, anger, drugs, or drink? *Leo Blair was a self-made man. Therefore, he had the strength that comes from experience and an ability to find a so-*

lution to any problem. These are great gifts to pass on to your children. They teach perseverance and confidence in a crisis.

Question Ten: Capricorn: Mother: What rewards did your mother expect from life? Did she achieve her goals? What did she fear? *Hazel Blair was probably afraid of illness and death because she lost her father when she was six months old and her husband's stroke changed their life forever. She didn't seem to have had high expectations, so she was able to accept whatever life gave her. Her faith helped her cope with her fears, so they didn't rule her. Where she had fear was in imposing her needs and desires on others. This could make Tony either indifferent to the demands of others or too sensitive to them. These are the seeds of great imbalance.*

The Twelve Questions About Yourself

Now, answer the twelve questions in terms of yourself. Write your answers on the appropriate lines below and in abbreviated form on the lines provided in Figure 1.2. How many of the answers about yourself are the same as or exactly the opposite of those about your parents? How many of the answers come from your own faith and beliefs? These are the gifts on which you can rely.

Question Eleven: Aquarius: How much freedom and uniqueness do you express in your life? What are the judgments that limit you or hold you back?

_____

_____

_____

Question Twelve: Pisces: What is your dream? Are you working to fulfill it or is it an escape? _____

_____

_____

Question One: Aries: What is your vision of life? In what position do you see yourself in that vision? Are you a leader? What do you believe you are worthy of having? _____

_____

_____

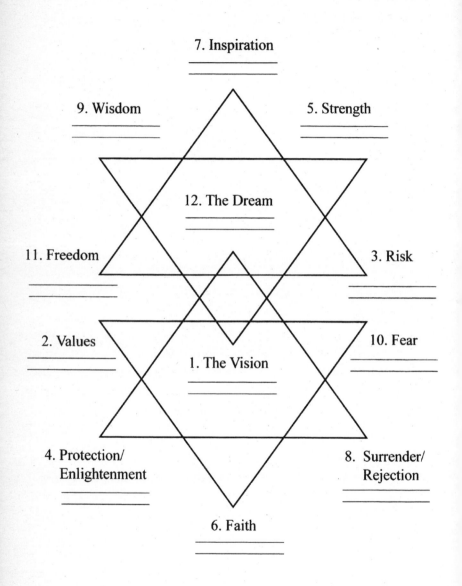

Figure 1.2. Your Personal Star

Question Two: Taurus: What are your values? Do you put joy and happiness at the top of your list? Or, do you give your power away by blaming life or others for your circumstances? _____

_____

_____

Question Three: Gemini: Have you taken any risks for your dreams or goals? If not, why not? _____

_____

_____

Question Four: Cancer: How much do you protect yourself and others from your truths and desires? Do you take on too much responsibility in one area and, in so doing, avoid it in other areas? _____

_____

_____

Question Five: Leo: How successful are you socially and professionally? Do you isolate yourself? Do others enjoy your company? _____

_____

_____

Question Six: Virgo: In what do you have faith? What values work for you in good times and bad? What do you believe is the one thing that will change your life? _____

_____

_____

Question Seven: Libra: What inspires you? What lifts your spirit and gives you joy? Is this a part of your life? If not, why not? _____

_____

_____

Question Eight: Scorpio: Can you separate yourself from friends and family members who hurt you or take advantage of you? Are you able to speak out when someone does something wrong to you? Or, do you protect other people from themselves? _____

_____

Question Nine: Sagittarius: How much of what you do comes from your-self? Do you copy others or do you find your own way? Are you able to accept in life what you can't change and find the courage to try to change what you believe you can? Or, do you always follow the rules and therefore find yourself looking for an escape? _____

_____

_____

Question Ten: Capricorn: What do you expect from life? What are you afraid of? Do you know why you have this fear? _____

_____

_____

I will use Tony Blair, the prime minister of England, once again as an ex-ample of how to answer the twelve questions from a personal and present point of view.

Question Eleven: Aquarius: How much freedom and uniqueness do you express in your life? What are the judgments that limit you or hold you back? *Tony Blair had enough strength and courage to follow his own heart before he be-came interested in his father's dream. He wanted to be a rock star, and he went for his dream and learned a great deal from the quest.*

Question Twelve: Pisces: What is your dream? Are you working to fulfill it or is it an escape? *Tony Blair's first dream was to be a rock star. Because he was able to pursue it, it evolved into a greater dream, one that included a deeper purpose. He entered politics when he felt he could make a difference. To know you can affect change in your environment is the beginning of real power.*

Question One: Aries: What is your vision of life? In what position do you see yourself in that vision? Are you a leader? What do you believe you are worthy of having? *Tony Blair has always seen himself as a leader. His vision has changed as he has, but he always tries to be the best or first at what he does. He was not afraid to seek the highest position in his country: prime minister.*

Question Two: Taurus: What are your values? Do you put joy and happi-ness at the top of your list? Or, do you give your power away by blaming life or others for your circumstances? *Tony Blair is not afraid to make himself happy because he is not afraid to use his voice and oppose what he doesn't believe in. His strength of character allows him to follow his heart, and his heart has led him to his destiny.*

Question Three: Gemini: Have you taken any risks for your dreams or goals? If not, why not? *Tony Blair has never been afraid of trying and failing. He has had enough confidence in himself and enough faith in what he believes in to have taken chances in school, pursued a music career, and entered the world of politics.*

Question Four: Cancer: How much do you protect yourself and others from your truths and desires? Do you take on too much responsibility in one area and, in so doing, avoid it in other areas? *Tony Blair was a rebel early on and had no trouble saying what he thought, even if he was the only one saying it. His ability to express his truth is one of his greatest gifts. The imbalance may occur in the area of loyalty. His desire to support the United States in the face of war has threatened his security and position in his own country.*

Question Five: Leo: How successful are you socially and professionally? Do you isolate yourself? Do others enjoy your company? *Like his father, Tony Blair has great charisma. It's difficult not to like him. Charm has helped him to achieve his goals.*

Question Six: Virgo: In what do you have faith? What values work for you in good times and bad? What do you believe is the one thing that will change your life? *Tony Blair seems to have faith in both himself and life. He seems to believe that you can change things. That's a powerful belief.*

Question Seven: Libra: What inspires you? What lifts your spirit and gives you joy? Is this a part of your life? If not, why not? *Tony Blair is inspired by the same things that inspired his father: politics and the ability to make a difference in the lives of others. He is living his dream.*

Question Eight: Scorpio: Can you separate yourself from friends and family members who hurt you or take advantage of you? Are you able to speak out when someone does something wrong to you? Or, do you protect other people from themselves? *Tony Blair is loyal to his friends and the people who support him. This is a great asset that can become a weakness if he doesn't know when to let go.*

Question Nine: Sagittarius: How much of what you do comes from yourself? Do you copy others or do you find your own way? Are you able to accept in life what you can't change and find the courage to try to change what you believe you can? Or, do you always follow the rules and therefore find yourself looking for an escape? *Tony Blair is not afraid to face his fears or shape life his way. He is, however, very idealistic. If this is not balanced by common sense and practical solutions, it will lead to trouble.*

Question Ten: Capricorn: What do you expect from life? What are you afraid of? Do you know why you have this fear? *Tony Blair expected a lot from life and he got it. He learned and grew, and took the risks that he needed to take. He may be afraid of letting down the people he loves.*

If your parents did not give you courage or faith, don't worry; you can give them to yourself. However, you will have to go beyond your parents' limits and step into the unknown. Study your answers and red flag the issues that need work.

Family Themes

Before we begin to analyze your answers, I'd like you to answer a few questions about your grandparents. Within every family is a theme, and that theme either empowers the family members or brings them down. Even if your legacy is a successful family business, this so-called gift could be the one thing that keeps you from becoming you. Whatever the theme is, it will have a powerful hook on your choices until you bring it into your consciousness.

A family theme is a pattern that is programmed through beliefs, emotions, and behavior. The pattern is in your genes, controlling your tendencies and your natural inclinations, until you consciously make a choice to change. When you probe your parents' and grandparents' lives, you begin to see the themes that run through all the sides of the family and it becomes obvious why the members of the various couples were attracted to one another. Is the theme in your family positive? For example, have all the men in your family followed their hearts and created their own successful businesses? Or, is the theme negative? For example, has someone always gotten pregnant, forcing a marriage and halting the pursuit of a dream? Positive themes help you meet life's challenges. Negative themes make you repeat mistakes and increase fear.

Ask yourself, "What keeps popping up in my family tree—actors, military men, or maybe alcoholics?"

Don't just blame family themes on genes; look at the reasons the themes are perpetuated. Themes can be patterns that either help or destroy, but what they share is the psychological grip they have on the family members who believe them. Don't be fooled by a flipped pattern, one that makes the experts think it has skipped a generation. What has really happened is that some courageous youth thought he or she could break the pattern by going to the opposite expression. For example, a father who gambled spawned children who didn't take risks. However, opposite behavior is just a necessary second step (opposition). It produces the same limiting results: you're not motivated from within and so are still responding to others instead of choosing with your own heart.

It is important to understand why your parents became the people they did. What were the events and environments that shaped them? When you understand, you can forgive. It's easier to forgive your mother for being critical when you realize her mother criticized her mercilessly. If your father had to work to support his parents when he was still a child, you can understand why he had trouble with responsibility and ran away from it later in life. The more information you have, the easier it will be to put the pieces together. So, before we tackle your childhood, let's see what you know about the circumstances that shaped your parents.

The following questions concern your grandparents and how your parents related to them (their authority figures). Look for themes in your parents' backgrounds that are either similar to each other or the exact opposites. To get to the truth, you must stop believing everything you were told. Instead, balance the so-called facts with your intuition. Some information is just a hunch, but those hunches are usually right. If your mother always declared that she adored her mother and yet she never called her mother and rarely visited her, something is missing from her story. When answering the following questions, put down everything you've been told, everything you've experienced, and everything your intuition tells you.

1. What were your mother's and father's relationships with their mother and father? Was there more love or more fear?
   Mother: _____
   Father: _____

2. To which parents were your mother and father closer and why?
   Mother: _____
   Father: _____

3. How many siblings did each of your parents have? Was a sibling like a parent to either of them? Was your mother or father like a parent to a sibling? Did a sibling die young?
   Mother: _____
   Father: _____

4. Were your parents the oldest, youngest, or middle children?
   Mother: _____
   Father: _____

5. Who was the favorite in each of your parents' families? Why?
   Mother: _____
   Father: _____

6. What was happening before your mother and father were born? Did either of their mothers have a miscarriage? Was there any drama, bankruptcy, or crisis going on either before or immediately after their birth?
   Mother: _____
   Father: _____

7. What was happening in the world either before or immediately after your parents were born? Was there a war or defining event like September 11, 2001?
   Mother: _____
   Father: _____

8. Did either of your parents' families have a family secret? Do you know what it was?
   Mother: _____
   Father: _____

9. At what ages did your mother and father leave home and why?
   Mother: _____
   Father: _____

10. How did your parents meet? Did they marry because they were in love or to escape their families or the limitations in their lives?

Mother: _____

Father: _____

Okay, have you identified a theme yet? If you've got one, ask yourself how it's been affecting your life. Have you been using it, or has it taken over your life and your choices? Do you feel you've had no choice with this issue and either surrendered without a fight or tried to escape from its clutches?

Use the following categories as a guide to help you discover your family theme:

- Freedom/judgment/isolation/forgiveness
- Escape/humanitarian or idealistic causes/dreams
- Visions/heroic deeds/deep unfulfilled yearnings
- Values too high or missing
- Risk/bravery/adventure/discovery
- Protection/fear of change/sorrow/new ideas/faith
- Success/charm/love affairs/recognition
- Service/responsibility/power
- Relationships/leadership/truth/desire to change the world
- Separation/selfishness/abandonment/transformation/regeneration/sex
- Perseverance/imagination/beliefs/religion/education
- Reward/fear/spiritual strength/expectations

Once you've determined your family's theme, just keep it in your mind and realize it may be an issue in your life. Did your parents repeat their relationships with their parents with you, or did they try to compensate for what they didn't have? Also, note how much attention they received as a child. If they didn't receive any, did they marry someone who kept the attention off of them or were they attracted to someone who put them first? Where are you in all of this? Are you repeating or flipping the coin?

Your Answers to the Twelve Questions

To help you quickly analyze your answers, I will briefly explain the issues that motivate each of the twelve questions. It's important to understand how these issues influence your life. For a deeper and more comprehensive explanation, go to the chapter that represents the question.

Question Eleven: Aquarius: Judgment and Forgiveness

Judgment is a tool to be used to help you slow things down, set limits and boundaries, or just eliminate from your creation or world what you believe doesn't belong. Unfortunately, most judgments are made unconsciously in an attempt to gain control. Judgments should be strong for children so that they can learn to distinguish between right and wrong. If children don't learn right from wrong, they can get very hurt. However, what most parents don't know is that things that are judged as bad create desire because they become mysterious and forbidden. Say no to a child and that child will want the item more. What is forbidden carries temptation. It goes back to the Garden of Eden and Adam and Eve. When something is denied, curiosity results.

Children also need judgments to have something to resist. If you are too accepting and lax, you have nothing to push against, nothing to oppose, and discovering who you are is more difficult. Opposition is an attraction for those who found it missing in their youth. The right amount of controversy is healthy, particularly if you can discuss your differences. If your family allowed you a different point of view, you're on your way to being a strong and healthy human being. If it was their way or no way, authority and opposition, as well as anger, are on your plate.

Children listen to what works. If your parents' judgments worked for your parents, you accept them more easily. If your parents' lives were a mess, why would you rely on their judgments? In fact, you might want to oppose everything they tell you, not out of defiance, but out of a need to survive. The more experiences you have, the more you understand why your parents made certain judgments or tried to protect you from what they believed was bad. Understanding leads to forgiveness, and forgiveness leads to a release of anger and negative emotions.

Teach your children how to make judgments of their own, respect their opinions, and encourage them to test their opinions when it will not bring them harm. There is nothing like experience to teach a lesson quickly. Have you overcome all the things you weren't allowed to do? It's important to be able to break the rules. If you never did, you're probably stuck trying to be a "good" person who always does the "right" thing. The path of perfection is a limited, self-destructive one. The quickest way to learn is to make mistakes. Mistakes are your best teachers. Being too good as an adult can get you into more trouble than it can get you out of. If your children can't stand up to you, they won't be able to stand up to other authority figures. Teach them how to express their truth, even if it opposes yours. When you can't rebel, you've got to lie. And when you lie all the time, you forget what you really believe in. And without a truth, you have no identity or uniqueness and nothing to offer the world.

Which of the following expressions shaped your choices?

- If your father was very judgmental, you will be either a rebel or very obedient. Remember, neither extreme is the answer. You've got to know how to take a position that is not a response or a reaction to someone else, but that comes from within you and supports your goals.
- If your father was all accepting, you will be attracted to judgmental people. You will seek resistance to help make you strong and help shape your identity.
- If your father shifted his position to suit his needs, you will not trust or rely on others and so will be either very reliable or unreliable just like him. If you are very reliable, you will have difficulty disappointing people because you have become the loyal, responsible person that was missing in your life. This will be a problem because you will attract people who lie and manipulate. (Opposites attract; you project what you repress.) You need to make your choices based on the needs of the moment, not by automatic response.

If you have issues surrounding freedom or judgment, read the chapter on Aquarius.

QUESTION TWELVE: PISCES: DREAMS

Dreams are what embrace a family and give it a sense of unity, meaning, and purpose. If your mother had dreams, her spirit reached out and embraced the family because she was using her imagination. If she couldn't dream because she was disappointed or fate had stopped her, she probably contained her desires and passion, or blamed others or the world for their lack of fulfillment. As a result, you might feel that this thing she didn't share, this disappointment, had something to do with you. If your mother's dream was to escape, you may try to escape life, too, instead of facing it.

Which of the following expressions shaped your choices?

- If your mother had a dream and she made it come true, you have a path to success laid out for you. You *know* it can be done.
- If your mother succeeded but her success left you out, you might be afraid or angry at success. This would stand in the way of your personal achievements.
- If your mother had a dream but never tried to make it real, you may remain stuck in fear, as she may have been.
- If your mother had a dream and took a risk that failed, she may not believe she is able or good enough to create what she wants. She will either push you to finish her quest or try to stop you from trying at all.
- If your mother didn't have a dream, you may find it difficult to get started in life or to feel supported by life, or you may feel afraid to go out into the world and follow your destiny.

Dreams are warm and embracing. They protect you in tough times and give you something to use to deflect criticism and judgments. If others judge your dream, they are not really judging you. You are not your dream, while at the same time your dream is you. Dreams are magical and you need one.

If you don't have a dream or your dream is stuck, read the chapter on Pisces.

QUESTION ONE: ARIES: ATTITUDE AND VISION

The big attitude, the one that frames your life, the one associated with your personality, is the interpreter of your experiences, the judge that either condemns your thoughts and experiences to prison or releases them to freedom. A great attitude has faith in the future and the possibilities, respect for the past and your limitations, and courage to meet the moment. "Life is about doing the work you love" is a great attitude. It helps you find the courage to follow your heart. The belief that "life is all work and no play" doesn't make you want to reach out and embrace the journey. An attitude that helps you cope with life rather than hide from it is an attitude worth imitating and keeping.

All attitudes are magnets: they attract others. The kind of attitude you have will attract someone who either shares it or opposes it.

Which of the following expressions shaped your choices?

- Idealists are often attracted to realists. They find criticism and judgment a source of security. If you are an idealist, you need to make your visions real by choosing experiences that bring your vision into the moment.
- Critical souls look for greater truths or for other people who have faith. However, they will test your truth and faith by challenging them over and over again because they do not believe—yet.
- Realists want power, so they are often attracted to partners with big and generous hearts. Remember, opposites attract.
- Truth needs a purpose. Therefore, people who are invested in truth often seek people committed to a cause.
- People with faith seek faithless people with whom they can share their faith.
- Creative souls need visionaries, people who are able to see their talents projected into the future.

Your father's attitude toward life was the first one you encountered. Did you accept it as the truth or did you oppose it, choosing the opposite position? If your attitude is in opposition to your father's, it's not quite yours either. You're still trying to overcome your father and his authority over you. Look at your attitude. Does it reflect faith and strength, or does it project to the world that you're a victim or a loser? If you don't believe in yourself, fake it. We learn from pretending; it gives us confidence. The way to get real confidence is to take risks that are connected to a goal. This allows you to build and learn, and to see your progress. Take your father's attitude and reshape it, or create one of your own.

If you need to work on your attitude or vision, read the chapter on Aries.

QUESTION TWO: TAURUS: VALUES

What kinds of pleasure did your mother enjoy? Did she gain satisfaction from pleasures of the senses, such as sex, food, music, or just being loved? Did she love success and power, or did she live a life of faith and helping others? If her life was filled with crises and challenges, did she meet them with courage or did she let them defeat her? Was she a strong individual who had causes for which she fought? If she followed her passion and that passion didn't destroy or paralyze her, you will find your passion a lot easier. If, however, she believed she had made a terrible mistake because she followed her heart or trusted it, she probably cut herself off from her instincts and did not trust them. This means she may have lived in fear, seeking security instead of pursuing her dreams, and you will be left feeling that life is full of loneliness, loss, and betrayal. Remember that your mother's bad experience was *her* experience; it doesn't have to be your defining experience. You should create your life around your choices and no one else's.

If you were fortunate enough to have joy around you, you will find that joy is not a difficult thing in which to believe. However, pain is a lot easier for people to share. Everyone can connect with suffering and loss; few can connect with success and joy. If your mother was miserable, was she able to use her sorrow to either create art or help others? If she was able to do either of these, pain won't paralyze you. If pain stopped her, it may stop you, too. It is the blend of pleasure and pain that creates a balanced emotion. When you can stay rooted in both your hopes and your fears and not separate from one or the other, you will find stability and satisfaction in life.

Which of the following expressions shaped your choices?

- If you weren't able to give your mother joy in life, you will feel powerless and worthless. You may relate to others only through pain and sorrow.
- If your mother's pleasures excluded you or took her away from you, you may avoid them. You may judge them negatively rather than see that your mother misused them.
- If your mother gave up on joy altogether, you will either seek it desperately in life or you won't believe in it at all.
- If your mother's joy (for example, an affair or an addiction) caused pain to the family or other people, you may associate her joy with pain.
- If your mother's joy caused *her* pain, you may not pursue a dream in the belief that dreams only bring suffering.

Ask yourself what brought your mother more joy than you? This is what you will seek to conquer; this has power over you until you face it, use it, or understand it. If your mother had no joy, you will have nothing to overcome and you will miss an important motivation in life. You'll have to get it from within.

So, the big question is: Did your mother include you in her joy? Did she share her joy with you? Was she happy with your gifts and the things you made for her? Did you make a difference in her life in a positive way? If you did, you will feel as if you have an emotional place in the lives of others. If you can't bring joy to other people, you may seek to bring them anger or pain. This is just another way to connect.

If your personal star is missing joy or values that support you, read the chapter on Taurus.

QUESTION THREE: GEMINI: CHOICE AND RISK

Risk is a key point in the twelve questions. If one of your parents took risks that changed his or her life in a positive way, you will not be afraid to reach out to the world and gain new experiences. Your father should have been the risk taker because he is the symbol of success in the outer world. Did your father's choices lead him to leaps of faith or did they take him back to safety and security? When you have enough love and faith in yourself, you are able to meet life's challenges and to look forward to the adventure of trying something new. If your childhood offered you nothing, risk was perhaps your only choice. To understand how you see risks in your life, look to your father and why he took them or avoided them.

Which of the following expressions shaped your choices?

- If your father succeeded at the risks he took, taking risks will be easier for you.
- If your father succeeded but then lost it all, you may not see the value of success because the final outcome for your father was failure.
- If taking risks made your father happy, you will open yourself up to adventure. However, if your father's joy at taking risks left you out of his world, you may not value it as you should.
- If your father was fearful of taking risks and the result was security and safety for your family, you could either value security or you could hate it if your life was boring and without joy.

Risk is the key to success. Through taking risks, you break out of old patterns and open yourself up to new possibilities. You can't get out of your childhood without taking risks. If security is the most important thing to you, you may be stuck in your past. You should take risks for a goal or to discover something new about yourself. If you just jump off buildings with a parachute to feel your spirit soar, you will get a quick thrill, but it won't move you forward in life. Connect your leaps of faith to your goals and you'll see your world change.

If taking risks is an issue in your life, read the chapters on Aries, Taurus, and Gemini.

QUESTION FOUR: CANCER: PROTECTION

Protection is a strange thing. You protect what you fear, not what you value. If you hold on to something, it's because you're insecure, not because you have faith. If your mother was too protective, you will have a lack of faith in the world and in yourself.

Which of the following expressions shaped your choices?

- If your mother protected your image more than your feelings, you may feel angry and abandoned. You may also have issues of self-worth. Emotions are the source of all power.
- If you had to protect your mother—that is, if you were the adult and she was the child—you will have trouble with responsibility and relationships later on in life. If you are male, you may have trouble relating to females because the most important female in your life smothered you emotionally and demanded too much from you. You may choose partners who can't express their emotions, which makes you feel safe from being smothered again but keeps you unfulfilled. If you're female, you will take on too much responsibility in relationships or you may avoid them or avoid having a family. You need to learn how to say no to those you love and balance giving and receiving.
- If your mother didn't protect you enough, you may turn inward and seek other ways to feel protected. If you turn inward, you may develop a rich inner world, but without confidence, you won't be able to connect that world to others. If your mother didn't protect you enough, you might also seek relationships that feature protection rather than love. The best scenario is to discover faith within yourself. Your faith will then take you out into the world and keep you safe.
- If your mother didn't protect you enough, you may fear taking risks. This means success will be more difficult.
- If your mother didn't listen to you, you may feel unworthy and unsafe. Paying attention to your child's hopes, desires, secrets, and fears is a form of protection. It makes the child feel worthy and safe.
- If your mother protected you only from the outside world and not from other members of the family—for example, an abusive father or sib-

ling—you may have trouble setting personal boundaries or expressing yourself in a relationship.

The summation of your mother's fear is found in what she protected in life. If your mother helped you reach out to life and pursue your dreams, she was telling you she had faith in you and the world. If she held you back with fear, you will be afraid and not understand why. Ask yourself what she gave more attention and protection than you. Where you had freedom and safety, you have confidence. Where you were overprotected, you have limitations. Where you felt abandoned because you were not protected and you should have been is where you have the most fear. You can learn to protect yourself. The most important protection is your voice, or the ability to set boundaries and say no. When you can express your feelings, you will move forward and reach out to life with faith. Support, not protection, is what you should give and seek. Most protection is an attempt to keep the truth from surfacing. Most of us have illusions about ourselves to which we cling to feel good, but these illusions keep us limited. The more faith you have in yourself, the more truth you can handle, the fewer illusions you will need to protect, and the stronger you will be.

QUESTION FIVE: LEO: SUCCESS

Success for a child is recognition and acceptance by others. Children who know how to connect with others are children who have it easier in life. If your father had charm, charisma, or talents that helped him become popular, you will see him as strong and important. If he was important only because he had money or power, you will seek these things because you believe they have power and, in so doing, avoid working on yourself; success will be all that matters to you. If your father knew how to cut a niche for himself in life and he included you in that niche, you will feel as if the world has a place for you. Children look to their father for their position in the world.

Which of the following expressions shaped your choices?

• If your father was respected or well liked and he loved you, you will have no trouble finding your position in life.
• If your father loved you but didn't have a place in the world, you will either protect him or surpass him. (If you protect him, it is because you are ashamed of his weaknesses.)

- If your father abandoned you, you may seek fame and group adoration to compensate for his lack of attention.
- If your father was successful but never paid attention to you, you may avoid success because it took the one thing from you that you valued.
- If your father tried to keep you down, rewarded you for doing wrong things, or criticized you, you will see authority as a threat and something to rebel against. This may also result if your father put too much pressure on you to succeed. Fathers should raise their children up and make them feel special and strong. If your father didn't, you'll have to give that to yourself.

Success is measured in two ways: inner and outer. If you were lucky enough to be the apple of your father's eye and your father was a man whom others respected, you will have both your inner and outer worlds validated and you will find your way in life with ease. If you loved your father and he loved you but he could not handle the world, either you will seek a partner who is exactly like your father, including his weaknesses, or you will flip the coin and seek someone who adds what was missing. Most often, the kindness and love are removed and replaced with a sharp business mind and a cold, calculating heart. This does not make you happy, but it may make you feel secure and protected. Don't give up one world for the other; know that you can have them both. You are meant to be successful and loved. You don't have to choose one or the other. If you want to know what you use to connect with others, ask yourself how you connected with your father. If you want to know what you will seek more than love, ask yourself what was either more important than you to your father or what he gave you in place of love.

If you feel that you don't deserve success or you want it too much, read the chapter on Leo.

QUESTION SIX: VIRGO: WORKING VALUES

What are values anyway and where do they originate? You should have gotten a set just for being a part of your family. Your parents may have believed that honesty is the best policy, that respect is important, or that giving to others is the key to life. It doesn't matter what they told you; what matters is what worked. If your parents told you to be honest, then cheated their friends or punished you for your honesty, you will not value honesty or trust your parents. If your parents believed in a spiritual life but were consistently taken advantage of by other people, you will not value spirituality, even if you go to church every Sunday. What is worse than not having any values is keeping values that you *know* don't work. Most values will work if they are used with faith or strength. The values you will take with you are the ones your mother supported in you and in others. If she didn't support them, she didn't believe in them and they won't serve you. Get rid of what doesn't work or what you don't believe in. If you don't, you won't have room for what does work.

Children tend to add what's missing. If your parents didn't have any spiritual values, you may find yourself on a spiritual path. If your parents didn't believe in money, you may want it and pursue success with a vengeance. This is where you try to make changes, where you try to fix the picture. You change the values. If you have taken on your parents' values and nothing else, it's time to take another look at them and start adding some of your own. What works for you? What's important to you?

Which of the following expressions shaped your choices?

- If your parents' values were totally spiritual and your parents didn't pay attention to your ego or your need for attention, you will have trouble grasping anything real. This lack of the personal will leave you seeking to be perfect or pursuing an outer dream instead of creating what lies in you heart.
- If your parents' values were based on images and acceptance, you will seek to add something spiritual or lofty to the pot.
- If you pursue values that don't work, you will increase your fears and insecurities in life.
- If you don't have your own values, you have nothing on which to rely in the big, competitive world. You'll seek a protector.
- If you don't have your own values, you will use your parents'.

Any value that is expressed to excess or extreme becomes disempowering, no matter how much good it represents. An overemphasis reveals fear, not confidence and faith. In analyzing your family's values, look at what was expressed the most. This is also an area of fear. You push out an image that is meant to hide or mask a weakness. If you feel unworthy, you may believe that money and a beautiful house will make others love you. If you are afraid of reality, competition, and negativity, you may seek out a spiritual life, not out of faith, but out of fear. What you truly believe in you use quietly and without fanfare. List your parents' values, list your own, then challenge the whole lot of them on a continuous basis. Values change as you change, and you should always be in a state of growth or greater understanding.

If your values work, you feel empowered. You don't feel empowered just because your values are good. Children look for love and power. They need something to support them and their dreams.

If you don't know who you are or what you believe in, read the chapters on Taurus and Virgo.

QUESTION SEVEN: LIBRA: INSPIRATION AND LEADERSHIP

Ideals are essential to the survival of the spirit. When you lose or give up your ideals, your soul has no way to rise above conflict and limitation. If your father was able to lift his spirit because he had something that inspired him in his life, you will have that in your life, too. This is a true gift. If your father's pleasures were watching television and drinking beer, his spirit suffered and so did his family. Did your father love nature, art, or music? Did he love to build things? Perhaps he sang in the church choir or loved to dance. What brought his spirit joy? This will be a strong point in your life. If your father had nothing that lifted his spirit, you may feel weighted down by life. You may feel imprisoned by work, and you may give up on success because all it offers is more work. Of course, you could add what was missing by seeking meaning in life and connecting to your spirit.

Which of the following expressions shaped your choices?

- If your father was inspired by something that brought him acceptance and success, you will value what inspired him and add it to your life.
- If your father was inspired by something evil, you may find yourself in conflict. You see its power to inspire, but at the same time you know it's wrong. Unless you can replace this evil inspiration with a greater inspiration, you will be attracted to the evil inspiration or you will hide from everything that lifts your spirits.
- If you have nothing that inspires you, you will be attracted to people with dreams and faith.
- If you are inspired, you will want to share your inspiration with other people or with people who have lost the connection to their spirit. You may want to make a difference in the world.

- If you have faith in life but not in yourself, you may seek out people who believe in you.
- If you have faith in yourself but not in life, you may seek out people who believe in life, change, and possibilities.

Inspiration is a spiritual form of pleasure. It goes beyond the senses and awakens joy in the heart. When one of your parents has reached a level of consciousness to be inspired by life, you will find it easier to be inspired, too. There is nothing more powerful than inspiration, for it brings together mind, body, and spirit and makes you feel whole. With it, you can overcome great odds. Without it, you will be stopped by simple problems. To identify what inspired your father, ask yourself what gave him pleasure or joy.

QUESTION EIGHT: SCORPIO: SEPARATION OR SURRENDER

Did your mother have limits to her love? I hope so. It's important for parents to be able to pull back from their children and let the children know that certain things are unacceptable. When unconditional love goes too far, it becomes abuse. If parents allow bad behavior to occur without a consequence, the children will suffer the consequences.

Which of the following expressions shaped your choices?

- If your mother punished or criticized you to excess and you didn't speak up, either you will be very critical and lack self-confidence and self-worth or you will be too loving and afraid to create disharmony, which could lead to abuse.
- If you spoke up to your mother and defied her and she listened to you, you will find it easier to have your own voice and power.
- If you defied your mother and she did not speak to you for days or weeks, you will be afraid of authority and unable to speak up.
- If you did not receive any resistance when you confronted your mother, you may find it difficult to create your own identity and values. You may find that you are attracted to difficult relationships or impossible projects. You are seeking resistance to test yourself.
- If your mother was too needy and you found yourself taking care of her instead of standing up to her, you will have an overdeveloped sense of emotional responsibility and find that you are attracted to relationships

that are either too needy or totally undemanding. Either choice leaves you feeling lost or disconnected.

It's important to be able to disconnect from those you love. There has to be a limit to the behavior parents will tolerate, and at the same time, children need to be able to stand up for what they believe in, even if it means disagreeing with their parents. So, if your mother could never separate from you, could never express her anger, you will have trouble separating from other people in life and you could take on too much. You will not know how to disconnect, and if you can't separate, you can't become intimate. You've got to be able to leave a room to enter it. If you don't know how to make others let you go, you will be very cautious about intimacy and connecting.

If you have trouble separating, read the chapter on Scorpio.

QUESTION NINE: SAGITTARIUS: ACCEPTANCE

Acceptance, not physical power, is strength. Only what you accept can you change. What you reject becomes the enemy and your opposition. To accept, you've got to be able to rise above an issue and encircle it with understanding. The more you understand, the more wisdom you have and the easier it is for you to face life and the troubles it brings. The qualities that give you strength are the qualities that help you cope with fear, fate, and the unexpected. You can't be a good problem solver without having faith in your ability to find an answer. It is this faith that is essential to the endurance of your happiness. Anger only serves you when it's useful—for example, when it helps you persevere against an injustice—not when it is used to inflict pain on others. The more creative you are, the more spiritual strength you possess. If your father felt defeated by life, you will not see him as strong. If he was able to persevere during difficulties and find a way, you could rely on him, and that is strength. When you can persevere, life is worth pursuing. Nothing that can be overcome will stop your happiness. You must face grief and integrate it into your life. You must see death as a part of living. Only by accepting these facts can your life truly go on.

Which of the following expressions shaped your choices?

- If your father handled problems with anger or abuse, you will be afraid of problems and anger and will hide from life. Or, you will handle problems the same way your father did.

- If your father faced his troubles and struggled for a solution, he will have given you a great gift: You know how to deal with life.
- If your father relied on other people instead of on himself for solutions, you will lack faith in your ability to tackle life.
- If your father always found an answer and a way because he had faith, you will have faith, too.
- If your father was controlled by your mother, you may have loved him but you didn't respect him and you may try to avoid men that remind you of him. If you are a man, you may avoid strong women instead of learning how to hone your voice.

If you have trouble accepting life, read the chapter on Sagittarius.

QUESTION TEN: CAPRICORN: FEAR

Fear is what stops you. To remove an old fear from your psyche, you need to go back to the moment it was created and see what you associate with it. What you associate with fear you will avoid in your life, and you may end up fearing so many things that you will have nothing to do with real fear. Separate your fears from the moments that caused them and the issues that surrounded them, and you will diminish the overall fear in your life.

What stopped your mother from fulfilling her dreams? What and who did your mother blame for her mistakes or failures? Whatever your mother feared is what you'll try to overcome. If the fears are too great, you could give up on power and your ability to create.

Which of the following expressions shaped your choices?

- If your mother was stopped from pursuing her dreams because she married and had children, you might think that families get in the way of dreams.
- If your mother was stopped by war or illness, you may give up on life because you can't control fate. Faith is your lesson. Everyone has his or her own destiny. Your mother's destiny is not your destiny unless you make it so.
- If your mother was stopped by her need for security, you need to take risks and open yourself up to life. She had a lack of confidence that she may have passed on to you.
- If your mother was stopped because she didn't feel worthy or good enough, you will either share her lack of self-worth or set out to make your mark on the world.

- If your mother was stopped because she loved being a victim, you will have trouble showing your weaknesses and may feel isolated and alone.
- If your mother blamed others for her lack of success or fulfillment, you may believe you are powerless in the face of people who are more talented or stronger. You may take on too much responsibility in an effort to overcompensate and thus create a similar lack of success by flipping the coin and expressing the other side.

Whatever stopped your mother is what you must overcome. If you can't overcome it, you must understand it and be able to use it in your life in some way. For example, many psychologists entered the field out of the need to understand the chaos in their own childhood.

If fear and expectations are strong factors in your life, read the chapter on Capricorn.

How to Hone and Integrate Your Answers

The best way to deal with each answer is to contrast it against another one. I have combined the answers in a way that will give a deeper understanding and meaning to the issues. For example, how much risk your father took is tied to how much fear your mother had. Fear stops risk; risk eliminates fear. How did these two issues work together in your life? Pay attention to extremes. When one answer is too strong, chances are the other answer will be passive. You want the two issues to be balanced for the best results.

- Questions Eleven and Two: Judgment and Values: What you judge and what you value form the backbone of your journey. Judgments give you something to resist, and values give you an anchor. If your judgments are too strong, your values will be forced to support the judgments and not your dreams or goals. This will throw you off. If you don't have enough judgment, you need strong values to make you feel confident in the world. You may have to make your values too strong to feel secure, and then you will find it hard to change them as you grow.
- Questions Three and Ten: Risk and Fear: What you fear is what stops you from taking a risk or what motivates you to move forward in an effort to overcome the fear. Too much fear paralyzes, and too much courage can lead to failure through overextension of resources or abilities.
- Questions Four and Five: Protection and Success: Success is how the

outer world sees you as strong. However, if you don't have faith in yourself, you won't be strong no matter how successful you are. What you are afraid of is what you will protect. Too much protection makes you weak. The ability to learn from mistakes removes the need to protect and frees you to gain strength, which leads to success.

- Questions Six and Seven: Faith and Inspiration: What works gives you faith, and the more things you have faith in, the freer you are to be inspired by your spirit. What inspires you lifts you above your worries and fears, and helps you get a greater perspective. If your fear is too strong, you will suppress your inspiration in an attempt to gain control over your feelings and emotions. Where you need to control is where you have fear. The more faith, the less fear and the more things inspire you, producing an easier life.

- Questions Eight and Nine: Separation and Acceptance: What you can separate from, you can accept. What holds you by either guilt or fear, you will reject or deny. The ability to accept comes when you have the strength to stand up to the authority in your life and risk rejection for your beliefs. As long as you feel dependent emotionally or otherwise, you will not be able to separate and thus accept. Your acceptance will be out of necessity, not choice.

- Questions Twelve and One: Dreams and Vision: When you have enough faith and love to imagine a life without fear, you are ready to dream and to place yourself in that dream. If you can envision yourself someplace else, you can dream; and if you can dream, you can envision yourself in a better world. Your journey begins and ends with the dream and the vision. The more love and faith in your life, the bigger your dream and the more power and position you have in your vision.

Changing Your Star

The following three questions will help you organize your Star Within. It is important to see what's missing, what's negative, and what's working.

1. List everything that is missing from your Star.

_____

_____

_____

2. List the areas in which you're negative and need to find a new, more positive expression.

_____

_____

_____

3. List the gifts that serve or help you.

_____

_____

_____

A Guide to Change

It's important to know how to begin the process of change. If you take the following steps, you can begin to change your Star and your life.

1. Observe yourself. Study your Star and observe yourself with new eyes. Begin to see how you operate in life. If you are a pleaser, determine why and when you please. If you are a rebel, watch for what makes you want to oppose others. Always return to your diagram and study it to understand yourself more and more. You need to see yourself and your choices with a more discerning eye.

2. Express yourself. You need a voice to begin your journey. Your greatest protection comes from your truth and your ability to express yourself. If you can't say no or put your feelings on the table, you won't be able to protect yourself and move forward. The chapters on Aries, Taurus, and Gemini will be very helpful. They discuss how you gain a strong voice by being able to please, rebel, and then reposition yourself closer to your intention. It's a process that develops your values and clarifies your motivation. Once you have this mastered, you are ready for almost anything. Remember that you need to be able to express yourself before you can learn to contain. If you reverse the process, you may head for a breakdown. In addition, it's important to remember that the ability to express your anger, worries, and fears is just as important as expressing your hopes and dreams and getting the approval of others.

3. Challenge yourself. Challenge your old ideas and choices by asking questions instead of accepting answers. Ask yourself why you do the things you do. Instead of accepting your behavior, challenge it with

your new understanding. You don't need to come up with an answer right away. Just confronting your choices will set a process in motion that will bring you greater self-knowledge.

4. Trust your intuition. You need to trust the answers you get from your gut, not just logic or what you are told. The greatest wisdom comes from your heart and soul. If you don't listen to it, learning will be more difficult for you.

5. Identify the problem and commit to changing it. You need to identify clearly and precisely what it is you want to change in your life and then you must commit to the effort. To change an old pattern requires vigilance and consciousness; you must be aware of what you are doing and stop yourself from making the old automatic response. If you can commit to the process and not get discouraged when life doesn't magically change, you will succeed. You need to know that the process will take you into discomfort. Until the new pattern is experienced with frequency, it will not "feel right."

6. Make a plan. To change a problem, you need not only a commitment but also a plan. You should know by now where fear stops you or how you try to control everything. If you've been observing yourself, you should be aware of your actions and choices. The point that keeps you stuck must be changed. You must build an imaginary bridge across the problem. Envision a solution. See yourself speaking out, and figure out exactly what you would say. If you can't figure it out, it won't happen. There is always more than one choice; there is always a way. Prepare by rehearsing your new choices in your mind. If you keep reprograming your mind through visualization, it will begin to make new choices on its own.

7. Choose differently. To choose wisely, you must be able to take risks and face your fears or at least try a new solution. You won't be able to take risks and face your fears if you don't have a voice or trust your instincts. Once you do, you will see that your choices will become stronger and you will be more ready to challenge others and their expectations of you. For help, read the chapter on Gemini and choice.

8. Stop protecting yourself and others. Once you can choose for what you want without worrying about others, you are ready to hear the truth. As long as you need to protect yourself and those you love from your desires and expectations, you will not allow yourself to hear the truth. If you hear the truth, you might have to act on it. And if you're not ready

to change, it's easier to remain in denial. Until you're independent, you won't discover how you really feel about yourself, your goals, and your life. Instead, you will accept whatever rationalization supports your fear.

9. Have faith. Faith comes from experience and taking risks for what you know you want. If you can learn from your mistakes, they won't be mistakes; they'll be lessons. The more you risk yourself for what you want, the more faith and confidence you will gain. Once you have these two magic energies, everything will happen on its own.

To change your life, you should begin with one issue—the easiest one. You want to build confidence, not prove to yourself how strong you are. One success builds on another. Take from your list one thing and become a master of all its possibilities. Get your friends to help you; let them support you. Tell them you're going to call them up if you begin to weaken and want to repeat an old pattern. Tell them what you expect from them. Tell them you want them to be tough with you. If you don't have friends, this is one of your major problems. Everyone needs support.

The Second Leg of the Journey: The Twelve Steps

Once you've answered the twelve questions and filled your personal Star diagram, you're ready for the second leg of your journey; you're ready to discover your truth, strength, and higher purpose. I have divided the journey into four levels of consciousness. Everyone lives in all four levels simultaneously. Some parts of you are well developed and capable of patience, forgiveness, and understanding. Other parts are still childlike, anxious for attention, power, and success. If your sun sign falls into the first level of consciousness, this does not mean that you are not as wise as a sun sign that is in the fourth level. Think of life as a spiral. Your level one may be way beyond someone else's level four. If you just keep bringing enlightenment to your life as you experience it with more and more faith, you will raise your understanding and your consciousness. So, don't worry where your sun sign is; concentrate on the steps given for your specific sign.

Each sign is broken into twelve steps and another four levels. Every step you understand and accept in your life increases the light and faith you bring to your world. It takes time to change, but once you make a new choice a part of your repertoire, you will find change occurring very quickly. Each sun-sign journey will help you identify the conflicts you need to face, the attitudes you need to change, and the fears you need to diminish through love.

To begin, turn to your sun-sign chapter. There you will find the twelve astrological houses turned into twelve steps or lessons. Astrological houses begin with Aries, thus Aries rules the first house in astrology. However, I am beginning with the sign of Aquarius, or astrology's eleventh house—this is my first step. I do this because every birth or beginning starts long before the idea arrives into consciousness. There is a whole process that goes on before you become aware of the idea's existence. This means that you are not always aware of what you are thinking or how you are feeling. I know this sounds crazy, but when you choose one way and tell yourself it's another, you are avoiding a feeling within yourself. For example, if you tell yourself you like Jane, but every time Jane invites you to lunch you don't have time to see her, there is something going on that you are not paying attention to. Once you can accept that you are not in touch with all your feelings, you will be more open to learning because you won't have a fixed idea of who you are or what you want. There is always something more we can learn about ourselves. The process can be fun, not just frightening. However, if you are hiding from your anger, you will have trouble with this concept. Until you're ready to deal with your anger, you won't want to know how you really feel.

Each sun sign has its own unique way of unfolding and expressing the challenges and fears that are encountered. The cycle ends with the tenth step, or the sign of Capricorn. Capricorn represents the reward you expect to receive at the end of your journey. What you expect creates the path. Therefore, it would be wise to look at or clearly define what you want. As your understanding grows, your expectations will change. Remember that you're not a static being. The eleventh house, or step one, is the point between your past achievements and your future desires; it is where the new dream enters to unite the two. This is your point of entry.

Each of the twelve journeys is similar and different. They are similar in that they all have a dream to fulfill, an authority to challenge, a truth to discover, a judgment to remove, and a reward to receive. They are different because the dreams and the challenges are different for each sign. What may be a struggle for you is easy for me, and what is easy for you may be what I fear. Thus, the process is the same, but the issues differ.

The first level of awareness in each sun sign represents the state of idealism or unconsciousness. You see your world through the eyes of other people, and if other people do not reflect back the image you have of yourself, you feel betrayed, lost, and unloved. You search for validation of your greatness, perfection, and goodness, and if you get it, you experience the first level of consciousness with love and joy. However, if you don't fit the images others value, you turn inward. Now you must choose who you believe: others and their judgments, or your own instincts and beliefs. The more you can listen to yourself, the stronger and healthier you will be. The more you try to please others, the more you will lose your power. Life in level-one consciousness is a struggle. Everything becomes a choice you don't want to make. It's you or them; you can't have it all, at least not until you learn to challenge the world around yourself and express the parts of yourself that others don't want to hear. This would be level two.

The first emotion the heart feels is freedom through love. Children are not afraid to imagine and explore. However, when you begin to form desires and yearnings from your explorations and they urge you forward so they can manifest, you encounter conflict and fear. Conflict shatters your perfect world and your beliefs. The desire to avoid conflict and keep your world harmonious forces you to hold conflict inside so that you can get the approval of others. When the inner tension becomes greater than the outer tension you are avoiding, you take a stand for what you believe in. The fear of being abandoned must be faced for the soul to go deeper within itself and find the path to its own heart. As long as your existence depends on others, you will feel powerless and helpless, and will not make your choices for your dreams but to keep other people loving and needing you.

Once you take a leap of faith and challenge the authority in your path, you have entered the second level of consciousness. Your initiation is the ability to face your fear of abandonment and go beyond the rules and fears of other people so that you can expand your world. If you had no authority in your life, your initiation is your newfound ability to stand up for what you want without the support or resistance of others, just because you believe in yourself and your path. It is much more difficult to gain strength when you have no opposition than when opposition is all around you. Without something to oppose, you will find it hard to bring forth what is inside of yourself. If you were born rich and famous, or your parents just didn't care, you will have to find your resistance from the obstacles in your environment or strewn on the path to your goal. Without a goal, you will find yourself attracted to the greatest resistance, such as a relationship that is unavailable, a job you can't have, or the path with the most debris. Resistance turns you inward, and it is only from within that you can connect to your inner calling and passion. This does not happen when you choose a big paycheck or a secure job. That's the lure, the deception, the temptation, for those of little faith. In the second step of the second level of consciousness, or the fourth house of Cancer, you are asked to let go of protecting the issue. What you protect is what you are afraid of losing or what you fear may hurt you. You cannot see where you are going until you release this issue. Once you do, you are ready for the third level of consciousness, which builds faith and the power of belief.

The third level of consciousness is experienced whenever you have enough faith in yourself to take a stand or to fight for what you believe in. Nothing is truly yours or something you can count on unless you are willing to stop protecting it. The risk you take gives you a gift, and that gift is faith. Faith is the initiation into the third level. Each time you stand up for yourself and what you believe in, you make a deeper commitment to your truth and you gain more faith. The more faith you have, the more power you will be perceived to have and the easier it will be for you to bring forth your differences and uniqueness without fear.

Whenever you're not afraid to be different, you're in the third level of consciousness. Parts of you can be in this level and parts of you can remain in a lower level. The more parts of you that have faith, the easier it will be for you to bring all of yourself up to this new level. To express faith, your ego must be willing to postpone its compulsion for pleasure and fulfillment of its immediate desires for a greater reward: the manifestation of your dreams. It must be ready to work without praise and to tackle even the toughest obstacles to bring forth the gold that lies within your heart. You must challenge all of yourself—your mind, your body, and your spirit—to bring out the best in all of you. You cannot neglect any one part. However, you must choose a leader, one goal, one dream to manifest, if you want to have the greatest strength and magnetism to complete your mission. The time has come to let go.

The third level of consciousness demands that you narrow the path. The easiest way to do this is to turn your choices over to your higher self, to God, and to the universe. To accomplish this, you must have faith that you are divinely protected and that you will have what you need if you can just accept what is offered and use it to get to where you believe you are going. This can only happen once you begin to see the synchronicity of life and experience the magic of letting go. When you let go, something greater always comes to you. You won't see the gift if you hold on to the past. When you let go of love, what is gone begins to appear all around you, in everyone else's life. If your desire is to have a baby, it seems everyone you know is becoming pregnant. Can you be happy for them even if you fear that you may never have a family? Anger, jealousy, and rejection only separate you from your desires, while love and honor empower your connection to these things. When you can share in someone else's happiness, you empower happiness within yourself and you master the third level of consciousness.

Once you have faith, you begin to accept, and through acceptance you acquire a greater understanding. What you accept you can use, shape, and mold, and what you reject becomes the enemy and what opposes you. Thus, it seems wise to see the value of what you like and dislike, and to choose for what you want without judgment. Choice that is free of judgment is choice that builds dreams with the least amount of struggle. Choice is the most powerful tool you have in your life. Make your choices with faith and you are ready to create.

It will be through the ninth house and the wisdom to accept that you will reach the fourth level of consciousness. When you can accept, separation disappears and differences merge. You no longer have to choose between this and that, and feel that what you didn't choose is lost. On the contrary, when you choose what unites rather than separates because you can accept differences rather than be threatened by them, you are ready to receive the greatest reward of all: your purpose and the ability to change the lives of others through love.

The ultimate reward of consciousness is the ability to see love everywhere and in everything. Each sign has its own judgments that it has placed on life. To go beyond what you were given, to begin to create something new, you must overcome your past and your limited vision and knowledge. To find your way out of your past, take the journey through your sign and meet the challenges I have just described. If you have trouble with one of the steps on your journey, go to the chapter that represents it and follow the twelve steps that express its journey. For example, if you don't have a dream, read the chapter on Pisces and dreams even if you are not a Pisces. The path to self-knowledge does not have an end; every new idea or awareness leads you to a new level with new challenges. Life is a spiral, not a linear road. There is always something to learn. However, the more you know the process and the more faith you can bring to it, the more you can accomplish in life and the happier you will be. Everyone has something unique to offer the world. If you never turn inward and listen to your heart, you will not find it; if you never go beyond what you were given and forge your own path, you will never fulfill your dream or manifest your destiny.

The Ingredients of Creation

BEFORE we begin our journey of shattering illusions and building dreams, I'd like to introduce you to the three realities you will face in your quest to understand and conquer your environment. They are the ideal, the shadow, and the gap. Each has its own reality, rules, and rewards. All three are present in every moment, but it takes experience and consciousness to see them as separate and to use them to your advantage.

To be able to negotiate all three realities, you must be able to recognize them. The ideal is everything that is obvious, the facts and issues that are in the light. The shadow is what's hidden, what's not said or revealed, the secrets below the surface. The gap is the unexpected, the empty space that invites surprise. How you combine and use these three realities forms the structure of your identity, intelligence, and style. Don't worry; this will all make sense as you read on. To help you maneuver through the three worlds, the universe has given you two guides, ego and spirit, which are both voices of the soul.

Ego, Spirit, and the Soul

When your heart and mind venture out into the world to guide you, they take the form of spirit and ego. Most people make the mistake of valuing one over the other, which creates an automatic imbalance. Both are equally important in the process of creation. Ego rules the world of "reality" and the mind. Wherever you place your ego, your mind will follow and support it. Because both the ego and the mind are motivated by fear, you need to balance their cautious natures with the intuition and courage of the heart. Ego creates the attitudes that separate you from other people and provides a vessel in which your uniqueness can take form. Its creative abilities are limited to illusion, and if you haven't anchored yourself in a truth or discovered your passion, you may find yourself seeking to reduce your world to a place you can control. Ego moves away from experiences that don't bring praise or victory; it avoids equal relationships because its positions are only superior or subservient, "with me" or "against me." On the positive side, it keeps the desires and expectations of other people at a distance, encourages you to be "selfish" and to seek your own yearnings and destiny. Ego has no trouble lying or being deceitful. In fact, its purpose is to use deception to protect you. When you feel weak or vulnerable, ego can help you *appear* confident and strong. It gives you the ability to manipulate and lead others away from your truth, so that you don't waste energy fighting unnecessary battles. Ego's style is linear, direct, and oppositional. It needs spirit to find the shortcut, the way around the problem, the creative solution. When your ego is leading the way, you feel that the world is against you, that you're not good, smart, or perfect enough, because ego always sees what's missing, not what it has.

Spirit, on the other hand, is motivated by love and the need to unite with others, or with anything else for that matter. It is driven to help, connect, and serve. It never has a plan, only an inner yearning for wholeness and unity, and so it is totally confident and spontaneous. Able to seize the moment and turn what is into what it wants it to be, spirit cuts through illusion simply by surrendering to the truth or by having the patience to let life unfold. Surrender is not difficult when you know that you can never lose yourself and that what you give always comes back. Spirit's favorite place is the unknown, a place without rules or limitations, a place where those with faith have the advantage. Following spirit brings you right to the edge of your confidence and makes you face your fears. Spirit *knows*, without words being spoken; it senses what's right and wrong, gains strength through helping others, brings love and harmony into your life through acts of kindness, and allows you to see the quality of something and not just its form. Together, ego and spirit keep you cautious in danger and courageous in opportunity. However, without a director, a third point behind which both can unite in a common goal, these two polar opposites will tear you apart, not guide you. That third point is your soul. As you learn to balance your heart and mind, your soul urge is heard, and both ego and spirit respond. They now have a common purpose. It's the end of division, and the beginning of true creativity. Once you follow one voice, life begins to flow and you are easily lifted above the mundane. Unafraid to look at your mistakes from above, you can now use the information, lessons, and new possibilities they reveal. Once you can learn from both victory and defeat, you're ready for success.

The Ideal

Ideals are symbols that resonate to the soul's innate desire for perfection, beauty, and love. Ideals either serve or demand. If they serve, it is because you have allowed them into your heart. There, they can inspire and empower you by offering images that evoke feelings of courage, peace, justice, freedom, and truth—eternal symbols that motivate you to rise above your present environment. In contrast, ideals that demand present themselves as outer images, insisting you measure yourself against their ideas of beauty, success, intelligence, and power.

In the beginning, these two worlds—the inner and the outer—seem to have conflicting desires and paths. Not everyone is ready to face fear and hardship for greater consciousness or even happiness. Therefore, the universe hides your spiritual path within the pursuit of your goals. When you hold on to your dreams and ideals, and pursue your worldly goals, your two worlds begin to merge. As you gain faith in yourself because you are able to stand up for your truth, you begin to shape and mold your destiny through the power of your skills and beliefs, you begin to see the invisible road—your purpose—on which you've been walking. It was always there, but only faith could bring it to light.

The collective majority always rallies around ego-driven ideals, which are there to placate the perpetual fear of never being perfect or having enough. It is easy to be a leader of the collective if you fit its image. People who are born beautiful, with a perfect body, or with a family that has money and social position walk through open doors. Children who don't fit in often find doors slammed in their faces. The experience creates poor self-esteem, and these children begin to erroneously believe that their differences are obstacles to acceptance, not the gifts they truly are. Differences are what make people strong. They bring lasting success and sometimes even change the world. For example, think of a high school reunion. It is seldom the class president who has become famous. It's the Bill Gates, the kid who didn't fit in, who has become the billionaire. *So remember that believing in yourself is more important than accepting the values of others*.

It's important to know that collective recognition is not lasting. Dare to be different, and the attacks will be harsh and constant. Ignore the criticism and believe in yourself, and the masses will turn around and raise you up as their new symbol of success. The accepted is in the light; it is the ideal. Everything else you can find in the shadow.

The Shadow

The shadow is where the greater part of you dwells waiting for its chance to be brought to light or to become the "ideal." In the embrace of its darkness, the shadow teaches the power of containment, opposition, and truth. What isn't accepted by the ideal goes directly to the shadow. The shadow is the war zone where the ignored and judged parts of you battle for love. They want you to love them enough to fight for them. When you do, something magical happens: they rise to the light. Love creates an inner necessity for expression. You can no longer turn your back on your own beliefs. The inner struggle that ensues creates frustration and anger. When the anger is strong enough to resist the outer forces that have rejected or judged it, it forces you to take a stand and speak out, breaking through your fears. Resistance gives birth to a truth and leaves you with an unexpected gift: sacred inner space. This space represents the love you have given yourself and is the beginning of inner faith and confidence. Through opposition, you discover a truth. It's up to you to choose for which truths you are willing to stand up. These will become your values.

Expressing your feelings and your anger can become addictive because it gives you the advantage over everyone who can't. Anger used to control others, rather than to serve a truth, produces emptiness, even when you win. You increase your feelings of nothingness because you take a stand for nothing (the absence of truth). Now you have a need for more power. It's a never-ending cycle.

Anger should be seen as a signal that something in you is asking for a voice. Not everything should be expressed. Only through experience will you develop an ability to discriminate and to know what to say and when. Each time you stop protecting others from your truth, you free yourself of unnecessary frustrations and feelings. The inner space you create allows you to hear your instincts more clearly, and it is these instincts that become your guide to safety and success.

The Gap

The dark, mysterious unknown is the gap. The gap can be entered safely only through love. Without love, being in the gap makes you feel unnoticed, unworthy, and totally disconnected from the world. With confidence and love, the gap is the place to create, discover, be surprised, experience miracles, gain wisdom, and invent things the world has never seen. This is where genius lives. To be in the gap is to surrender all control. Whatever you surrender, you give over to faith, inviting God to co-create with you. When He joins you, there is always a way to get things done. The more you surrender, the more faith you receive and the easier it is to live in uncertainty, or without the guarantee of a particular result. When you can do this, your life takes on an excitement you never thought possible. For example, inventors find themselves in the gap all the time. It's one reason they love to invent. It's that place they enter when they make a mistake. If they can be in that place, accept the mistake, and go with it, the magic begins and they discover or learn something new. Einstein's mind was addicted to the gap. His mind took him to far-off places where no one else had ever been. To use the gap, you must be ready to play with the unknown. The gap is either all fear or all faith. Either way, your feet never touch the ground.

The Inner Voice

If you're wondering if you have an inner voice, the answer is yes; everyone does. But not all inner voices are based on personal beliefs. When your inner voice is critical, you've brought the judgments of others into your safe place and then being with yourself is no longer peaceful. Your inner voice should be connected to your instincts and your heart, not to the logic of your mind. The mind is naturally pessimistic. Its mission is to warn you of danger, so caution is what it seeks, and judgment and criticism are its allies. To access your positive inner voice, you must listen to the first message you hear, the little voice that rises up before your mind jumps in and challenges it. *Your first thought is the voice of your heart and your instincts.*

You need your inner voice at turning points, times of change, and when you are about to make a life-direction decision. In a crisis, a critical inner voice increases fear; it does not support you. A critical voice sounds like this:

"What are you doing going after that job? You're not smart enough. You'll make a fool of yourself." If that's your voice, it's time to change it. A supportive inner voice speaks with love: "Go ahead and try it. You can do it. You're talented and wonderful."

Your inner voice should help you create a bridge from where you are to where you want to be. It should say whatever you need to hear to get you through the moment. Good ones use humor, inspiration, and love. Remember that in times of fear, it's more important to be confident than right. Your voice should express its faith in you, in what you can do and in what you hope to do. Belief is everything. "They can because they think they can" is one of my favorite sayings by Virgil. People who develop a supportive inner voice find the strength to persevere no matter what they have to face. The Beatles, the famous rock band, had a routine they would do to make themselves feel better when times were bad. John Lennon would say, " 'Where are we going, fellows?' And they would go, 'To the top, Johnny!' in pseudo-American voices. And I would say, 'Where is that, fellows?' And they would say, 'To the toppermost of the poppermost!' I would say, 'Right!' And we would all cheer up."*

How to Create a Supportive Inner Voice

The first step when taking charge of anything is to observe it, to see how it works in your life. Pay attention to the thoughts that arise when things don't go well. Are you filled with self-criticism? If you are, you'll seldom listen to helpful suggestions from other people because you're already overloaded with thoughts of what you did wrong. I'm not telling you *not* to analyze a situation. Just don't do it right away. First, give yourself credit for whatever you did right, even if it's not apparent. You must become your own very best friend. Honor yourself for having the courage to look at a problem. If you have a goal or a dream, hang on to it. Call forth the part of yourself that believes in you. Your belief in yourself causes others to believe in you. You are the most important person in your life. If you cannot be your own best friend, you will never have another person as a best friend, because how you treat yourself is how you teach others to treat you. A belief, no matter how small, can be enlarged through attention, kindness, and support. Give those things to yourself and you'll see your strength grow. If you can't give them to yourself, be pre-

*This quote is from *The Lives of John Lennon*, by Albert Goldman (New York: Bantam Books, 1988).

pared for criticism, deception, greed, anger, and competition. They're all out there waiting to attack anyone without self-confidence.

Muhammad Ali had a great inner voice. The only difference was that he shouted it out to the world rather than keep it to himself. He constantly said that he was the greatest. Floyd Patterson, also a heavyweight champion boxer, observed this about Ali: "I never liked all his bragging. It took me a long time to understand who Clay was talking to. Clay was talking to Clay."* So, whether you hold it in or shout it out doesn't matter. What does matter is what you say to yourself when you meet your fear. Which voice will you lean on—the voice of your heart and love, or the voice of fear?

*This quote is from *King of the World: Muhammad Ali and the Rise of an American Hero,* by David Remnick (New York: Vintage Books, 1998).

PART TWO

The First Level of Consciousness

"Men were born to succeed, not to fail."

—Henry David Thoreau

The first level of consciousness supports new beginnings. It divides the world and its concepts into manageable parts. The first level is useful no matter what level of consciousness you have already reached because it helps you enter new situations and feel secure when you are caught by surprise or in an unknown place.

The first level is symbolized by the child. Infants feel connected to everything and everyone. To see themselves as individuals, they must learn to define themselves through division—by discarding or keeping, labeling, and organizing whatever they encounter. The more people and areas of your life to which you can say both yes and no with equal mastery, the clearer your identity and goals will be. The abilities to say yes and no are your primary tools for chiseling away the stone and revealing your uniqueness and purpose. Saying yes allows you to please and receive praise from others but the ego is sacrificed. Saying no separates you from others and allows you to see your own truth. If you never go beyond division and see that life is not really about good and bad, or right and wrong, you will never find true peace or inner satisfaction. The ability to divide is an essential step to unity. Don't become stuck on one side of your life. Mix up your different sides and watch the magic happen.

AQUARIUS: Freedom
(January 21 through February 18)

Aquarius brings us back to play.
It loves the nonsense of the day.
Fate is a challenge that must be met.
You conquer it when you forget
What terrible deeds you have done.
Forgive yourself and you have won.
Whoever can rise high above,
Whoever can see life as love,
These sweet souls get their surprise.
What you love never dies.

Question Eleven

About Your Parents: How much freedom and uniqueness did your father choose to experience in life? What were the judgments that limited his self-expression and experiences?

About Yourself: How much freedom and uniqueness do you express in your life? What are the judgments that limit you or hold you back?

Freedom is a universal ideal, and its powers are many. Nothing inspires the heart more than the call of freedom, the desire to be who you are, the liberty to express what lies in the depths of your heart. Freedom promises to rid you of the weight of responsibility, guilt, and love, which bring along compromises

that can kill the spirit and paralyze the soul. But freedom without consciousness is not freedom at all. It's a prison built by fear.

Freedom Is the Conquest of Fear

How much freedom do you trust yourself to have without self-destructing
or losing control? Freedom is the most desired energy on the planet, and yet
few souls ever contemplate just how difficult or dangerous this world would be
without self-discipline, consciousness, or a goal. Freedom cannot be experienced or discovered without resistance, and so the initiation into its bliss
takes you through conflict and tension. When you have no opposition, you
must be compelled from within or you will become lost without a direction or
a dream to give your world unity and a sense of wholeness. Without opposition, you will not find or bring forth this inner world. Instead of on an open
road, you will find yourself in a small place, locked away from others, perhaps
isolated from life. Freedom happens when you make the connection to the
heart, for it is the heart that guides you in the unknown. If you have not made
this connection—that is, if you do not feel worthy of love—you will seek
someone stronger and more confident than yourself to take charge. You give
away your power, and without your power, you remain dependent and childlike. The uniqueness within you will never find its way out. Another way to
express your unworthiness is to take the position of strength. You do this by
trying to save those who feel more lost than you. Every lost soul pulls you to
him- or herself and asks to be rescued. But what you are really doing is avoiding your own yearnings and desires. It is easier to fix someone else's life than
to live your own.

Uniqueness Makes You Special

Aquarius is the sign of uniqueness. You are here not to express what others
tell you to express or to be what the world admires, but to show everyone who
you are, what makes you different and unique. Freedom is the ability to express who you are whenever you desire. All people, deep down in the bellies of
their souls, want to find this uniqueness because what makes you different
makes you special.

The first way you experience being special is by pleasing others. You feel validated as a child when you make other people happy. This is how you begin life: with love and the desire to change the lives of others through that love. What you need to learn is that the only way you can change anything is through self-love. Until you have the power of love within yourself, you are powerless in the world. Without belief and confidence in your own opinions, ideas, and feelings, you cannot hold your boundaries, create a safe place, or express anything unique at all.

How do you begin to discover this wonderful part of yourself? Through your imagination. Aquarians are some of the most imaginative and inventive people on this earth. They have no compunction over dressing differently, doing things their way, or standing out in a crowd. The ones that are truly unique, and are loved for it, are the ones who love themselves and their creations. What you love attracts love. The more you love who you are and what you do, the more love you bring to yourself. If you are not sure or confident about what you want, you have a gap, and in this gap, others will pounce on you with comments and judgments. This will increase your insecurity. To be unique, you've got to move beyond the need for approval from others. To find yourself, you've got to listen to yourself and give your inner voice respect and love.

Freedom Is the Ability to Imagine

Let's go back to imagination. All children are born with the power to dream and to create in their minds. However, if your life is a crisis, if you are more concerned with survival, then you will believe you need acceptance and approval, not dreams. And if you don't know that dreams are important, you will not waste your precious time letting your mind spin fantasies that seem out of your grasp. *What you need to know is that the most important and essential part of your journey is your imagination. It is through the ability to imagine that hope is born.* If you have no dreams, you have no hope. Without hope, you will not accomplish anything. You have no motivation. Take away a person's dreams and that person becomes powerless. If you had a traumatic childhood, you are probably still in crisis. The first step out of that crisis is through your imagination and your ability to dream. It's not difficult to dream, but you do need a safe place. That safe place can be your bathtub with the bathroom door closed, the sidewalk in front of your house, or your closet. Be alone with yourself and set your spirit free. Just give it permission and it will begin to work for you. Observe how you judge your creations. You must stop judging. Let your spirit take you where it needs to go. It will begin small, but little by little, it will lift you up and show you what to seek and how to feel happy inside. The magic is within you, not without. You do not need anything or anyone to begin your journey. All you need is yourself.

When you are safe and free to imagine, you can get in touch with your inner yearnings and desires, and you feel compelled to express those feelings in the outer world. How well the people you love and the people in authority receive those expressions is the key to how easy it is to be unique and how much confidence you have in your uniqueness. More often than not, when you were a child, your feelings were judged and dismissed, leaving you afraid to express them again. You held your feelings inside and, if no one was around to hear them, you then may have dismissed them yourself. When this type of disconnection happens, you are on your way to a life of work and accomplishments without satisfaction or inner fulfillment. You cut yourself off from your dreams. Inner yearnings can be expressed only when you face the authority (fifth house), which for Aquarius is Gemini and Choice. To break through the limits of your life, you must take risks, go beyond the fears of your parents, and travel into the unknown. Doing this requires faith, in you and in a higher power. The more you believe the universe is on your side and the world is a loving place, the easier it is to take risks. If you do not feel this way, don't worry; just follow the steps one at a time and you'll get there.

Judgment Is the Enemy of Freedom

Judgment is the enemy of freedom. Most people make judgments and leave them there, never to remove them or look at them again. This is the same as building walls of stone around your imagination and freedom. Judgments stop the mind; they halt the process of evolution. Judgments are there for you to build and shape with, not to create fear and limitations that stay forever. Once you know the territory you have chosen to explore, you can remove the judgments that are protecting you. If you are in a new job, you will not feel free to do anything you want right away. You need to limit yourself until you *know* or *understand* what the company's policies are and how things are done. Once you know the rules, you can either accept them or stretch them based on your own inner knowledge, confidence, and wisdom. This is what judgment is for: to protect you for the moment, not forever. If your mother doesn't want you to date someone she doesn't know and you are twenty-one years old, you don't need to abide. By now, you should know how to discriminate by yourself. It is hoped that you trust your instincts and listen to them, which enables you to take safe steps in choosing whom you date and with whom you hang out.

Your freedom has been limited by the judgments of others. You need to decide which judgments to keep and which ones to let go. Why are you afraid to do this or that? What is stopping you? Remember that having too much freedom as a child can create the same fear as not having enough. With too much freedom, children don't develop the abilities to compromise and to accept limits. What they do develop is a fear of losing freedom through commitment. Understanding is the way out of judgment.

The Father Passes Along His Judgments to You

Your father is responsible for the judgments in your life. Ask yourself what judgments stopped him. He expressed his fears through his judgments and then imposed those fears on you through his rules and beliefs. What did he judge as bad? This is what he feared. This is where he felt the need to put restrictions on his life and yours. Did those restrictions help him to express himself or did they keep him locked in fear and afraid of taking risks? Look at the judgments that either he imposed upon you or that were missing. If you had too many judgments imposed upon you, you might be a rebel who wants to oppose anyone who stands in your way, or you might be passive and just accept everything that others tell you to do. Either way, you're stuck on what others are doing and not looking ahead to your own dreams and path. If you had no judgments imposed on you, you will seek resistance through relationships that are unavailable, difficult goals or jobs, anything strong and impossible to have. Your inner being is seeking someone or something to stop you, to force you to turn within and reflect on what you are doing. Without resistance, the soul continues to seek the outer rewards of life and never discovers the inner joys of passion and dreams.

Aquarians are afraid to judge. Their hearts are big and filled with understanding. Too much understanding doesn't help you or others. It just takes you off your path and keeps you stuck in your fears. The only way out is to accept conflict. You must be willing to face the music, the anger from those around you, the disappointment of those you love, and continue down your road, the one that calls your heart. Your heart knows your destiny and your purpose. Listen to it, follow it, and you will be guided and protected the whole way. (See Figure 3.1 for the Aquarius Star.)

The First Level of Consciousness

The first level of consciousness divides the eleventh house and first step, and the third house and fifth step. It brings the soul into conflict by pitting the heart and instincts against the need to make a tough choice. Until you see that hurting other people by not protecting them is sometimes the best thing for their spiritual growth, you won't be able to let go of protecting those you love and you won't be able to make the tough choices you need to make to begin your journey.

Step One: The Eleventh House

Sagittarius: Wisdom Is Freedom of Choice

I know that I am smart, and that if I wanted to see the wisdom in something, I could. But a part of me refuses to look because I also know that my feelings of freedom will be spoiled. I'll see that I have to oppose other people and challenge their choices for me, something I'm not quite ready to do. I'm protecting myself by remaining innocent, but being that way works only when you're young. I have to grow up and make the tough choices sooner or later.

The unconscious side of Sagittarius allows the soul to escape by rising above a situation or ignoring it. Your need for unconditional love holds you back from choosing for yourself. When you find your own dream and want your own rewards from life, you will find the strength to face criticism and risk love. Protection is the tool the Aquarians have to master. It can be used to either protect or hide from the truth. Own your ego and don't be afraid to challenge what other people try to impose on you. They know you have a good heart and that you don't want to hurt them, but they have no problem hurting you. Silence makes martyrs; it doesn't support freedom or independence. You must recognize that sometimes it's important for you to judge, even if your judgment hurts others. Just express your judgment with your heart and good intentions. Making a judgment will destroy your illusions of uncondi-

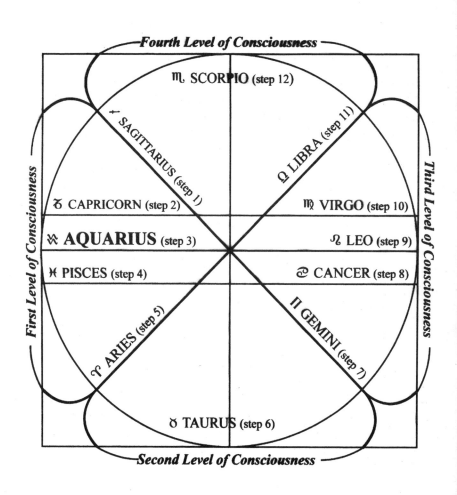

Figure 3.1. The Aquarius Star

tional love and your need to give and receive it, but these things have to go anyway for you to grow up. If you don't challenge the voice of authority because it's either too weak or too strong, you will never find your own path or live your own life.

> You are in level one if you believe in unconditional love.
> You are in level two if you believe that those in authority hold the wisdom.
> (Levels three and four are listed at the end of step one in the fourth level of consciousness.)

Step Two: The Twelfth House

Capricorn: A Reward Without Freedom Is Not a Reward

It seems to me that I have two choices: I can please others and feel unconditionally loved, give up my dreams and my freedom to be me. Or, I can accept my dreams and have my freedom, but give up the idealistic love that is so important to me. There must be a way to have it all. Until I figure it out, I'll hold on to my dreams, but I won't share them with anyone.

The desire for unconditional, idealistic love is the stumbling block of the Aquarius. This desire can be met only through giving, but the return is seldom equal to the gift and you are always let down. You need to learn to receive. To do this, you must let go of the ideal and realize that love must be built through opposition and conflict as well as caring and harmony. The way to stay on your path is to acknowledge your dreams and give them your unconditional love. Then others will love and accept you because you are doing the most challenging thing on this earth: you are living your dreams and expressing your uniqueness. It may take others some time to come around, but the more committed and dedicated you are to yourself and your destiny, the less opposition you will get from others. Doubt and uncertainty are projections that mirror your own inner fears. Love yourself and your dreams, and the reward will be everything your heart desires.

> You are in level one when the reward you get is too much protection (no freedom) or abandonment (too much freedom).

You are in level two when you are willing to express your point of view and risk love.

You are in level three when you have faith in your dreams.

You are in level four when you realize the reward is the journey.

Step Three: The First House

Aquarius: Freedom Is Accepting the Ego

I have always been afraid of my ego because I see that the problems of the world are caused by selfishness and a lack of compassion for others. However, what I am learning is that it is not the ego's fault. I abandoned my ego, and myself, when I didn't stand up for my dreams or my feelings. Once I made the commitment to be me no matter what others think, my ego also made a commitment, and now we work together as a team. I am so much stronger with an ego.

Aquarius is in love with freedom, the freedom to express all sides of the person, not just what everyone wants to see. You love to reveal the many facets of your soul. Change is something you value; it is no longer something you fear. With change come new ideas, greater pictures. However, the Aquarian also judges the ego to be the source of the world's problems, and in so doing removes its strength in the world and its ability to express itself safely or deal with opposition and conflict. What you must ask of your ego is to have faith, not control. You must give up saving others or the world to make yourself feel strong and realize that it is through example that we teach. If you become the successful, unique individual you were meant to be, you will help others every day of your life.

You are in level one when freedom is something you seek in the future.

You are in level two when freedom is something for which you fight.

You are in level three when freedom is something in which you have faith.

You are in level four when freedom is everything you do and say because it comes from your heart without fear.

Step Four: The Second House

Pisces: My Dream Is the Path to My Truth

I love to dream, but to make dreams real requires that I have faith in myself and in my truth, not in the truth of others. I now know that I will never discover my own truth and express my dream in the world if I don't accept that I must sometimes disturb the peace and fight for them. I must give up the child in me who wants to be protected and loved, and start risking myself for something I believe in.

Dreams are what you are made of. You live for them and by them, and they serve you well when you have your own voice and are guided from within. If you don't have your own voice, you will use your dreams to escape life and keep you protected. In your dreams, you are magical and free. You can be free in the real world, too, if you can just tame your compassionate heart with the wisdom of knowing that courage is what you need to be free. You must face your fears, anger, rejection, and anything else that comes your way—this is true freedom—to be free of fear. Until you can give up your need for the world to be perfect, you won't be able to begin creating that better world. You don't need to be protected from the judgments of others; you are protected by your faith.

You are in level one when dreams are what help you to escape the tension of the moment.

You are in level two when dreams are what help you to express yourself and take a stand.

You are in level three when you have faith in your dreams.

You are in level four when your dreams are your truth and your truth expresses all of you, even what others have judged as unworthy.

Step Five: The Third House

Aries: Judgments and Choices Are One and the Same

I have always been afraid of hurting other people and of expressing a truth in conflict with that of another person, so I don't always tell others what I think. The problem is that others are not afraid to tell me what they think. I realize that I present myself as weak when I don't have a voice.

This is a hard one for most Aquarians. Hiding your judgment or opinion is how you show other people love and protect them from their ignorance. You do this because you're not strong enough to stop protecting yourself from the world of tension and conflict. Once you're ready to meet life head on, you'll give up protecting others from the truth and will start challenging them. Then your mind will get the feedback it needs and the strength it desires. In addition, the competition in which you're afraid to participate won't be painful because you will truly know that it is only through risking yourself and learning from your mistakes that you will grow and become great.

You are in level one when you want to protect everyone you love.
You are in level two when you want to discover yourself and your uniqueness.
(Levels three and four are listed at the end of step five in the second level of consciousness.)

The Second Level of Consciousness

The second level of consciousness divides the third house and fifth step, and the fifth house and seventh step. The first level is expressed through fear and safe choices; you enter the second level when you are strong enough to challenge the choices of the authority in your life. You must be ready to accept that conflict is essential to growth and that unconditional love is not possible unless you first give it to yourself. So many times, you must stand in conflict to bring out love. If you are always avoiding conflict, you will never have the chance to make the most important choices in your life. You need to realize that giving others everything they want and need does not create a loving environment. On the contrary, it creates an abusive one. Without a voice to protect and stand up for yourself, you are a doormat for anyone with the courage to ask you for a favor. Learn to say no, learn to say what you feel, and let others deal with your truth. Your mission is to find your truth, pursue your dream, and take a stand for what you believe in.

Step Five: The Third House (Second Level)

Aries: My Truth Is in My Choice

I found the courage to make a selfish choice when I realized that no one was really going to take care of me and that I had to start standing up for myself. It made me stronger, and now I'm doing it all the time. It does become easier each time you meet the moment with truth and faith.

Once you're able to be selfish, you won't always be selfish, not with your heart. The ability to own your ego is essential to the ability to take your power, and once you feel strong, you want to share with others. To take your power, you must be able to stand up to the authority in your life, or the fifth house, which for Aquarius is ruled by Gemini and involves the issue of choice. You must let go of your image of being perfect and accept the judgment that comes when you displease other people. It's okay to displease others; they'll get over it and so will you.

Here's a simple procedure to follow when you want to make a good decision:

1. Take the position of the heart first. What feels right? Don't worry about the consequences; just focus on your desire.
2. Look at the facts. What are the limitations that you must consider?
3. Combine your answers to steps 1 and 2, above, and compromise as necessary.

If you do not take the position of the heart first, you will never know what it is. Fear and the facts will prevent you from understanding its deepest yearnings.

You are in level three when you have faith in a vision that is based on your dreams.

You are in level four when you know that life always has a greater vision waiting to manifest within you.

Step Six: The Fourth House

Taurus: Unconditional Love Is What I Need to Give to Myself

I have been avoiding love because I've been afraid that I'm not perfect enough. I have been choosing to give the love that I've wanted to receive. Instead of being rewarded, however, I have been overlooked, rejected, or ignored. Now I know that perfection is a personal thing. If I express myself and my truth, there is nothing else for which anyone can ask.

Love is what you live for, but it needs boundaries and limits when you give it to humans and not to Gods. To take the most loving position means you don't overprotect or overexpose other people. You need to support others' strength, not their fears. You can't love completely unless you accept the negative, too. You have to look at your anger and your fear. No one can be perfect all the time, and if you try to be, you will have a nervous breakdown. Love means you can be real. It means you can have an ego and your ego can make demands on others. It means you can have a different opinion. It means you can have your own dreams.

You are in level one if you are seeking and giving unconditional love.
You are in level two if you are confronting the rules and expectations of love.
You are in level three if you are giving unconditional love to your dream.
You are in level four if you are giving yourself unconditional love.

Step Seven: The Fifth House

Gemini: Whoever Makes the Choices Has the Authority

I am attracted to people who have the ability to take risks and say how they feel. I am more worried about hurting other people's feelings than I am about myself. This is not good. I am beginning to see that protecting the ideals of others doesn't help them. In addition, it keeps me in the role of their protector, which prevents me from being free. I have to learn to let go.

The people to whom you give your choices have the power, not you. Without choice, you can't take action or build whatever it is you want to build; you can only follow. Thus, the need to own your power through choice is essential to your happiness. The fifth house is the house where you meet your fear, and your fear comes in the form of authority. Of course, it is your own judgments that have created the monster that sits in your fifth house, and if that monster is weak, it is hard to fight. How can you fight something you need to hold up? If you don't find someone to resist your desires in life, you won't be able to bring forth your voice and you will spend your life taking care of others who are weak. If, however, you witnessed someone become strong by giving up on love, you won't trust strength and you'll hide from it. Just because one of your parents gave up love for power doesn't mean you have to do the same. Love and power do not necessarily conflict with each other. Change the underlying motivation and intention, replace the fear with faith, and see power as the ability to change the world, and you will have love and power together.

> You are in level one when you allow others to make your choices for you.
> You are in level two when you challenge their choices.
> (Levels three and four are listed at the end of step seven in the third level of consciousness.)

The Third Level of Consciousness

The third level of consciousness divides the fifth house and seventh step, and the ninth house and eleventh step. It challenges you to face your fear of losing unconditional love if you choose for either yourself or the truth. When you realize that you are not loved unconditionally no matter what you do, that those you love use you to fulfill their needs, you begin to make choices for yourself and your dreams. You enter the third level when you are ready to pit your newly exposed ideas and ideals against those of others. You will be challenged and attacked. The competitive world is filled with sharks that are eager to inhibit your talents and eliminate you as competition. Your mission is to test your strength and courage against them. What you will learn is that you don't have to be smarter or better than others. You just have to believe more deeply than they do, and you'll have the advantage.

Step Seven: The Fifth House (Third Level)

Gemini: I Seek the Choice That Will Keep My Dreams and Vision Safe and Give Me the Best Reward

I have been protecting myself and other people from my choices. Now I need to protect my ideas and dreams from others until I know that those people can be trusted. Will I ever feel free?

You are at an early stage of your journey and protection is still important. It will remain important until you have the skills to discriminate, an instinct you trust, and the ability to stand up for yourself and say no. Until you learn how to protect yourself and your ideas, you will have to be cautious and careful of what you share and with whom you share it.

> You are in level three when you choose for yourself and recognition. You are in level four when you choose to face judgment and criticism because you have faith in yourself and your dreams.

Step Eight: The Sixth House

Cancer: I Must Let Go of Protection

I know I am naturally overprotective of the people I love, but I stopped protecting them when I started making my own choices. I know I feel better when I don't have to rely on others. It's great to be independent and to have confidence in my feelings.

You survived your childhood by taking care of the people who were less wise or loving than you. It is time to have faith and trust that if you let go, these people won't fall so far down that they will be lost. Your destiny is not to hold up others out of fear; it is to inspire them through faith. Do not be afraid of the truth. It may hurt for a moment, but it also has the power to heal. Sometimes we must dig out the rot to allow a wound to heal. Truth has a way of cutting through illusions and leaving you to face the neediness and fear of your ego. You can't begin to change until you acknowledge that change is necessary.

> You are in level one when you need to be protected.
> You are in level two when you need to protect others.
> You are in level three when you seek a greater truth than the one you know.
> You are in level four when you believe wherever you are is where you should be.

Step Nine: The Seventh House

Leo: My Ego Is Responsible for My Freedom

I have renewed faith in my ego. I used to believe that ego was good for nothing or responsible for the problems of this world. Now I know that it is a lack of ego that is the problem. Most people have trouble being selfish or standing up for themselves. Until you can be selfish, however, you can't truly be generous with your heart.

You judge the ego incorrectly. A strong ego does not interfere with love or life. Rather, the lack of an ego creates problems. Until you can take care of your own needs, you will never be able to help others for the right reasons. You will continue to protect people to please or avoid them, not because the desire comes from your heart. Your ego expresses the pain of your mistakes. It feels loss and fear when it is disconnected from your heart and dreams. Include your ego and you will be free.

> You are in the level one when your life revolves around the needs of others.
> You are in the level two when you stand up to others and speak your mind.
> You are in the level three when you believe in yourself and your dreams.
> You are in the level four when you see freedom as your choice.

Step Ten: The Eighth House

Virgo: Letting Go Gives You the Control

I thought I had trouble letting go because I didn't have faith in others. In reality, it was because I didn't have enough faith in myself. I thought the only way to get love was to give it unconditionally. To be loved, you must not need love. You must be willing to let love go. When you do, it comes back to you stronger than ever.

When you take back your ego, letting go becomes easy. You erroneously thought that life would be easier if you just ignored your needs and desires. What you have learned the hard way is that when you please too much, no one is happy. You make the people you please feel weak, needy, and wanting more of you and your time. If, instead, you share your journey with them and let them help you, you allow them to give to you. This is a gift of love and power, which they will return to you.

> You are in level one when you give to please others.
> You are in level two when you give to strengthen yourself.
> You are in level three when you see that what you want is everywhere around you.
> You are in level four when you have what you want all the time because it is within you.

Step Eleven: The Ninth House

Libra: When I Accept My Truth, I Am Free of Judgment

I avoided my truth to protect other people, but instead of love I received rejection. When I accepted my truth and let go of other people, the opinion and judgments of others no longer bothered me because I knew what I believed in and that gave me strength.

Truth—now there's a confusing idea. Whose truth rules? What is truth anyway? By now, you should realize that truth is what inspires you. Whatever lifts your spirit and your heart, whatever motivates and ignites your passion, is your truth. Yes, truth can change because you change. Once you stop protecting the truths of other people and pay attention to your own, you stop dividing things into right and wrong, and instead seek the power of inspiration. Then you will always be guided by and open to a greater truth and a new level of awareness. Now that's the wisdom of truth.

> You are in level one when you believe what you are told.
> You are in level two when you feel betrayed by what you were told.
> (Levels three and four are listed at the end of step eleven in the fourth level of consciousness.)

The Fourth Level of Consciousness

The fourth level of consciousness divides the ninth house and eleventh step. In the third level, you were asked to have faith in your voice and your dreams. In the fourth level, you are asked to accept the wisdom of the universe instead of your own. You are asked to turn things over. You have fought for your truth and realize how important it is to accept conflict and stand up for what you believe in. Now you are asked to turn it all over, not to a person or a dream, but to your higher self, to God, and to the universe. You know that there is always a greater consciousness and idea to be had. Turn your fate over to that unborn idea within you, to the unknown. Trust that there is a better way and that you can find it. When you can rely on what you don't understand or on what has yet to happen, you have reached the level of pure faith.

Step Eleven: The Ninth House (Fourth Level)

Libra: Truth Is Not Truth Until It Has a Shadow That You've Owned

I was able to reconnect with myself when I stopped worrying about hurting other people and saw how much I was hurting myself. This allowed me to look at the anger I had for the sacrifices I had made that were never acknowledged. When I give to myself, I acknowledge myself and all my feelings.

You no longer fear the shadow. You have faced the struggles of life and survived. You have let go of those who love you, faced their anger and rejection, and taken your own path, one that took you far away. Strangely enough, that same path has brought you home. You have changed and so has your truth. Gone are the innocence of youth and the inspiration that comes from ideals that can call you only from a distance, a distance that allows the ideals to stay perfect in your eyes. Instead, you now have an inner wisdom, a truth that does not judge, but forgives and understands. After all, you've done it all, and you did it with your heart. It didn't prevent you from hurting others or causing them pain, but then pain and sadness cannot be avoided. You need, instead, the strength to endure, to look for the bigger idea, the faith that tells you nothing is lost. It only passes through a stage of darkness to once again be reborn.

You are in level three when you have faith in your truth.
You are in level four when you realize truth is whatever you choose it to be.

Step Twelve: The Tenth House

Scorpio: Self-Mastery Is My Reward

I used to be afraid to reveal my talents, genius, and true intentions to others, but now I'm not. If they really love me, they will want to know how I really feel and they won't want me to tell them a lie.

Your fearlessness is your reward. You are not afraid of the judgments of other people and so can let your imagination soar. You are an inventor, a master, a game player, and you have a wonderful weird sense of humor. Life seems ridiculous from your point of view. It is absurd to be serious about things you can't control. Pay attention to what you can do and turn everything else over to your higher self. It all works out in the end if you just have the faith and the courage to surrender to what you want. What you want then speaks to you and tells you what you have to do to get it. You have learned to learn from your desires and from the objects you desire. See love in the object or person you want and surrender to that love, and you'll magically get your reward.

> You are in level one when you believe in good and bad.
> You are in level two when you can hide your truth from people who are negative.
> You are in level three when you know that you are both good and bad.
> You are in level four when you know that your intentions are what make you good.

Step One: The Eleventh House (Fourth Level)

Sagittarius: Wisdom Is the Ability to Accept Pain with Joy

I must forgive myself for not having the consciousness or wisdom to know all the answers. When I do, I will be able to accept it all.

You have true wisdom when you are strong and wise enough to accept your pain with your joy. Don't cut yourself off from what will make you strong. It is through suffering, not victory or success, that you gain your greatest knowledge. What you lose you value, and now you know to look for meaning and love before it's too late. You embrace the moment because it's all you have. You know that it's up to you to choose what you see and what you highlight in other people. If you choose to see love, you will. If you choose to see pain, you will. The power is in your hands. Don't be afraid to mold your life your way. That is freedom.

> You are in level three when you listen to your inner wisdom and stand up for it.
> You are in level four when you find wisdom in each moment because you have courage and faith.

The Cross

The cross is composed of the eleventh, fifth, ninth, and third houses and is where change must occur. (See Figure 3.1 on page 69.) The two fixed houses represented by Sagittarius and Gemini challenge each other to see a greater truth:

Sagittarius (eleventh house): *I will not be able to listen to my inner voice or wisdom until I come to terms with myself and the fact that I will challenge and hurt the feelings of other people when I bring out my own wisdom and truth.*

Gemini (fifth house): *When I own my inner wisdom and truth, it will be easy for me to make tough choices. I will accept that life has both pain and sorrow, and that when you judge quickly and for the right intentions, you create something wonderful in the world. My ego will become strong and my world filled with love and fairness.*

The two mutable houses represented by Libra and Aries must anchor themselves in this new truth by taking a stand:

Libra (ninth house): *I must accept my truth and my right to judge for myself what I want in my life and what I want the world to be like.*

Aries (third house): *If I am not able to own my own opinion, I'll be ruled by people who can make strong and sure choices. I must stop being the hero for others and take a stand for what I want and believe in.*

PISCES: Dreams
(February 19 through March 20)

Dreams are magic, they ignite our hearts.
Their mission is our unhealed parts.
They trap our wounds in a sweet embrace,
Then let them soar, and off we chase.
For glamour and glitter, we go through the fire.
Each fear encountered takes our spirit higher.
Their power is distance, remaining beyond
Our capacity to hold, our need to bond.
As we close the gap to this ethereal goal,
We hear more clearly the voice of our soul.
"You are much more than you think you can be.
Follow me," they say, "and truth you will see."

Question Twelve

About Your Parents: What was your mother's dream? Did she fulfill it? If not, what stopped her?

About Yourself: What is your dream? Are you working to fulfill it or is it an escape?

You are a dream, and you live in God's dream and in His creation. Dreams are what compose the world, and without a dream of your own, you have to live in someone else's creation and abide by that person's rules and enjoy that person's choices. That's fun for a while, but sooner or later you feel a yearning, and a voice within you asks you to create your own ideals, express what's in your own heart, and live your life according to your own rules. Until you are tired of what is, you will not seek to change it or move out of where you are.

Learning how to dream is the most important step on your journey. If you don't have a dream, you will not feel protected, safe, motivated, or inspired. Dreams are what give your work satisfaction and your moments meaning. They are the links to your heart and to God's love. God speaks to your soul through your dreams. Open up to these ethereal clouds of the imagination and you will rise above the harsh realities of life and discover that the world can be an exciting and loving place.

Without Dreams, Your World Shrinks

Dreams should be as important to you now as they were in your childhood. Your lost spirit is merely your disconnection from your dreams. You have let life and its responsibilities, labels, and images become more important to you than your ability to create and imagine the world into a greater place. When you give up on your ability to change yourself and your environment, you give in to fear, limitations, and restrictions, and open the door to depression, which is the loss of your dreams. Don't worry, it's not difficult to find your dreams again, but you may have to fight to keep them in your life. Your dreams challenge other people who have lost their dreams, and these souls need to protect themselves from inspiration and yearning so that they can stay safe and protected in their lives. They are afraid to feel and be inspired because if they do, they will have to make different choices and disappoint the people they are protecting.

It's easy to dismiss dreams as nonsense and unimportant, but if you take the time to look deeper, you will see that they are the blueprints of life. Before you can put an idea down on paper, you need to imagine it, dream it, and see it as complete. Children don't question their imagination. They are filled with it. They can play in dirt and laugh their sides out. What a great joy, and it comes from so little. How did you lose your capacity to love and laugh over nothing? You lost it by allowing other people to impose on you a set of values that didn't include inspiration, joy, or love. Your own values probably encourage you to behave well, pursue success, and act responsibly. Wow, that's inspiring indeed. Make no bones about it, dreams inspire you to go beyond your feelings of worthlessness and urge you to take a risk for what lies in your heart. Ignore your dreams and you ignore your inner voice, your intuition, and your guide in the unknown.

If you can't take risks and accept change, you will become a prisoner of the reality in which you're living right now. That reality, if it doesn't expand, will contract. Nothing stays static, no matter how hard you hold on. If it contracts, it will fall apart, and if you hold on to the parts, you will be pulled apart. Let go. Move forward with the rhythm of life and your inner calling. Let yourself be guided from within and led by your dreams without. Dreams inspire because they are the messengers of the heart. They lift your soul up out of the trenches of tragedy and keep you going when nothing else can. Dreams remind you that another reality is waiting for you if you can just keep moving forward and have faith in what you want. The people who succeed in life and live with love are the ones who hold on to their dreams no matter how bleak or tragic life becomes. The faith they develop by holding on to their dreams is what helps them manifest their dreams. They choose joy and dreams over depression and sorrow. Joy and dreams don't stay if you don't attend to or believe in them. They leave as soon as you begin to focus on fear and sadness. If you are not happy, it's because you choose to be unhappy. The good news is you can choose to be happy. But joy takes faith. Dreams take faith. And that means you must have faith in something, someone, or in yourself.

When Fear Is Great, Dreams Are Small

Dreams are lost out of fear. Unfortunately, not too many people believe in dreaming. Parents tend to encourage their children to find jobs that bring a good paycheck or guarantee security. However, dreams should not be used as a way of escaping from life. To make a dream real, you must actively make choices for it, not sit in front of the television and hope it'll arrive with your dinner. Dreams require passion, desire, imagination, fortitude, and faith. If you are not willing to give your dream your all, you might as well give it up. Risk your faith for what you believe in, but learn from your mistakes. Fortitude and perseverance don't mean continually repeating the same mistakes. They mean learning from everything you do and improving upon it as you go forward. Almost everyone will discourage you from taking a leap of faith, from believing in yourself. Instead, they will encourage you to follow a path that leads to routine, the graveyard of spirit and dreams. So many people want to give their children more things, better clothes, a fancier bicycle, a newer computer. What children need is their parents' time, laughter, joy, and dreams for them. Children whose parents see them as great, successful, and independent will follow that vision into the unknown.

Mothers Are the Keepers of Dreams

It is the mother's dream that embraces the family and makes the members feel safe. Her spirit and faith bring all the divergent emotions together and unite the various members into one unit. If a mother doesn't dream and enjoy life, what does she give to her children? A path strewn with unappreciated, discardable objects that do not come close to replacing the words of love and faith that children need when they fall, that they need to make them feel safe. Love, not possessions, give a sense of security. When you are loved, you can get through ridicule, disappointment, and loss. When you don't have a connection to your parents' hearts, you don't know how to connect to your own heart. Dreams are a simple way to reach anyone's heart. Parents need to share their dreams with their children and support their children's dreams. Parents need to find out what lies in their children's hearts and not judge or ridicule them. This is what gives children the power to dream and to believe in themselves.

Since only a few dreamers survive childhood, the world has more dream poppers than dream creators. Many dreamers lose their faith once they find success because they make the mistake of trying to hold on to what they have created instead of allowing themselves to evolve and change. When you get stuck holding on to an old dream, you lose faith in your power to create. You pursued a dream once; you know the way and can do it again. It will be easier if you don't try to repeat yourself, but instead take a risk for a new idea. The courage to take a chance is at the base of all dreams that succeed.

Risk is essential to dreams. If you are afraid to take risks, you will not have a dream, unless it's one into which you can escape and that you have no intention of ever pursuing. Did you lose your faith because you fell when you tried to pursue a dream and no one was there to pick you up and tell you to try again? Was there no one to tell you that everyone fails the first few times they try something new, until they get the hang of it? If a supportive person was missing from your life, you have to become that person yourself; you have to become your own best friend. You have to support yourself. Give yourself the encouragement to keep going, to face your fears, to not fold. Learn which friends you can call for encouragement and get rid of the ones who make you feel worse.

The Mother Brings You the Dream

It is your mother who brings you the dream, and through her vision of you in the world, she gives you faith and love. Her vision should not be based on a perfect image of you, but on one that sees you as happy and successful because you're living your dreams. When your mother believes in you and your desires, you find your life easier to manage. Your hurt and pain are decreased when someone understands you and points the way to the next step, the one that will take you out of the rut and into a greater experience of yourself. If your mother gave up on her dreams, she won't believe in dreams and she may not support yours. Then you will have to give yourself this gift.

To create a dream, you must yearn for one and you must learn how to listen to your heart. Your heart will release a dream for you when you are ready to accept one. Pay attention to your inner voice, listen to your needs, and give yourself the chance to imagine and play with your visions. Do not judge what comes up, but let it lead you forward into crazy, unknown places. From the journey, you will feel a spark. The light of passion will be ignited, and you will suddenly have a dream that speaks to you with such power, you won't have to ask anyone if it's possible, if it's real, or what you should do. You will know without question that this is your destiny, and you will commit your desire and soul to manifesting it. (See Figure 4.1 for the Pisces Star.)

The First Level of Consciousness

The first level of consciousness divides the eleventh house and first step, and the third house and fifth step. The first level begins with the desire for a new dream. The fourth level, which you will encounter at the end of your journey, ends with the realization of your dream. Once you have achieved your reward, or dream, you have a choice: you can take the current dream a step higher and use your success to help mankind, or you can choose another journey (dream) and seek a new reward. When choosing a new dream, you must decide how much freedom you want to express and how unique you will

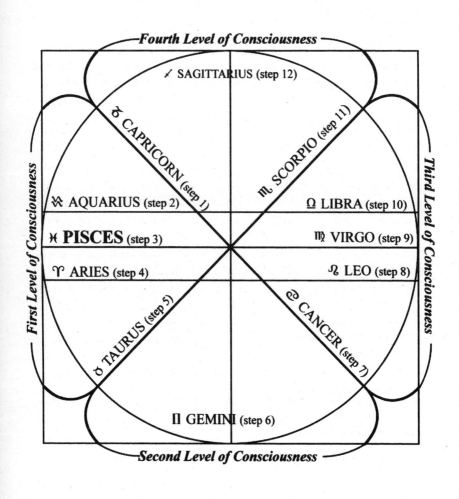

Figure 4.1. The Pisces Star

dare to be. Thus, it's the reward you choose to seek that will shape the path you take. What will the reward be for you: success, fame, and fortune or the discovery of your higher purpose? There's no right or wrong answer, only the experience your heart desires.

Step One: The Eleventh House

Capricorn: My Reward Is Love and Protection

I have faith in love and the ability of the universe to protect me, and so I am able to let go and dream. When I do, I discover new ideas and visions that inspire me. Now I am in a dilemma: Do I pursue these visions? They will take me beyond protection and challenge the love I have in my life. What is more important? What should I do?

The first choice a person makes is always for protection. You cannot seek a new world until you feel secure in the one you're in. However, even though you may put your dreams off until you're stronger and more independent, you should know their value and not dismiss them. There's nothing more powerful than a dream. Allow the dream in yourself to grow and expand. Let it change its vision and face, and when it's right, you'll be ready to reach for it in the outside world through your heart. You'll be ready to let it guide you beyond protection and safety, to a love greater than the one you know now.

> You are in level one if your reward is what others tell you it is.
> You are in level two when you challenge their reward and seek your own goals.
> (Levels three and four are listed at the end of step one in the fourth level of consciousness.)

Step Two: The Twelfth House

Aquarius: Freedom Is Not Enough to Balance Truth and Ego

I feel free when I just let go and follow my heart. However, others won't let me do that. They try to protect me or they abandon me for not taking care of their needs. So I hide my truth, and then my ego either expresses itself like a tyrant or it lets go and allows others to walk all over me. I'm so afraid of losing love that I cannot feel secure with just my truth to protect me.

Your desire for freedom and your need for protection are at odds with your dreams. You must be strong enough to persevere and let go of your outmoded ideals concerning love. Love on a first-level basis has to do with survival and pleasing, not with expressing the feelings in your heart. The yearnings you want to express will get their chance when you get your voice. You need to begin to take risks in your life and experience different choices. Don't let fear be your leader or the authority that stops you. When you discover what you truly believe in and commit to it, you will have the strength to balance truth and ego.

You are in level one if freedom is something you hide or put off for the future.
You are in level two if freedom is something for which you need to fight.
You are in level three when your truth and your ego give way to your uniqueness.
You are in level four when freedom is everything you choose to do because you do it through choice.

Step Three: The First House

Pisces: Life Is a Dream

I live in a dream, and it protects me from the harsh realities of life. The longer I hold on to my dream, the more I want to make it real. All the people around me have dreams, and I try to support all of them in their quests. When I do, something wonderful happens: I feel stronger and more committed to my own dreams.

The Pisces dream—the ability to be free, to choose from the heart—is yours as soon as you understand the sacrifice. What you choose to manifest in the world will require you to let go of something else. It will also require you to put certain parts of yourself in the light and to restrain or contain the rest. Right now, your dream is innocent because you are not aware of any consequences or sacrifices you will need to make. This is the only way the universe can get you to commit. It all seems so wonderful and perfect at the beginning. But as you move forward, something else in you will be challenged. You must be willing to meet those challenges to continue. Only a dream of the heart will hold you through to the end. Early dreams may come and go. You'll know you have the right dream when it wakes you up and gives you the strength to take responsibility for your life and give up what stands in the way of its manifestation.

> You are in level one when the dream is an escape.
> You are in level two when you are following your dream, not someone else's dream or the road to safety.
> You are in level three when you have faith in your dream even though no one else does.
> You are in level four when the world is a world of dreams.

Step Four: The Second House

Aries: For What Will I Stand Up?

I learned what was important to me by doing what others thought was important to them and thereby discovering what I like and what I don't. However, when I wanted to do those things but do them my way, others rejected me. I must somehow learn to accept myself and all of my feelings so I do not have to rely on others to protect me, so I do not have to follow paths that do not make my heart sing, and so I will not be afraid to lose love because I made a choice that spoke to me.

What is important to you when you are young is what brings you attention and from what or whom you can learn. As you gain experience, you learn your own truths, and then you have to stand up for them to use them in the world in which you've been living. People don't like change when it doesn't originate with them. When you bring in new ideas, you impose change and other people resent you at first. But if you hold to what you love, these people will start respecting you for what you believe in.

A dream, one of your own, is the easiest way to begin the process of separating your values from those of your parents. Until you start separating, you won't be able to see yourself as different, and if you're not unique, you won't have anything new to offer the world. When you use a dream to separate, you can finish the process with unity, especially if your parents support your dream. Without a dream, you must pull in something that opposes your parents' values, like a relationship they dislike. This way, you become a victim of your needs, forcing them to cast you out, and although you have separated from their values, you have not accomplished your goal; you still don't have a clue to what your own values are. You are now dependent on this new person's point of view. Until you can find the strength to stand up for yourself and your beliefs, you will never feel powerful or in control of your life.

> You are in level one when your vision is to please others.
> You are in level two when your vision is to challenge others.
> You are in level three when you have faith in your vision.
> You are in level four when you know a greater vision is always waiting
>   for you.

Step Five: The Third House

Taurus: My Choice Is Love

I used to believe unconditional love was the only thing that mattered. However, if I give that kind of love, I must give up choice and hope the people I love unconditionally will protect me. When someone else is in charge of my choices, I get either too much freedom or not enough. There must be a better way. I must find the courage and strength to risk myself for my dreams. I must go beyond their fears and mine.

Unconditional love exists only on the higher planes. It's not your fault love has betrayed you; it was your image of love that let you down. That image has to go. You need to create the image and the world you want, and you do it through choice. Your choice now is either to protect yourself or to try again. Learn from your mistakes. Don't trust so unconditionally. Know that others have ulterior motives and that fear stops them from keeping their promises and fulfilling your needs.

> You are in level one when you believe in unconditional love.
> You are in level two when you desire the power of choice.
> (Levels three and four are listed at the end of step five in the second
>   level of consciousness.)

The Second Level of Consciousness

The second level of consciousness divides the third house and fifth step, and the fifth house and seventh step. You enter the second level when you're filled with enough inner tension that you accept yourself and what has been judged as bad or inadequate, and choose for what you want even though you're not perfect. What you discover is that no one is perfect and that choice has power. People who make choices are looked upon as strong; people who avoid choice are looked upon as weak. What you must give up to discover your strength is your need to be protected. If you can persevere through the loneliness, mistakes, and troubles life always places on our path, you will find something greater than what you left behind. There is always a new idea and a better way. In the second level, you seek to find it.

Step Five: The Third House (Second Level)

Taurus: I Love Myself Enough to Try

I have learned through experience to have more faith in myself. I realize that others pay more attention to me when I pay attention to myself and when I don't expect them to love everything I do.

You have reached an important point of growth. You are beginning to see that you can give value to yourself and that when you pay attention to something, others do, too. So if you pay attention to yourself and take your eyes off others, you will begin to see the power of belief and faith. Believe in yourself and others will accept you. Don't be afraid to take risks or make mistakes. No one is perfect. Learn to laugh at your mistakes and others won't give them that much importance either.

> You are in level three when you have enough faith to let go and allow life to unfold.
> You are in level four when you find love in every moment.

Step Six: The Fourth House

Gemini: I Accept the Power to Choose

I used to be afraid to choose because I was afraid of being rejected or judged for my choices or mistakes. However, the more I took the chance and made a choice, the more experienced and confident I became and the more faith I had in myself.

Commitment can be frightening when you don't have faith in yourself. If you make a commitment when you don't know who you are or where you're going, you'll be imprisoned by that commitment and unable to set yourself free. That's why it's essential to get as much experience as possible without worrying about results. Let go and learn from everyone and everything. Don't be afraid to experiment, since even a commitment can be changed. If you made a choice you see isn't working, let go of it and make a new and better one.

> You are in level one when you choose for unconditional love and pro-
> tection.
> You are in level two when you choose to risk yourself for your dream.
> You are in level three when you can let go of the dreams of others and
> have faith in yours.
> You are in level four when you turn all your important choices over to
> a higher power.

Step Seven: The Fifth House

Cancer: I Am Afraid of Being Abandoned

I want to take a risk and do things my way, but I feel other people will abandon me if I don't meet their expectations. They pull back their approval and emotions when I do something that displeases them and so I become frightened. What I have to do is stick to my guns.

The fifth house is where the line is drawn between love and fear. To change your consciousness, you need to transform the fear of the fifth house to faith. The fear of Cancer is abandonment and betrayal. All children experience loss of support from their parents when they begin to disagree with them. The severity of this loss, in proportion to the act, determines the amount of fear a child has when it comes to abandonment. If you were punished for every little thing, your fear of abandonment is great and could, in fact, be a neurosis. You certainly aren't able to make mistakes, which, of course, everyone does. If others don't punish you, you punish yourself because your self-worth and self-esteem are so low.

Cancer is your wound, the hurt and pain of being neglected when you listened to the rules—that is, when you were "good"—and still didn't get love or a reward. When this happens too often to children, they begin to believe there is something wrong with them. To change this attitude, you've got to share it. Secrets have power because there is nothing to challenge them. Open up, look at your wound, and allow others to look, too. It's sometimes easier to do this with a stranger because a stranger is less invested in your response or the results. It's a simple act of sharing. When you can share your sorrow, you can heal it. Ending the isolation caused by pain and sorrow requires opening up to God through prayer or to others through sharing.

> You are in level one when you choose to be protected rather than follow your own path.
> You are in level two when you are willing to risk abandonment to experience life.
> (Levels three and four are listed at the end of step seven in the third level of consciousness.)

The Third Level of Consciousness

The third level of consciousness divides the fifth house and seventh step, and the ninth house and eleventh step. Your ego is afraid and wounded. It has been diminished by rules, judgments, and ideals that require perfection, and so it's afraid to try. What it accepts instead is protection, which appears the same as love but, of course, is not. Children need protection; adults need to be shown the way. To let go and risk yourself requires faith. You cannot enter the third level of consciousness without faith. You cannot have faith without a dream.

Step Seven: The Fifth House (Third Level)

Cancer: When I Have Faith, I Don't Need Protection

I learned to have faith in myself by having faith in other people and by seeing that it is only fear, not ability or talent, that holds other people back. Once I saw this, I began to open myself up to more experiences and to risk myself in new ways. This gave me the confidence to let go of protection because I now had faith in myself.

The easiest way to learn is through others. Protection will be there as long as you are afraid. However, the more new experiences you have, the more you let yourself make mistakes and test yourself in the world when the consequences really don't matter, the more confidence and faith you will have in yourself when it really does count.

> You are in level three when your ego feels confident and you have faith in yourself.
> You are in level four when you know you are always protected by God.

Step Eight: The Sixth House

Leo: Faith Makes Me Strong

I have gained faith in myself by ignoring the judgments of others and listening to my own inner voice. My intuition is the best source of knowledge on earth and it never lets me down. I now feel protected and guided, and have patience and the ability to let go.

You have reached a wonderful point in the journey when you begin to rely on yourself for knowledge and know you will find an answer when you are seeking one. The answer may even find you! The more you open up to the wisdom and guidance around you, the less you have to do to accomplish your goals and the more you free your spirit to become a creator.

> You are in level one when your ego feels judged and hurt by others.
> You are in level two when you are willing to take responsibility for your choices.
> You are in level three when you have faith in your strength and ability to choose.
> You are in level four when you turn your choices over to a higher power and know that they will be successful.

Step Nine: The Seventh House

Virgo: What Is Real?

I hold on to everything I can because the world seems so uncertain. Nothing is as it seems. I feel that I'm floating and lost in a world in which all people but me know what they're doing and where they're going. This forces me to be opinionated and judgmental, since I'm trying to create something through the sheer force of my being.

You are living on faith, and it's up to you to choose the boundaries for your world. Your choices and thoughts are powerful now. What you want the world to be is what you will see. Therefore, try to be positive no matter what the circumstances. If you believe you deserve to be abandoned or unloved, your thoughts and choices will reflect that. If you believe you deserve more, the world will give you more. You are in a powerful place to decide your destiny by what you feel you deserve.

> You are in level one when you believe that letting go means losing.
> You are in level two when you care more about the reward than what you are doing.
> You are in level three when you see your dreams in others and honor them.
> You are in level four when you see your dream and vision all around you.

Step Ten: The Eighth House

Libra: Truth Is the Light

Truth, to me, is the light and everything in the world that is good. But when I own the light, I also bring in darkness and have to deal with other people's negativity, greed, and jealousy. What's going on here?

You have chosen the light—half the picture. You can't create a painting with just the color white; you need some shadow to bring the picture out. You are avoiding half of life by trying to be perfect and good. When you become tired of everyone else being bad, you will begin to see that you can't reject the shadow; you must embrace it. When you embrace your anger and fear, you can use them your way, not the way others have. You can use your anger as motivation to change yourself and the world. You can use your fear to understand the fear of others. Everything has a purpose.

> You are in level one when you see truth only as the light.
> You are in level two when you oppose the truth of others.
> You are in level three when you have faith in your truth.
> You are in level four when you see the world as one truth.

Step Eleven: The Ninth House

Scorpio: I'm Either Perfect or Nothing

I am caught between feeling that I can be perfect and that I'm nothing. Since perfection is a difficult position to maintain, I feel mostly like nothing. The way I feel is completely based on how much attention and validation I am given by others. I have no idea what I really think of myself.

You will remain caught between perfection and nothingness until you learn to create yourself through your own image. Other people judge you to control you; it has nothing to do with love. You receive approval when you please others or meet their expectations, and you don't receive it when you violate their rules. Your approval has nothing to do with you and yet you base your whole identity on other people's opinions. It's time to take yourself back and accept you are both light and shadow, you have both good feelings and bad feelings, and both have a place in the world, in your art, and in your heart.

You are in level one if you think the world is divided between good and evil.
You are in level two if you oppose one or the other.
(Levels three and four are listed at the end of step eleven in the fourth level of consciousness.)

The Fourth Level of Consciousness

The fourth level of consciousness divides the ninth house and eleventh step. It asks you to own and accept the parts of yourself that have been judged. This includes your anger and your negative feelings. When you begin to realize that you should love all of yourself, not just what others like or dislike, you will begin to love and accept all the different parts of yourself. This is the beginning of real power. The more you can accept love in yourself, the more strength and love you will receive from others. The more you seek to be perfect, the more empty and abandoned you will feel.

Step Eleven: The Ninth House (Fourth Level)

Scorpio: What's Perfect Anyway?

I have come to realize no one is perfect and perfection for many is based on some silly outer image that changes all the time. I'm going to seek a deeper and greater perfection, one based on eternal principles, truths on which I can rely.

You have just moved from seeing only the surface of life to seeing what's hidden, to seeking the mystery or the greater truth. This is where the journey really begins. You will start to find answers that make sense to you, and these answers will have nothing to do with what you expected to find out or what others have told you. You are awakening to your higher self and it's an exciting moment.

> You are in level three when you see yourself as both good and negative, and you accept and use it all for the right intentions.
>
> You are in level four when you see no difference between goodness and negativity, just a difference between intentions.

Step Twelve: The Tenth House

Sagittarius: I Have a Voice That Guides Me

As soon as I decided to seek a greater understanding of myself and the world, I began to hear my instincts speak to me. It is this very subtle inner voice that makes me feel either good or anxious about the decisions I am about to make. If I listen to that voice, I am okay. If I rely on how things seem, I run into trouble. I feel so much more loved and safe when I am connected to this voice.

Once you have your inner voice, you're ready to face the world. Your inner voice will be your guide for the whole journey. Listen to your inner voice and it will become strong and will actually stop you from doing unproductive things. Don't listen to it—instead, override it with rationalization and excuses—and it will become too soft and difficult to hear. Your inner voice will not impose itself on you; you must choose its wisdom over the wisdom of the world. When you do, your life will begin to change.

You are in level one if you rely on the opinions and judgments of others.

You are in level two when you have the courage to go beyond your need for protection and take the power of choice.

You are in level three when you base your choices on your inner voice.

You are in level four when you turn your choices over to a higher power.

Step One: The Eleventh House (Fourth Level)

Capricorn: My Reward Is Faith in Myself

I have come a long way. I used to depend on others because I thought they were wiser and stronger than me. No one knows better what lies in my heart or what's good for me than I do. If I have faith, I have power and I can achieve my dreams.

You are on your way to achieving the greatest reward of all: seeing love in every moment. If you can love, you can feel free and life will be wonderful. Remember that you can choose to see love or hate, good or bad; the choice is yours. Don't wait for love. You can have it now.

You are in level three when you have faith in your goals and feel the reward is unimportant.

You are in level four when life is the reward.

The Cross

The cross is composed of the eleventh, fifth, ninth, and third houses and is where change must occur. (See Figure 4.1 on page 88.) The two fixed houses represented by Capricorn and Cancer challenge each other to see a greater truth:

Capricorn (eleventh house): *My reward is always a promise in the future, but I want joy and happiness now. When others are in charge, I have to wait. When I make my own choices, I can choose for what I want now.*

Cancer (fifth house): *I was afraid to ask for what I really wanted or to be who I really am because I didn't have faith in love; I thought it would leave if I* didn't do the right thing. I have faith in myself, though, and the more I believe in myself, the less I need to please others and the more I realize that other people's rules protect me from their fears, not from my own. I need to go beyond being protected and see what my own fears are. I must go to the limits of my faith. When I do, I will discover that I have my own dreams, and that my dreams will allow me to see the dreams of others and to hear my own voice. I will have my reward now. I will have my dream.

The two mutable houses represented by Scorpio and Taurus must anchor themselves in this new truth by taking a stand:

Scorpio (ninth house): *I am either good or bad, and it is becoming more and more difficult to always be good. I am beginning to see that love needs to include all of me.*

Taurus (third house): *I thought love demanded I be perfect, and because I couldn't be perfect, I gave up my choices to other people. That was a mistake. I received neither love nor protection in return. I now know that I must make my own choices.*

ARIES: Vision
(March 21 through April 20)

Aries divides right from wrong.
It struggles to sing its own sweet song.
The hearts of others are in the way.
They all have a sadness that wants to stay.
What needs to be known is the dark and light.
They are connected; this is the plight.
To seek one out is to find the other.
They are as close as brother to brother.
Not even the sword of truth can divide
Fear and love, they're on the same side.
Only together do they have great power.
Apart they become a fragile flower.
Your voice lies beyond values and truth.
It's the rebel in you that will find your proof.
She'll tell you that seeking—it has to go.
Believing in you—it's the way to know.

Question One

About Your Parents: What was your father's vision of life? What attitude supported this vision? Was he positive; did he believe that life was worth living? Or, was he negative and depressed because he gave up on his dreams?

About Yourself: What is your vision of life? In what position do you see yourself in that vision? Are you a leader? What do you believe you are worthy of having?

As a child, you were taught to obey, to follow the rules, and to be good. You believed that if you behaved, did the right thing, and put others first, you would be rewarded. You were taught to believe in a perfect world; in goodness, kindness, honesty, and loyalty; and that your talents would be recognized and applauded. Your parents were probably the first ones to break these rules, and it was downhill from that point on—or was it? What no one bothered to tell you was that these rules are ideals that should serve as buoys on your river to remind you not to venture too far out until you have the skills and knowledge to navigate unknown and dangerous waters.

Ideals inspire us when we don't have anything to measure up to. Their purpose is to make us reach higher than we think we can, not to defeat our soul and make us feel unworthy or hopeless. If you try to become a perfect replica of what others value, you will disconnect from your own heart and uniqueness. What you don't realize as a youth is that this uniqueness that everyone tries to take out of you is what will make you great. Give up your uniqueness for acceptance and approval and you become lost in the crowd. Don't let others define you. Rather, learn from them. When you're young, you don't know what you want or who you are, so it's easy to become lost, especially when there's no one around you to guide you.

You grow up when you realize that pleasing all the time is a fruitless, unrewarding job. It's important to be able to put your needs aside and extend a helping hand to others. If you do that all the time, however, others will not only take advantage of you, but they will disrespect you and you will live in anger. Your anger will come from wanting them to realize that you have needs, too. But, as you already know, that will not happen. You must value your own needs over those of others to move forward in life and be happy. Selfishness is a necessary step on the road to happiness and enlightenment. In fact, it's a primary step.

When you can let go of pleasing and following the rules, but always know your own limits and value, you are ready to cut through the desires and opinions of others and see your own path. Having a vision is an important step in the act of creation. It helps you to divide the world your way. When you cast your vision across the moment and into the future, you make a new cut and put your mark on the world. The more you hold on to that mark with faith, the deeper the impression you will make and the more you will polarize the people around you. They will either be for or against your vision. To cast a vision and challenge the old takes strength, ego, and courage. Without a doubt, your vision will be criticized and attacked. Until you are ready to risk rejection and face the judgments of others, your vision will remain hidden within you.

Judgment is the mind's way of controlling you, the people around you, and the natural flow of life. When things move too quickly, fear, caution, or criticism result, and you begin to worry. This slows you down or brings your choices to a halting stop. If other people's judgments do this to you, you may perpetuate the crime by negatively judging yourself. What you need to do is bring some faith into your life, and you can't do that until you stop listening to others and begin to listen to your inner voice. Teenagers get into trouble not because they don't listen to their parents or they break a few rules, but because they listen to their peers and not to themselves. If you just switch whom you please, you still are not self-directed. You are just listening to a different set of rules, and you stay as disconnected from your own wisdom as you were before.

If your parents never broke out of the pleasing syndrome, you will either follow their path or be very selfish. You may harbor a fear of others taking advantage of you because you witnessed the selfishness of others and saw sacrifice as a miserable thing. What you need to realize is that giving must come from a self-sufficient being, from a free heart, from a person who can say yes and no. When it does, it creates love, not anger, and the rewards can be great. To break away from your past, you must go back and look at it to see where and why you made judgments about life, ideals, and issues. Pay attention to the fact that you are basing the whole world on your parents' choices. When you were a child, your parents were, of course, your whole world. But you're not a child any longer, and you can improve upon or change what your parents saw.

You release judgments by challenging them with new and better ideas. If you expose yourself to new situations, people, and places, you will not remain stuck in old patterns because you will learn and see the value of better ideas. People who are stuck in their life are stuck in the pattern of their life and are afraid to open themselves up to new experiences. If you feel stuck, you've let fear keep you from making friends, from sharing your feelings, and from hearing the exciting and new ideas that others have to offer. Isolation insures that you keep your limiting thoughts. If you stay isolated, you begin to disintegrate from within. If you can't create, you destroy.

Lessons of Pleasing

The first step to hearing your truth is to let go of the truths of others. However, life is a process, and pleasing others is the way we learn what's important to us and how to please ourselves. If you are never allowed to give a certain person pleasure because that person is just too miserable, you feel powerless and unable to change or affect the world. Thus, pleasing is important. But moving beyond pleasing is even more important. The following are some of the things you learn from being a pleaser:

- When you give, you get. Pleasing shows that when you fulfill the needs of another person, that person often turns around and gives you what you need. Thus, it is one way to get your needs met: giving to someone else means you'll improve the odds of receiving. (But you have to be open to receiving for this to happen.)
- Pleasing creates harmony and unity. When you repress the desires that conflict with the desires of another person and hide your ego, allowing that other person to feel important, you create harmony and a sense of unity. It's important to be able to do this; you just shouldn't do this all the time.
- Being accepted is temporary happiness. If you had the good fortune of fitting in at school, you felt happy, but it didn't change how you felt about yourself. If you put pressure on yourself to fit in all the time, you deny your individuality, lose your power, and live in anxiety.
- Pleasing is a way to hide or protect truth. If you're still pleasing and you're more than ten years old, you're using pleasing because you're afraid to express your truth or your differences. You're protecting yourself. Nothing is wrong with that as long as you know it and are working toward standing up for your truth.
- Pleasing brings temporary support. When your support is based on image, it lasts only as long as you fit the image. Real friends stay with you beyond approval. Real friends are people who value what is going on inside you, rather than how you look on the outside. The friends who connect to your emotions, hopes, and dreams are the friends who will be with you for a long time.
- Pleasing leads to lying. If you must please someone, you'll eventually have to lie to that person. When you are truthful to yourself, this often places you in conflict with the truths of others. If you must please, you

must find other ways to do what you want to do, and the easiest way is lying.

- People say one thing and do another. How big of a gap was there between what your parents said was true and what they really chose for? If there was a big discrepancy between what they believed and what they did, you will be confused unless you saw it consciously. You won't know what to follow. If you listened to what they said, you didn't satisfy them, but if you listened to what they did, you made them angry. You were caught between their lack of consistency and consciousness.

- You learn what your needs are. You discover your needs when they aren't met. There is no better way of learning what you want or need than by missing it.

- Pleasing creates the desire to be a rebel. When you have to follow rules, you dream of breaking them. When you can never display negative emotions, you are attracted to them.

- Pleasing out of necessity is the least powerful position. When you become really good at pleasing, you realize how easy it is to fool someone who wants to be pleased. All you have to do is pretend to give people what they want and they believe you. Pleasing has deception built in: if you need to be pleased, you will recognize only what you want to see. Thus, being good all the time, and wanting others to be good all the time, creates an environment in which deception and lies can survive.

- You can connect with anyone. When you put aside your differences, you can learn how to connect with people who are not like you.

- You learn to listen. When you learn to listen, you learn. There is so much to learn from other people if you can just be quiet and hear what they have to say.

- Pleasing makes you feel special. When you please someone, you become special, even if it's for just a moment. That's why pleasing is so addictive.

- Pleasing teaches responsibility. To please, you must do something or take responsibility for it. If you are successful at it, you'll begin to value effort and responsibility, two skills essential for success.

What happens if you never learn to please? The following result when you are not allowed to give someone else pleasure.

- You feel that you have nothing to give. This is crucial in the development of self-worth. When you stop others from giving to you, you are trying to control your pleasure and to avoid the expectation that arises in you when you feel the tug to return the gift once you have received it.

- You don't learn about others. You know things only through your own point of view. This can make you misjudge the responses of others, as well as distort your reality and ability to see the truth.
- You develop a strong inner world. An inner world is essential for your growth, but it won't serve you if you keep it cut off from others and life.
- You don't learn how to receive. The ability to please comes before the ability to receive. If you can't please, you won't be able to receive.
- You don't learn what makes you happy. You learn how to make yourself happy by making others happy.
- Your timing is off. If you can't please others, you will either give up too fast or hold on too long.
- You don't feel comfortable with attention. If you always put someone else first, you will be uncomfortable when the spotlight is on you.
- You are not able to take orders. Pleasing gives you power. When you can't please, you feel powerless. When you feel powerless, you rebel against authority or resent it.

How to Stop Pleasing

The following are three techniques I have used to help people learn how to say no and begin to set boundaries in their lives. You need something to interfere with your automatic yes, and you need to practice and accept the discomfort that comes from valuing your needs over others. It's tough at first, but it's amazing how quickly the discomfort vanishes. Practicing these techniques works better if you do it with a friend who has the same problem. You can share the results and encourage each other.

1. Postpone your answers. Get back to people. You need time to think about your answers because your automatic answer is yes. You must place a monkey wrench in the path of your need to accommodate. Have a list of evasive responses you can say instead of yes. Acknowledge your weakness and be prepared to overcome it. This is what being conscious and responsible is all about.
2. Practice several responses. There are certain situations that occur repeatedly, and you fall into the same trap each time. Have an answer ready

and rehearse it in your mind. The more you rehearse and struggle with something, the better you teach your mind to follow a new pattern. If you want to heal this you can. In the beginning, it will be difficult, but it won't take long. It's amazing how quickly you feel the power of no and reach for it over the anxiety that is produced by your fear of saying it.

3. Fix your mistakes in your mind. At the end of the day, or immediately after you say yes when you wanted to say no, figure out what you could and should have said and go over it several times in your head. Visualization is a very powerful tool. Once again, you are training yourself to respond differently.

If you practice these three simple techniques, one day sooner than you think, "no" will pop out of your mouth and you'll wonder where it came from.

The Father Holds the Vision

It is your father who guides you to your vision through his attitude toward life. Did he see life as a challenge to be met with courage and excitement or did he feel defeated by responsibility, fate, or lack of love? Did he keep going when he experienced loss or did he take it out on you or your mother? Was he able to regroup from mistakes and still risk himself for his beliefs? If your father gave you an empowering attitude, you can take it and use it as your starting gate, and it can form a strong foundation from which you can see and reach beyond. If your father was depressed or defeated, you may oppose his attitude, but what you are really doing is just flipping the coin. The problem with opposition is that it prevents you from finding your own center, or vision, and causes you to attract depressing relationships that represent your father. *Know that how you interpret what happens to you is more important than what actually happens.* When you can find meaning in or learn from an experience, it won't defeat you. Learn from your father's mistakes; don't repeat them. You do not have to be defined by your parents. Their issues are your building blocks. Build a better and stronger house with what they gave you. You can do this by choosing a strong and positive attitude that will serve you in life. (See Figure 5.1 for the Aries Star.)

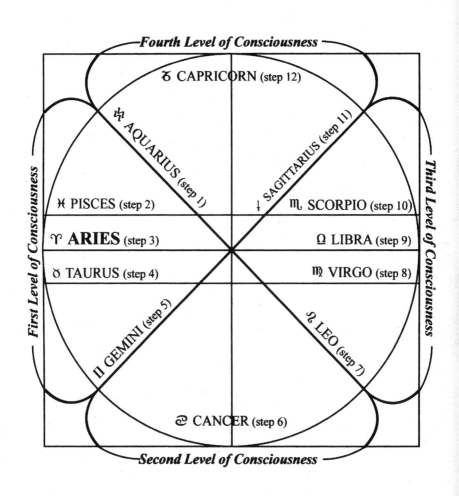

Figure 5.1. The Aries Star

The First Level of Consciousness

The first level of consciousness divides the eleventh house and first step, and the third house and fifth step. Success and freedom seem to be in conflict because success to you still means receiving recognition from others, not from yourself. You must discover through trial and error that the only way to feel strong and valued is to love and believe in yourself. When you do, the world pays attention and begins to give you the support you desired through pleasing other people or meeting their expectations.

Step One: The Eleventh House

Aquarius: Freedom Comes with Success

I used to think that freedom was being adored and loved, but when you are then others expect you to keep pleasing them. I have discovered that I can be free only when I'm alone, but then I miss the attention. I'm so divided and neither choice makes me totally happy. However, when I am alone I find that I am free to imagine and dream and that makes me feel good.

Your fear of losing the comfort of love and its protection keeps you living a compartmentalized life—you are emotionally dependent and you act independent and free. Until you are willing to let go of comfort and attention, you will not be willing to look at what is holding you back. All the adventure you want, all the rewards that lure you will not be yours unless you can deal with being alone. When you can be alone, you can be with others. When you can be alone you are free.

> You are in level one when freedom is the need to escape the moment.
> You are in level two when freedom is your ability to be different.
> (Levels three and four are listed at the end of step one in the fourth level of consciousness.)

Step Two: The Twelfth House

Pisces: The Dream Needs My Protection

When I shared my dream, others attacked it, and so I felt as if I should hide it and protect it. What I learned is that I don't have to accept the judgments of others,

I don't have to protect my dream, it is there to protect me. If I surrender to my dream and believe in it others believe in me.

The dream is there to serve you, not for you to serve it. If you can't connect to your dream it's because you don't feel good enough to imagine a perfect world. Imagination is the building blocks of the creator—if you can't imagine you can't create. If you protect and hide your dreams you will never make them real. Don't accept the criticism of others, they are basing their ideas on their own experiences and dreams. What judgments have you made on dreams?

> You are in level one when your dreams offer you an escape from reality.
> You are in level two when you oppose the dreams of others and pursue your own.
> You are in level three when you have faith in your dream.
> You are in level four when the world is one big dream.

Step Three: The First House

Aries: My Vision Divides My World

I see everyone else going along with a truth they believe in, how can I impose my ideas on them? What right do I have to tell them what I think?

The world will never invite you to express yourself; it will be happy that you keep quiet. Everyone's ego is competing for time and space. If you're going to be heard you're going to have to get in there and make them listen. The more you believe in yourself and your dreams the easier this is. Without a dream you are just another ego that wants attention. With a dream you are a creator, and everyone wants to listen.

> You are in level one if your vision is to save others.
> You are in level two if your vision is to become independent.
> You are in level three if you believe in your vision.
> You are in level four if you know that there is always a greater vision waiting for you.

Step Four: The Second House

Taurus: Love Is the Most Important Thing to Me

I used to feel that being totally loved all the time is what I wanted, but the truth is that it is too demanding to always have someone think you are perfect. I find I can't be me. It makes me want to be different from those I love just to create separation so that I can discover who I am.

You get what you want and you don't want it. I think there is a song like that. Anyway, once you realize that it is not always to your advantage to be the center of attention you are on the way to taming your ego—a major shift. Once you can begin to hide your truth, or what you are doing, you are actually removing your ego from being the center of attention because you have given it another focus—a goal. Now you know that if you give the ego a goal, it will learn patience and wait for its reward. In fact, it loves to be your buddy and support you in your quest to deceive those that expect way too much from you.

> You are in level one if you give unconditional love.
> You are in level two if you confront the authority and risk love.
> You are in level three if you have a goal or a dream that you give your passion to.
> You are in level four when you give unconditional love to yourself.

Step Five: The Third House

Gemini: What Should I Choose?

I used to avoid choices and let everyone else make them because I thought it made my life easier and everyone else happier. But the truth is no one ever thought of what I might want, they never asked me. If you give up your ability to choose, you give up your freedom. I'm learning to say what I want and I'm getting it.

Choice is the key ingredient to change, growth, and knowledge. When you give your choices away, you give your power away. Those who can make decisions, the tough ones, are the people who will move ahead and be leaders. It doesn't even matter if your choice is right or wrong, the person who is not afraid to take the risk and follow his or her instincts is the person who will succeed. You can't define yourself and create an identity until you own your ability to make a choice.

You are in level one if you choose to please others over yourself.

You are in level two if you choose to face the authority that is in the way of your dream.

(Levels three and four are listed at the end of step five in the second level of consciousness.)

The Second Level of Consciousness

The second level of consciousness divides the third house and fifth step, and the fifth house and seventh step. It separates the fearful child who wants to be protected from the empowered young adult who wants to take charge of his or her own choices and life. To enter level two you must find the strength and courage to stand up for what you believe in. What must go are the ideal images of your past, and you must be willing to stand alone and feel the coldness of a new truth that has not yet become your friend. Persevere and you will survive your first winter of little faith until your faith is strong enough to build a roaring fire.

Step Five: The Third House (Second Level)

Gemini: My Choice Is for My Dream

Life used to be a tug of war; I could not decide which path I should take, or what I should do. As soon as I gave up or let go, it all came to me, my dream, my path, and that I had to face those who love me and tell them what I want to do. There is no other way except through the fire.

Once you have your dream you find the courage to meet the opposition. The more you believe in what you are doing, the less opposition you will receive. Others feel the gap of faith and when you don't have faith they attack you and try to control you. But when you do, they know you've already made up your mind.

You are in level three if you choose to make your choices based on your inner voice.

You are in level four if you turn your choices over to a higher power.

Step Six: The Fourth House

Cancer: I Protect Myself from Fear and Criticism

I hate to be criticized because I want to be perfect and I'm afraid I'm not. I also want the truth. The truth hurts, but it makes me strong. I have learned that if I have a dream, then not being perfect is okay because I can make my dream perfect. This gives me confidence and reduces my fears.

When you can shift the criticism of others off you and onto a goal, then it doesn't hurt so much. It is important to be able to detach from your feelings and your beliefs so that you can use them in many ways later on. The dream gives you the means to do this. When you have a dream you only need to be perfect for it, and you're in charge of your dream. At least the one you hold in your heart.

Protection is a powerful issue for the Aries. You are either not protected or overprotected growing up, so there is a great fear of emotional abandonment. You want independence but you are afraid that if you have it you won't find love. It's all based on self-worth and the need for the hero in you to take care of others, particularly the mother. However, you must let go and move forward, you will not find the strength or support you need without expressing and owning your dream.

> You are in level one if you are protecting yourself or others from life.
> You are in level two if you are taking risks and meeting your fears.
> You are in level three if you have faith in your ability to endure the gaps in life, when no one is around to give you support.
> You are in level four when the only protection you need is faith.

Step Seven: The Fifth House

Leo: I Have Trouble Taking Orders from Anyone

It seems I was born unable to listen to others who try to limit and control me. I want to make my own rules; I want to go farther than others want me to go. My greatest desire is to be independent enough to make my own decisions and find my own way. I stand up to authority all the time and that causes conflict and fights. There has to be a better way.

You don't know how to take your authority yet, so you battle. What you are trying to do is prove to yourself that you are strong or stronger than those trying to tell you what to do. When you have enough confidence and experience in life, your independence will come naturally. What is standing in your way is your emotional dependence on those you love. You are afraid if you go they and you won't be happy. If the dependence is too strong, you may create trouble so that you will be pushed away.

> You are in level one if you feel that strength lies in success and attention.
> You are in level two if you are seeking to be your own authority.
> (Levels three and four are listed at the end of step seven in the third level of consciousness.)

The Third Level of Consciousness

The third level of consciousness divides the fifth house and seventh step, and the ninth house and eleventh step. It asks you to have faith in your vision. The choice is yours; you can keep your vision close and perfect or you can risk destroying its perfection by making it real. The illusions of your vision must be let go of and the love that created it must be held on to for you to begin to make it real. What you will discover as you move toward this vision is your truth, that is, what inspires you and what you want to include in your world. Don't give up when others give up on you. Faith calls God to answer your prayers. Faith is how you make the invisible link to your future, the one you have chosen to live in. When you can let go, you create the space God needs to give you what you want. Let go and have faith in your vision and in love.

Step Seven: The Fifth House (Third Level)

Leo: I Am Not Afraid of Fear

It has always been important for me to receive recognition and praise from others, but when I received it, love became a burden—I just had more people to please. I gave up trying to make the right choice and I started looking for answers, not re-

sults. As soon as that happened I became stronger and I was able to see more possibilities in my life.

Once again you reach a turning point. When the ego can see the benefit of not just seeking praise, but looking beyond it, then it is ready to commit to hard work and a goal. Until the ego is willing to work for a greater reward, one that will require it to labor without profit or attention, then you are ready to see your real possibilities. Until this happens you are stuck. You must choose only what brings praise and attention. Not only is seeking praise unsatisfying, but it is also extremely competitive and a waste of energy.

You are in level three if you find strength in faith.
You are in level four if you find strength by turning your desires and
   problems over to a higher power.

Step Eight: The Sixth House

Virgo: I Accept Love the Way Others Choose to Give It

It is so easy to think that you are not loved when you have a certain notion of what love is, and that notion usually includes what was missing in your past. I now realize that there is always love around me if I can just open myself up and experience it different ways.

Everyone wants you to love them their way, not the way you feel like expressing love. It's one reason you don't feel loved. When you associate certain behavior with love you begin to limit your options. Of course, some limitations are essential for a choice to happen, but too many limitations that are not based on true emotions but images that can never be real are dangerous. Women believe that flowers and romance equal love. Men believe that sex, lots of it, means love. Everyone has their own view on it, and finding someone who believes the way you do is part of the process. If you can remove the behavioral choices and recognize the emotion you are seeking, you will increase your chances for love. If flowers and candy make you feel loved, perhaps someone doing the dishes can also make you feel loved. Honor how others want to be loved and you will be loved the way you want it in return.

You are in level one if you feel that doing things for others their way is
   a sacrifice.
You are in level two if you can receive love in a variety of ways.
You are in level three if you can give and receive with equal ease.
You are in level four when you accept whatever you are given and share
   whatever you have.

Step Nine: The Seventh House

Libra: Truth Is in the Vision

*How could I have thought that all I am is what others see in me? Others see what
I do and how I behave, they don't see inside and feel my love and faith, or know
what secrets lay in my soul. If they did, they would know that I am and will be great.*

Once you understand that you are more than the vision of others or what
they see in you, you are on your way. You will now start to investigate what
they have judged and you will pick up the parts of yourself that you let go of
just because someone else didn't like them. What about *your* likes and dis-
likes. Isn't this *your* dream and your world? If it's not, it should be. See beyond
what others see, see into your own heart.

You are in level one if your truth is what others have told you.
You are in level two if you oppose the truth of others.
You are in level three when you have faith in your truth.
You are in level four when truth is the moment.

Step Ten: The Eighth House

Scorpio: I Surrender to the Shadow

*If I am more than what others see in me, I must look at what they have judged. I
am not afraid to see my anger; it was the voice of my truth that saw injustice happening to me. I see that my so-called negative emotions are the parts of me that
refuse to accept the small images and truths that are demanded of them. Perhaps I
should listen to them more closely. They seem to believe that I am greater than I
think I am. Wouldn't it be something if they were right?*

You are so much more than you believe you are, and the only way to get to your greatness is by listening to all of you—the good, the bad, and the ugly. They all have truths to tell you and something to say. When you're not afraid of your negative feelings you will get in touch with a new kind of strength and power, one that goes beyond judgment and fear of abandonment, it's a strength that comes from feeling whole.

> You are in level one when the world is divided between good and bad.
> You are in level two when you are strong enough to look at your anger or negativity.
> You are in level three when you accept it all and use what you desire to build your truth.
> You are in level four when it is your intention that creates good and evil, not your actions.

Step Eleven: The Ninth House

Sagittarius: Wisdom Is Listening to Me

I used to depend on others to point out what I should learn and what was unimportant. Once I realized, however, that my vision of my future was different from others, I knew I needed to take charge of my knowledge. When I did, I discovered so much more and now I determine what I learn and what's important.

Experience is the best teacher. When you learn something firsthand you don't forget it. When you can learn from your mistakes as well as your victories, you will learn in leaps and bounds because you are learning from everything. In fact, mistakes can teach you more than success can. When you make a mistake it is easier to see what went wrong, what was missing; when you know what is missing you can add it to the pot. It may take some time to hone your talents or your timing, or to increase your courage through risk and practice, but you can if you commit to it.

What happens when others don't value the lesson you learned because they wanted you to win? Now you are faced with a problem: you can deny the lesson to make others feel good, which gives you a false sense of harmony. Or can you take the lesson and honor it. By learning even when others don't or when they don't want you to, you take the first step of real defiance, you accept what makes sense and is useful to you. No one has power over this, only you. You have found something no one can control.

> You are in level one if you believe that wisdom is pleasing others.
> You are in level two if you believe that wisdom is confronting others.
> (Levels three and four are listed at the end of step eleven in the fourth level of consciousness.)

The Fourth Level of Consciousness

The fourth level of consciousness divides the ninth house and eleventh step. To enter the fourth level of consciousness you must turn inward and begin to hear your own inner voice. When you do you see your vision and the reward you will seek for your journey. You must participate in your destiny to bring it forth.

Step Eleven: The Ninth House (Fourth Level)

Sagittarius: Wisdom Is Choosing Truth as My Goal

I used to feel that wisdom was the ability to be free to choose whatever I wanted, but that's not true—freedom is a burden and a responsibility when you don't know what to do with it. Once I had a goal I began to see that being able to understand what happened is more important than what actually happened. I now try to go beyond victories and defeats and learn something from them; it's amazing—now I win more often.

When you can go beyond winning and losing and learn from whatever happens, nothing will stop you. You have removed your ego from the situation and it is learning along with you. This will make you confident and give you the courage to take risks, because you're not invested in results. You are choosing truth rather than moving forward with a predetermined perspective.

> You are in level three if you are listening to your inner wisdom.
> You are in level four when you go beyond wisdom and seek your answers in the unknown.

Step Twelve: The Tenth House

Capricorn: My Goal Is My Reward

I used to avoid my fears by thinking they would go away, but they didn't. In fact, they got worse and started to take over my life. I've learned to face fear when it's small and not let it get out of hand. Having a goal and a dream gave me the motivation to do that. A goal helps you stay centered, believe in yourself, and keep moving when things get tough. My goal is everything to me.

Goals are not simple things at all, they come from your inner struggle and the desire of your soul to express its uniqueness in the world. You find your goals once you acknowledge your right to be different. Goals that are created for you don't have the same power, nor do they bring out your passion. When you follow a path that someone else paved for you, you will be more concerned with the reward than the journey and so you will miss the best part. When you pave that path, and know every stone on it, not only are you proud of what you have accomplished, but no one can take it from you, you can do it again and again because you've done it before. You're not dependent on others to do the work.

> You are in level one if you are seeking the reward of instant gratification.
> You are in level two if your reward is fighting or avoiding others who want to tell you what to do.
> You are in level three if you have faith in your dreams and your goals even when others do not.
> You are in level four when your reward is life and the moment.

Step One: The Eleventh House (Fourth Level)

Aquarius: Freedom Is the Wisdom to Have a Goal

It's so easy to use freedom to escape a moment, but the truth is escaping is a temporary reward, and it makes things worse. True freedom comes when I am able to face my fears and go through them, and I find the strength to do this when I have a commitment to a goal. This is wisdom.

When you love freedom with all your heart you won't let fear invade it, you'll want to face that fear and remove it from your life. When you keep things hanging over your head, the problems you tried to avoid become a continuous source of anxiety. Do not be afraid of commitments—the ones you make to yourself free you; the ones you make to others imprison you. Make a commitment to a goal today.

> You are in level three when freedom comes from standing up for your truth.
> You are in level four when freedom is having the courage to open up to a new experience.

The Cross

The cross is composed of the eleventh, fifth, ninth, and third houses and is where change must occur. (See Figure 5.1 on page 109.) The two fixed houses represented by Aquarius and Leo challenge each other to see a greater truth:

Aquarius (eleventh house): *Freedom to be me is found when I can be alone with myself; this allows me to feel connected to my heart.*

Leo (fifth house): *I can be me when I find the courage to express myself and challenge those that disagree with me. The more I believe in me the more others listen. I gain courage and strength and my voice begins to carry authority; when it does others see me as having my own truth. Truth comes to you once you have a vision of what you want to be.*

The two mutable houses represented by Sagittarius and Gemini must anchor themselves in this new truth by taking a stand:

Sagittarius (ninth house): *I must learn that there is truth and knowledge in the part of me that has been judged as unworthy by others. If I listen to this I will gain wisdom and strength.*

Gemini (third house): *I must choose to listen to all of me, and express myself even when others don't want to hear it. This gives me courage and makes me strong.*

TAURUS: Values
(April 21 through May 21)

The hero's heart has made it seem
That you're not real; you're just a dream
It's easy for you to be the ideal
You know how to please, just block how you feel
Don't be afraid to express your pain
It's freedom you seek, not fortune or fame
Hold on; give up—it's a state of mind
Let go of results and you just may find
The vision you're seeking is in your soul
Learn the lesson of pride and you'll see your goal
Let go of your yearnings; give Him your desires
Offer fate and your dream to the heat of the fires
Let them burn and smolder; as they die you are free
When the smoke disappears, your path you will see.

Question Two

About Your Parents: What were your mother's values? Did she live with love and joy, and follow her desires? Or, did she live with fear, which drove her to choose security and live with sorrow?

About Yourself: What are your values? Do you put joy and happiness at the top of your list? Or, do you give your power away by blaming life or others for your circumstances?

Taurus is love, and Taureans' lives are about the pursuit, acceptance, and rejection of this magical, ethereal energy. When they feel loved, Taureans are invincible; when they feel rejected, they are lost and depressed. The lesson of Taurus is to compromise, to accept that love can exist in an imperfect environment. But ideals are not so easily dismissed when they have been your only true and faithful friends. However, your world is changing, and to survive, you must change, too. You must be aware of consequence, of anger and betrayal. You must realize that goodness is not always rewarded, that it must be fought for. Those without power or a voice will be devoured by those who have strength and are hungry or just want to be entertained. Hold on to perfect images and ignore your anger and feelings of disappointment, and you will be on a path that's headed straight for betrayal. The ideals you have chosen to have in your life are images that will disappoint you. You wish to find these images in the world—wrapped, sealed, and perfect from day one. Ask yourself: If that's life, wouldn't life be boring? You've got to see the pieces around you and put them together. You've got to learn to separate what you want from what you don't dissect and eliminate in little pieces rather than take an all or nothing attitude. Yes, letting go is your biggest challenge and you admire anyone who can be tough, heartless, and even cruel. If you're not careful these become your relationships—at least until you learn that loving yourself often means saying no to others. Until you can set boundaries to love, you are its prisoner.

Ideals are created to be shattered. At the core of all ideals is a truth that you can love and take into your heart. If the truth stays in the realm of images, you may sacrifice your life trying to become what is impossible. Your mission is to see beyond the shell, the veneer, the gloss, and the promise. You need to ignore what others say, and see their real intentions and motivation. When you can, you won't be deceived. Solve the mystery in you first; understand your own motivation and the truth of others will become transparent.

How do you discover your own truth? The path is inward, not outward. You must stop chasing your desires and ask yourself what you expect from them, why they are important to you, and how they will change your life if you fulfilled them. Experience will teach you that most desires are dead-end streets. Instead of making you happy, desires increase your discontent; to be satisfied means you need more. If more is based only on quantity, you will increase what you eat, the drugs you take, and the desires you seek. Before long you'll be an addict of something. If you are fearful of following your desires because you're wise enough to know that they can take away your power, you may hide from your feelings and passions in an attempt to be in charge. Either choice is not going to work for long. Sooner or later you will have to give up on holding on or pursuing and just let go; you'll have to let yourself fall into yourself and be alone with you.

The most important thing you can do for you is learn to be alone. I don't mean isolation, I mean time without distraction: walks down a tree-lined road, a moment in a hammock, or twenty minutes in a warm bath. You've got to get to know you—what you feel, think, and desire—and you've got to give yourself time to spin dreams, to imagine, and to fantasize about life. You are never too old for dreams. Most people have trouble being alone because they are afraid of abandonment, that is, if they are not getting attention they fear no one will know they're alive. They are also afraid of their anger. Within you is a great deal of anger for not being heard, for love that was used or discarded, for judgments that hurt, and actions that abused the spirit. If you face this anger, you shatter your ideal images, what would you have then to keep you going, to make you feel warm and safe? What you would have is you. Inside you is an inner voice that wants you to hear it. If you keep ignoring it others will ignore you. When you connect to your inner voice, your attention is redirected—it shifts away from others and the world and turns the focus on you fulfilling your desires. Imagine that: you in charge of you—you relying on you and you making commitments to you—not you expecting things from others and being disappointed. Once you turn within and listen to your instincts you begin to feel noticed and strong.

Let's look at love or your concept of it. Did you know that too much love is as bad as not enough (it's not really love when it's given in excess, it's need)? If your parents doted on your every whim, you expect life to respond to you in the same way. If it doesn't, you may find that you don't want to live in a world where you are not the center of attention, and so instead of moving forward and risking yourself and your dreams, you cut yourself off from those dreams and stay the loving, needy child. Or if your ego is tough enough and your confidence great enough, you may just convince the world that you're a genius to be reckoned with. It's up to you how you use your need for love, but love will be the motivation that drives you forward in life.

What you choose to pursue and protect becomes the bases of your values. If you are protecting yourself from love because you were hurt, you will choose values that are without emotion—they will express the importance of possessions, money, or power. If money replaced love in your household, you may judge it as an evil and a hindrance to love. Ask yourself: What prevented my parents from loving me enough or more? This is the thing you seek in life; this you believe will be your magic wand.

Unfortunately, you discover there is only one magic wand, and it is not a substitute for love, it is self-love. Your mission is to emotionally separate from the love you were given or not given as a child (this does not mean you have to stop loving your parents, you just need distance). You will not be able to begin to love yourself until you are emotionally independent. This is why children who have a tough beginning sometimes get ahead faster—they must turn to themselves for support and listen to themselves for advice—they make that connection to their inner voice early on, and even if they don't see it as love, they are being directed by faith in themselves.

If you are going to separate from the idealistic love you were promised as a child you will have to deal with your anger. Anger is the most misunderstood emotion in the world. Anger shows you where you have given up your truth, where you are living in denial, and where you are afraid to take a stand. You must listen to anger but not act on it. You must give it a voice, but do not direct it at others or yourself. If you learn to deal with your anger when it first arises, you won't have excessive frustration that only knows how to explode.

Let's follow the path of anger (see Figure 6.1):

1. *Accept.* When you are a child you accept, but your acceptance is not based on choice—it is based on necessity. You must accept what your parents offer you, you are dependent on them. As you move forward toward your own desires you begin to discover that some of them are in opposition to your parents' wishes. Now you are in conflict: If you please them you become angry, because you have to give up what you want; if you please yourself they are angry and you have to deal with their anger and disappointment in you. Perfect children are perfect because they give up on pursuing their dreams. Most children are not ready to oppose their parents early on, so they accept the anger and give up their desires.

2. *Rise above.* To avoid anger you can rise above the situation and choose to understand what is going on. If you understand, you can forgive and you can avoid your anger. If you understand, you can show compassion. If your ego is in charge, you may rise above by feeling superior to others.

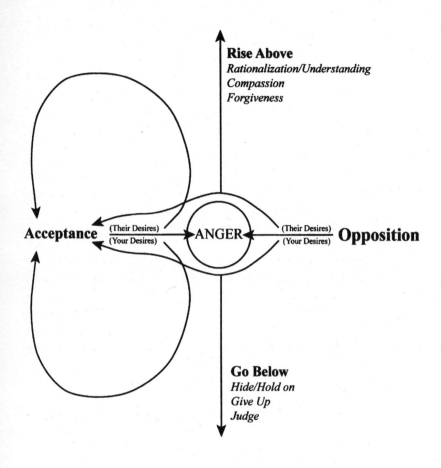

Figure 6.1. The Path of Anger

Opposition Creates:
1) Understanding about self that leads to greater acceptance
2) Understanding about others that leads to greater acceptance

Whichever choice you make without first facing your anger is a choice to escape—not a path to your higher self. When you escape you don't become strong, you become weak and fearful.

3. *Go below.* If you go below to avoid anger, you choose to hide your emotions in the shadows, or you overcompensate for even having these feelings by trying to please more, which only makes you angrier. After all, you're feeling the pull to separate (anger gives distance) and that separation makes you insecure. Now you can judge your anger as terrible and bad. Of course, it's you you're judging and this increases your fear and lack of self-esteem. You can give up and let go of what you want and then tell yourself you didn't want it after all. This creates denial and a wall between your instincts and your desires. If it becomes a pattern, you will totally separate from your inner voice.

4. *Oppose.* There is only one way out of this vicious circle and that is by acknowledging your anger and taking the position of opposition. You must be able to express what others don't want to hear and what they have judged as bad. At first you may just oppose their point of view, but eventually you'll begin to have one of your own. When you begin to stand up for your truth instead of opposing the truth of others, you can begin to see your identity and sense of self emerge. Remember, nothing is truly yours until you're willing to take a stand for it. Dreams stay in fantasyland until you are willing to fight for them.

Until you can face your anger and listen to it you will be ruled by it. If you hide your anger you will bring anger into your life through your relationships, or a boss, or friends. If you always rise above and understand, others will take advantage of you and even abuse you. The only way out of anger is by learning to express what's in your heart without fear. When you stand up for yourself even when no one else listens, *you* listen, you learn about you, you learn about others and what they really believe in, and you learn that anger can be a messenger of truth.

Opposition Is the Path to Truth

Rebelling is probably the most important thing you will ever do in life. Many adults have never achieved this goal. If you don't rebel, you must become a master manipulator, you must know how to get around the demands of others, you must know how to lie and deceive, and in the pursuit of your desires you will lose touch with your truth, the source of your strength, power, and uniqueness. To rebel is really to stand in your truth and be willing to accept the consequences. It's called rebelling because when children do it, it seems they are just being ungrateful, but what they are really doing is finding their own way and their own voice. If your parents encouraged you to express your differences and challenge their rules with reason, rebelling can unfold without too many crises. Unfortunately, most of you won't experience this smooth transition from their rules to your rules. Instead, you will believe that to be heard you must do something outrageously wrong. What you need to do is believe in what you are doing and learn to move out of your emotions and into your head. *You've got to listen to your emotions to know the truth and use your head to express that truth.* No one is going to listen to an emotional outburst.

To stand in your truth you must have the following:

- *The ability to say no.* When you can't say no you can't set limits or shape your own truth. You will be a victim of the desires and expectations of others.
- *A voice.* You need to express your feelings.
- *The ability to take risks.* You must be ready to risk approval and face rejection.
- *Self-worth.* If you never express your feelings you won't discover their value and you won't have self-worth.
- *Faith.* Give up the control. When you know what you want or need and you have expressed it, the next step is faith. Just believe it is possible.
- *Endurance.* You must be able to endure disappointing others. There is no other way to own your own truth.
- *The ability to face obstacles and resistance.* You need obstacles and resistance to find out who you are.
- *The ability to face the unknown.* You've got to be able to put yourself in new situations and learn something new about yourself.
- *The ability to stop asking for permission.* (I'm speaking to adults here.) No one is ever going to give you permission to be you.
- *Awareness of the consequences.* Know the consequences and the price of your actions. If you're not willing to pay the consequence, don't do it.

Why the Rebel Has More Power Than the Pleaser

If you are a rebel you have an advantage over pleasers, even though you still do not know who you are or where you are going. The power you feel is temporary; when you oppose just for power it loses its strength. Real power comes when you can connect your anger and your need to oppose to a goal. So if you are the rebel you've taken an important step, but you will become stuck and disillusioned if you don't continue to grow and make new choices. The following is a list of gifts you have gained for finding the courage to rebel.

- Rebels learn how to face their fears, an essential step in the process of self-development and empowerment. For starters, they're not afraid of losing approval.
- Rebels are willing to step into the unknown. This gives them an advantage.
- Rebels are ready to confront. They have an edge over all the pleasers in the world.
- Rebels learn something new—what you *really* believe in and hopefully what they do too.
- Rebels are not afraid of anger. They do not stop their pursuits because continuing will make someone angry. They are willing to experience your anger.
- Rebels discover how strong their opponents are by challenging them to walk their talk. Knowledge is power.
- Rebels make a deeper connection to their inner voice. The pleaser is more concerned with others. Rebels must rely on their intuition so they begin listening to themselves—a very important step.
- Rebels discover people's secrets and motivations. When you challenge someone, you usually discover something you didn't know. The more you push, the more the truth comes out.
- Rebels are not afraid to stand alone. When you are willing to separate yourself from the group and take a stand for what you believe in, you begin to develop an identity and sense of uniqueness. This is what will make you great.
- Rebels get admiration from others for being able to do what most people can't. When you can stand up for the truth—any truth—others applaud because so few do it. You become a hero just because you have the courage to face the status quo.

- Rebels take the magic out of the forbidden fruit. They're not afraid to be selfish. Everyone wants to say the truth and be selfish—that is, pursue their own dreams and not worry about others. But to do this means you would have to risk your good image and be labeled as bad.

The inability to stand up for yourself or what you believe in is the cause of much depression, anger, abuse, judgment, and injustice. It's the number one step that most people are missing. Those who are angry and confront all the time usually have an area of their life they are protecting, or hiding from.

If You Can't Oppose

When you can't oppose others, so much of your effort and energy is spent in finding ways to get your message across. Your fear of hurting someone's feelings probably comes from your own pain, and your need to protect others is your need to protect you. When you begin to speak up and risk hurting others for your truth, you learn that you actually hurt them less. When your truth comes from your heart it will be heard, even if others don't acknowledge what you say. Silence gives consent, so keep talking. The following problems can enter your life if you refuse to face your anger and stand up for yourself:

- You will learn to manipulate.
- You will need to wait for what you want.
- You will receive only what others believe you deserve or should have.
- You will remain dependent.
- You will be able to express your truth only in an environment of "similarity."
- You won't be able to learn anything different.
- You won't be able to discover how important your ideas are to you.
- You will remain in the world of the unformed, undefined.
- You will work for others who *can* confront.
- You won't get a chance to release the superfluous from your life because everything will be of equal importance.
- You will hold on to anger, which is self-destructive.
- You will never feel strong, certain, or in control.
- Anger and control will be part of all of your relationships because anger is projected.

I hope this little review of the pros and cons of confrontation will help you understand just how important it is. In fact, this is the major turning point. If you can't stand up for yourself, you can't go forward beyond this point.

The Value of Love and Fear

There is a reason your mother and your father don't have joy in their life, and that reason is not you. Just because you weren't a boy doesn't mean you were the cause of their unhappiness. If they needed a boy to inherit the family legacy, they have valued money and tradition over love and you. Taurus is your values, and what you believe you need to either support your dreams or to hold on to what you feel is important. Your dream needs values to hold it up, or it will collapse as soon as there is conflict. Look at your parents' past and their disappointments; look to the reasons they gave up. This is where they lack faith, and this is where you will need faith. Those who can persevere and believe in themselves are the souls that get ahead. Don't blame marriage, children, or other responsibilities for your choices; you decided what was important or should I say fear decided for you. Face your fears. Go for your dreams, it's never too late to turn your life around.

Fear is often created through association. For example, you ate a chocolate chip cookie and got sick, but it might not be from the cookie—maybe you had the flu. If it was the first time you ever tasted a chocolate chip cookie, however, you may continue to associate it with getting sick. We all connect experiences through association—they happened together so they must be related. Not true. You must go back and look at why you are afraid, why you lack motivation, or why you have certain fears.

The Mother Supplies the Values

It is your mother whom you must look to for values. If she believed in love, the family had values that supported love and emotions. If she lived on fear and a need for security, perhaps the family values may be based on image, money, and possessions. If your mother was unhappy, you may find it hard to be happy, because you've taken on *her* depression. If your mother had joy but kept you out of her life and her joy, then you may not trust joy. You will see it as separating. You value whatever brought you closer to your parents or what you believe would have fixed your relationship with them. Your values need to be challenged. This is the path of Taurus. (See Figure 6.2 for the Taurus Star.)

The First Level of Consciousness

The first level of consciousness divides the eleventh house and first step, and the third house and fifth step. It challenges you to stop putting off your dream so that you can pursue more instant pleasures and desires. You are seeking freedom and unconditional love and you can never get it by ignoring responsibility and commitment. What you need to make you feel strong and secure is a goal that builds self-discipline and confidence through work that gives you respect for yourself. Once you are free to make your own choices you will see that to make them wisely requires knowledge and strength of character.

Step One: The Eleventh House

Pisces: My Dreams Are for Tomorrow

My dream used to be all that I lived for, but I realized that everything I was promised was a lie. How can I have love if truth is not there too? So I protected my dream by putting it off into the future and in so doing, I gave up its rewards. This left me feeling weak and without the drive to succeed.

The dream is on hold while you discover the shadow side of your truth. You need to know what your fear limits are, that is, how far you can go on faith when you're afraid. The more you test yourself, the more confident you become and the more you are able to follow your inner voice that is leading you away from what is comfortable and into the world where you can make your dreams real.

> You are in level one if you have given up on your dream or see it as something in the far away future.
> You are in level two if you are willing to let go of love and seek your dream in the unknown.
> (Levels three and four are listed at the end of step one in the fourth level of consciousness.)

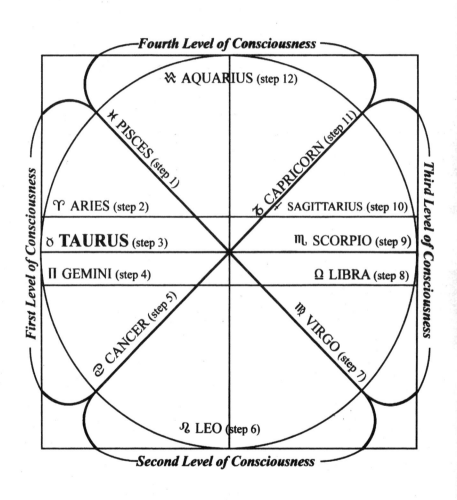

Figure 6.2. The Taurus Star

Step Two: The Twelfth House

Aries: I Need a New Vision

I thought I had a vision of myself and my life, then I learned that I'd have to compromise on that vision, so I didn't want it. I realized that it is ridiculous to think that there are not priorities to life and that I couldn't be happy with some of my desires most of the time and others on occasions. It's my insatiable appetite: it wants it all, and having it all is like having nothing—there is no distinction. I now realize that difference is what makes us special and that it is my uniqueness I must hold on to, not everything else.

The vision gets defined and reduced. It's so much easier to see what's important when you get rid of what you obviously don't need. The more you can reduce your vision to the bare essentials, the easier it will be for you to get through the difficult times, because you will know exactly what you can let go of and what is essential to success or your happiness. This information is sometimes the difference between success and failure. Experience life without luxury, and let go of being perfect—you need far less to achieve and be great than you realize.

> You are in level one when your vision comes from the desire to be free of the expectations of others.
> You are in level two when your vision is to separate or learn how to let go of those you love so that you can move forward in life.
> You are in level three when you can accept criticism without making you feel stupid.
> You are in level four when freedom is living and working toward your dream.

Step Three: The First House

Taurus: Can Love Survive Fear and Darkness?

I used to believe that if I was bad or made a mistake I wouldn't get loved, and in fact sometimes it seemed that way. If you love yourself unconditionally, however, then you can forgive yourself for whatever you do, and with forgiveness you allow love to triumph over fear.

The Taurus is the hero of the shadow. The first house brings only one-half of the circle to the light. You see the other half in others. Whatever you were given at birth, there's another half to discover. Don't feel deprived if you didn't have a loving family, the other side of the journey is waiting for you. Don't look back at what was missing, look forward and see your dream as possible. You've got to see love in yourself to find it in others. Too much love has a shadow, and that shadow is a lack of discipline, laziness, lack of motivation, and a feeling of depression because you have become disconnected from your truth and your goals. Do not be afraid of your shadow, love, or lack of love: they both exist in you—and neither one defines you—together they give you freedom of choice.

You are in level one if you are giving and seeking unconditional love.
You are in level two if you can oppose anyone who impedes your truth.
You are in level three if you are giving love to your dream.
You are in level four when you give unconditional love to yourself.

Step Four: The Second House

Gemini: What I Want Is the Freedom to Choose

It seemed such a simple solution to rules— break free. I thought if I had the freedom to choose, everything would be okay; I'd get to have all the experiences I wanted to without other people putting their fears and limitations on me. However, once I had freedom I realized why the rules were there—they gave me a feeling of security and provided boundaries so that I could see where I was going. Once I accepted limitations as necessary, I could choose where I wanted to limit myself and I could commit to a goal.

The soul sees the easy solution—if I were free to make my own choices, I would have things my way and I wouldn't need a dream at all. That sounds good on paper, but the reality is that to have total freedom is scary, especially when you don't have a goal or understand the consequences. You're dangerously lost in your ego's need to feel strong and powerful, and you still think that that's accomplished by conquering others or doing what they are afraid to do. When you don't have a goal, those with goals can grab you and use your need to be powerful to get you to do their dirty work. This will not be hard. To use choice with power requires you to take responsibility for yourself and that choice. You need to know where you are going and what that choice is meant to accomplish. If it's only getting you a quick high, or an instant pleasure, you will get hooked on highs and pleasure and never learn about real satisfaction or know the joy that comes from commitment and work that brings results.

> You are in level one when your choices are based on your need for love.
> You are in level two when your choices challenge you to let go of love and seek your own path.
> You are in level three when you can go beyond criticism and still believe in yourself and listen to your inner voice.
> You are in level four when you see freedom as the ability to accept rather than choose.

Step Five: The Third House

Cancer: Protection Is for Chickens

I hate being protected and I love being spoiled. It didn't seem to be a problem for me to have both until I realized that my fearlessness was easy as long as someone else was around to clean up the mess. I need to learn how to protect myself and make wise choices.

You have not been able to bridge the gap between feeling fearless and letting others do your work. Fearlessness without accepting consequences is just plain stupid, not courageous. You've got to look ahead and see what effect your choice can have on your whole life, not just this moment. It's time to see the bigger picture; when you do you will be ready to bring to a close your childish need to live without restrictions. If you were born into a family or life that didn't protect you, you seek protection and could get stuck in the quest. The step beyond protection is letting go. Know that you can't let go because you didn't have a choice as a child, things were just taken from you. The adult in you, however, must come to terms with faith and trust. You need to rely on you and the universe—you'll never be let down.

> You are in level one if you need to give protection and receive it.
> You are in level two if you are seeking a goal beyond the boundaries of comfort.
> (Levels three and four are listed at the end of step five in the second level of consciousness.)

The Second Level of Consciousness

The second level of consciousness divides the third house and fifth step, and the fifth house and seventh step. You are being asked to go beyond your need for comfort, protection, and unconditional love and learn to let go. Once you can say no to your ego, and free yourself to pursue things other than physical pleasure, you begin to feel the satisfaction that comes when your spirit is allowed to express its power. Your spirit has the courage to say no to what is not good for you. Once you can say no to pleasure you gain inner strength through discipline and you feel free. It is self-discipline that gives you freedom of choice. When you have self-discipline you are free to follow your heart and your dreams because you have broken through your attachment to your desires.

Step Five: The Third House (Second Level)

Cancer: There Is a Reward That Comes from Faith and Sacrifice

When others said no to me it made me angry and so I never said no to myself. If I wanted something I got it, even if I had to lie. However, once I realized that it's my choice, that I get to decide what's good and bad for me, and that those choices lead to consequences that either shape my life or screw it up, I started paying attention to them and exercising my right to say no. It made me feel empowered. Self-discipline has set me free.

Once you realize that you are in charge and the creator of your life, and once you stop fighting to make your choices and just make them, you begin to own your power. It is more important to say no than yes, at least in your formative years. You need to eliminate choices so that you can experience those that will teach you and prepare you for what you want to do. When there is less to choose from, you can see what lies beyond the sacrifice—it's your truth.

You are in level three if you rely on your inner voice for protection. You are in level four when faith protects you.

Step Six: The Fourth House

Leo: My Ego Is About to Fall

Strength—I thought it was my ability to be selfish and get my needs met, win, be popular, and stay in the spotlight. Boy was I wrong. It takes strength to hold in your need for attention and focus on the problem at hand. The more attention my ego got, the more it wanted. It made me feel like a slave to my desires.

The Taurus has spoiled its ego. You've been good and bad, cruel and kind, strong and weak, and nothing seems to satisfy your worldly needs. Your ego has let you down and you need to let go of taking care of its whims and wishes. It's time to say no to the beast and tame it with a dream and a goal. There are rewards other than instant gratification or fleeting pleasures. It's time to grow up and commit to work, the kind that brings real praise and a lasting sense of satisfaction.

> You are in level one if you see strength as freedom or idealistic love.
> You are in level two if you see strength as power over others.
> You are in level three if you see strength as faith.
> You are in level four if you see strength as the ability to accept and turn things over.

Step Seven: The Fifth House

Virgo: I Accept Sacrifice When It's My Choice

Sacrifice—it used to be the word I hated the most. Everyone would always tell me you have to give this up to have that, or they would force me to give up something I wanted for something I didn't want. Once I took charge of my choices I was able to choose what had to go and what stayed. It made all the difference in the world.

Only choices that are made with faith have power. When you can let go and not be afraid of losing that which you have let go of, you're on the way to true strength. You must learn to let go of your need for others to see you as special in order to enter the tough and competitive arena of life. To succeed you've got to be able to do without attention, and just get the job done. When you waste your choices by rebelling against authority you go nowhere. See beyond those who are in your way. You need a goal to give you vision and strength. Without a goal you will find it hard to have the discipline you need to conquer your desires and to discover the greater rewards of life.

You are in level one if you see letting go as a sacrifice or being weak.
You are in level two if you see letting go as power.
(Levels three and four are listed at the end of step seven in the third
level of consciousness.)

The Third Level of Consciousness

The third level of consciousness divides the fifth house and seventh step, and the ninth house and eleventh step. It wants you to face your fear of criticism and judgment—your fear of not being perfect—and accept yourself for who you are. Your life changes when you can you begin to have faith in yourself. When you go beyond the judgments of others, you discover what they are afraid of and this information gives you power. Now you will be asked to use this knowledge with wisdom—that is, for a good intention, not a selfish one. The beginning of real responsibility and greatness is the ability to use someone's fear and vulnerability to create something good and useful for all.

Step Seven: The Fifth House (Third Level)

Virgo: I See That Dreams Make You Strong

I let go of my dream in the pursuit of my desires and now I see that those who have a dream are strong and those without one are lost and easy to manipulate. I find that I look up to those who know what they want and where they are going. I need a dream of my own.

It is so important to realize that goals and dreams give one strength to move forward in life and make the tough choices. Without a goal why wouldn't you want the choice that brings the greatest pleasure? Once you begin to yearn for some distant reward, you will begin to postpone your desires and choose ones that will get you to where you want to go.

You are in level three when you can go beyond the judgments of others
and hear your inner voice.
You are in level four when you let go of anything that stands in the way
of love and joy.

Step Eight: The Sixth House

Libra: Truth Evolves with You

Everyone always talked so much about truth and yet all they did was lie. No one lived their truth, so how important could it be? I just gave up on truth—which was a mistake. When I felt strong enough to make my own decisions, I realized that I needed a truth to represent me. I could change that truth when I changed. Now that's freedom.

The Taurus often feels that truth stands in the way of love. So often others have denied you what you wanted for some silly truth that meant nothing to you or them. Only when you didn't have a truth did you realize that what you hold on to for protection is what you believe can take away the fear. Truth is your protection against fear. If you are afraid to be angry, you may choose an angry religion or organization to express your truth. Now you have an excuse to do what you couldn't give yourself permission to do or feel. It's all rationalization until you can face your fears and rely on what is really motivating you—it is hoped that it will be love and faith.

> You are in level one when truth is what others have told you it is.
> You are in level two when you confront the truth of others and you seek a greater one.
> You are in level three when you align your truth with your goals.
> You are in level four when truth is found in every moment.

Step Nine: The Seventh House

Scorpio: My Negativity Has Value and Power

When you can use anger and fear, and let go of those who don't belong in your life, you have power. I find myself attracted to those who have little compassion because I see them as strong. What I needed to learn is that when you are tough for a reason and not just to control or have power over someone, you can be tough and have love, too.

The ability to be tough for the right reasons is the hardest thing to do. Those who can speak their truth even when it hurts are souls that get respect and get ahead. When you face your fear of being rejected for trying to express what really lies in your heart, you can open up to the synchronicity and mystery of life. You begin to wonder at the magic or luck that saves you from your own stupidity and ignorance. You become interested in anything that's hidden, mysterious, or in disguise. Seeking to solve the mystery, to unravel the truth, to follow the music or the rhythm of life—this is what catches the Taurus heart. When you listen to yourself you hear the heartbeat of society in rhythm with your own dreams and desires. When you oppose others or try to please too much, you disconnect from yourself and the voice that can lead you to your destiny and your truth.

> You are in level one when you believe all the criticism and the judgments of others.
> You are in level two when you can hide your true intention.
> You are in level three when you accept the good and the bad and use it all in pursuit of your dream.
> You are in level four when you surrender to the love in you for you.

Step Ten: The Eighth House

Sagittarius: My Wisdom Lies in My Ability to Hear Myself

I used to believe that I would be strong and wise when I didn't listen to anyone or anything. Now I know I am wise when I can listen to myself, or the voice within me. Sometimes that voice agrees with others and sometimes it challenges me to change my position. What I've learned is that whatever it tells me, I can trust.

It all becomes very simple: the battles you fought, the people you opposed, the fears of others you faced to show your strength was all just so you could hear yourself and the voice within.

> You are in level one when you listen to what you are taught.
> You are in level two when you challenge what you know.
> You are in level three when you have faith in what you don't know.
> You are in level four when you have faith.

Step Eleven: The Ninth House

Capricorn: *My Reward Is My Dream*

I used to seek the reward I could grasp and count on because there was so little that was not unreal or taken away. Now I know that if I can let go and have faith in what I want and work toward it, I will get the reward I deserve. It all depends on me.

When you begin to depend on yourself and not others you won't be disappointed, and you find that you don't have to stop when others give up, you don't have to slow down when others are tired, and you don't have to hold on when you know you should let go. It is important for you to do your own thing *your* way. When you do, you become a leader, not a follower.

> You are in level one when the reward you seek is before you.
> You are in level two when you let go of protecting what you have and risk yourself and your rewards for a goal.
> (Levels three and four are listed at the end of step eleven in the fourth level of consciousness.)

The Fourth Level of Consciousness

The fourth level of consciousness divides the ninth house and eleventh step. It wants you to see freedom as the ability to pursue your dream and accept whatever reward comes your way. Both freedom and reward are found in the moment as by-products of the things you do, not end results that add to your position or possession. There is nothing more rewarding than following your heart. But to follow your heart takes courage. You must be able to go beyond the fears of others (who will try to stop you) and discover the power of self-discipline and self-acceptance.

Step Eleven: The Ninth House (Fourth Level)

Capricorn: *My Reward Is Seeing Freedom as My Dream*

I now know that the real reward is doing what you love, not seeking pleasure in the moment. When you do what you love you feel good inside and you don't need a reward—you have it. The freedom I sought so desperately was hiding in my beliefs and commitment to my dream.

You have reached a great truth when you realize that doing what you love is what it is all about. To do what you love you must stop protecting yourself, learn to let go, have faith, and own your strength and ability to pursue what you want in life. You can do this when the judgments of others no longer bother you, because you meet them with a greater truth—you are a good and loving person and no one can take that from you.

> You are in level three when you are not afraid to expose your dream to others.
> You are in level four when you are living your dream because you do it every day.

Step Twelve: The Tenth House

Aquarius: My Reward Is the Freedom to Be Me

In my past I thought freedom was the ability to do anything I wanted. Was I wrong? Instead of being free I found myself controlled by everyone who offered me something I wanted. I needed self-discipline to be free and I needed to be able to feel so good about myself that it didn't matter what others said.

Stop seeking love and look to yourself for support and validation, and your life can begin to turn around. As long as others can make you feel badly about what you are doing or who you are, you will be controlled by their ability to be negative. It takes great strength to be joyful and strong. You must hold on to joy and good feelings even when others are trying to take them away or control you. Commit to joy and you'll find freedom.

> You are in level one if freedom is an escape.
> You are in level two if freedom is the freedom to choose.
> You are in level three if freedom is the ability to express what makes you different.
> You are in level four when freedom is the reward of your pursuit of truth.

Step One: The Eleventh House (Fourth Level)

Pisces: I See My Dream in the Choices I Make Each Day

Putting things off is different from sorting them out. A quick fix works in an emergency. When you use quick fixes every day, you avoid problems. Instead of fixing them, you give them power. They won't go away. I used to put things off and think that they would work themselves out. What I've learned to do instead is to do what I can now and turn the rest over to my higher self. If I'm willing to face my fears, I get help from everyone; when I hide from my fears, I live in them.

The more faith you have in your dream the more faith you have in yourself. Choose for your dream every day and feel good about yourself, and you can begin to see results almost right away. When you have a goal and a dream it is easier to be self-disciplined and it's easier to accept criticism without taking it to heart. Your ability to accept and let go has given you the freedom to pursue your dreams.

> You are in level three when others don't believe in you and your dreams but you do.
> You are in level four when you choose for your dream every day in all that you do.

The Cross

The cross is composed of the eleventh, fifth, ninth, and third houses and is where change must occur. (See Figure 6.2 on page 133.) The two fixed houses represented by Pisces and Virgo challenge each other to see a greater truth:

Pisces (eleventh house): *The dream will be seen and accepted once it is not protected—once it can be shared or viewed as a source of strength, not a place to escape.*

Virgo (fifth house): *You see dreams as weak when you are young and unable to see beyond desire and ahead to consequences. Dreams slow you down and don't give you quick rewards. You've got to work for dreams and postpone gratification. When you're wise enough to see dreams as a source of power, you will own your own dreams and align yourself with those who are committed to theirs.*

The two mutable houses represented by Capricorn and Cancer must anchor themselves in this new truth by taking a stand:

Capricorn (ninth house): *When you have self-worth, you are ready to accept its rewards, not its substitutes. You are no longer satisfied with just sensual pleasure or quick fixes; you want something more lasting, something with meaning and purpose. The judgments of others don't bother you, and this sets you free—free to see where your spiritual path is leading you and where your destiny calls.*

Cancer (third house): *When you stop protecting your dream, you begin to choose for truth, you hear your inner voice, and you gain the self-discipline you need to begin to see your self-worth.*

PART THREE

The Second Level of Consciousness

"The virtue of all achievement is victory over oneself.
Those who know this victory can never be defeated."

—A. J. Cronin

The second level of consciousness is reached when the inner voice has gained enough courage to risk itself against the authority. You must have built within you enough frustration or passion to want to go beyond the boundaries that hold you back. These boundaries may include your parents, an authority figure, the town you grew up in, and the environment you know, and now you want to go beyond these limits and risk yourself in the unknown. This happens in Gemini, the third house and the fifth step on your journey. To move forward, old ideals and images must be left behind. It's time to let the perfect picture shatter and begin to listen to your heart. Know that there is always a way when you follow your heart, but that way may not be a straight road or a clear path. What is being asked of you is faith. Can you believe in your own abilities and stand up for them, risk them in the competitive arena, and move forward through disappointment and fear? What lies ahead is not easy. The second level is the hardest to navigate because the waters are filled with sharks. These sharks are the desires, greed, jealousies, and expectations of others—their need to control you and keep you from the prizes they are seeking. If you have talent they will want to squelch it; if you have passion it will be doused with water; if you have faith it will be tested; and if you don't believe in yourself—if you do not have a connection to your instincts and inner voice—you will be stopped by the fears and failures that are not yours. Your path is unique: Learn from others, but know that you have your own special destiny to fulfill.

If you have faith in your dreams and are connected to your instincts and listen to them above all else, if you can persevere when others abandon you, and if you are unafraid to go into the shadow and see someone's real intentions and motivations rather than their promises, you will survive this part of the journey—with help, magic, good friends, and many surprises. It is not how talented you are that will get you to the top—though talent is important once you get there—it is how committed and dedicated you are to your journey, how versatile you are in dealing with life's obstacles, and how quickly you learn and see opportunity. You win the race with faith. You win the opportunity to express your uniqueness with commitment. If you don't have these two qualities, go back and study the first four steps again.

GEMINI: Choice
(May 22 through June 21)

Gemini is the sign of choice
To use it well you need a voice
One that's anchored in intention
One that goes beyond protection
To find the truth you need to choose
Both good and bad, win and lose
In every moment you can learn
There's something new at every turn
Don't seek just praise or rejection
Don't choose failure or perfection
Follow your heart, it knows the way.
And please add play to balance your day.

Question Three

About Your Parents: Did your father have enough faith to take risks in life? Did his risks pay off?

About Yourself: Have you taken any risks for your dreams or goals? If not, why not?

Some of you were born wealthy and famous, others had to struggle to survive, but what lies in both your hands makes you equal—the first equalizer in the universe is choice. It may seem like such a simple ineffective tool because each person has the ability to choose and does so every day of his or her life.

But few pay attention to the power of choice and therefore choose wisely. The advantages you begin with are important only when you use them to serve either yourself or your dreams. The soul with money and opportunity may end up on drugs or dead, and the soul who had nothing but chose with conviction and faith may easily be the owner of a multi-million-dollar business. It is not usually one choice that changes our lives, but one choice has that kind of power.

Choice is what creates your world. You have chosen your way into your present dilemma. Choice surrounds you; it is the voice of creation that wants you to participate in the game. You make a choice even when you choose not to choose. When you avoid a choice you invite someone else to step in and make it for you. You've just given your power away. There are hundreds of people anxious to take your power and use it for their own purpose. The collective voice refuses all the time to choose and express their opinion, this allows anyone, even a madman, to step forth and make decisions for the majority. It happens all the time. It's how tyrants live and survive.

Kinds of Choices

There are four kinds of choices you can make in your life and each one rules a level of consciousness.

Choice One: First Level: Pleasing

The choice to please is the choice of the first level of consciousness. When you please others you give your power away unless you are using this level after completing all the rest. When you choose to please because it comes from your heart and not because you need something from someone, this choice has power. However, most choices to please are made out of fear, fear of being rejected, fear of disappointing those you love, fear of being abandoned, and so on. You are afraid to own your power when all your choices are about others. There is nothing spiritual about leaving yourself out of the picture. So if you have told yourself that the reason you give up your choices is to make others feel good, you're lying to yourself. When you can say no without guilt, I'll believe you. The inability to include you comes from a lack of self-consciousness, or self-worth. You do not know enough about you because your world has revolved around others and you don't know how to get out of it. It takes a commitment to yourself and the courage to try, to get the job done. If this is your problem, read the chapter on Aries.

Choice Two: Second Level: Self

The choice for self is difficult to make for two reasons: rejection and confrontation. You don't get praised for making a "selfish" choice, at least not in the beginning. When you begin to succeed because you are taking care of your own needs, however, others will pay attention and the recognition that was denied will return with something more—respect. It is only through the self that one becomes self-less. Imagine a world where everyone didn't expect others to fulfill them? When you have enough you want to share, and giving comes from the heart. Once you give from the heart, connecting to hearts is easy. Loneliness is eradicated because you feel the link to others and yourself and now you have the power to have that feeling whenever you desire—just make a choice to give.

Conflict is more difficult to deal with than selfishness. To stay in the second level you must stand up for your choice and oppose the authority in your life. The more dependent you are emotionally and physically, the more difficult this stage of the journey will be. How can you create dissatisfaction in others when your security depends on making them happy? You won't. The more you take responsibility for yourself, the less you *need* others and the easier it will be to choose for you and your dreams.

Choice Three: Third Level: Truth

Once you can choose for others and yourself you are ready for the next step: the choice for truth. What you will learn is that choosing to please yourself gets you only a little further than pleasing others; all you've done is flip the coin. The sea parts and the obstacles are removed when you are ready to choose for the truth and let go of protecting them or you. You are protecting your images and ideals, the world the way you saw it as a child. Go beyond your illusions that keep you a prisoner of your past and accept a truth that is greater, one that will encompass the new you that is emerging. When you are ready to see what may shatter the beliefs that have protected or limited you, you are ready for success, and the path that leads to faith. You cannot get strong, really strong, until you are capable of adjusting the beliefs that support you. As you grow they should change, but all too often they stay the same and growth stays compressed inside a container that does not allow it to do its best. Open yourself up to the truth, to a greater truth than you now hold dear, and your path will unfold and your spirit will soar and be happy.

Choice Four: Fourth Level: Faith

The best choice all the time is the choice of faith. When you reach a level of consciousness where you can see just how wonderfully you are supported by the universe, how much all your needs are truly heard and met, when you have the faith to let go, then you're ready for the choice of faith. The choice of faith invites the magic and miracles to participate in your journey. When you have faith you allow God's creativity to come into the picture. You are learning from the Master and He enjoys anyone with the spirit and faith to let Him play. When you don't have faith you don't have adventure, excitement, change, and growth. Life stays the same and you begin to die instead of thrive. Try to have faith in your small choices: Turn them over and let go of the control. Stop yourself from panicking and trying to make something happen when everything you do only leads to a dead end. Don't give up: allow faith to participate. If you didn't get a return phone call, don't think it's because you've done something wrong. Everything has a reason and if you have faith and patience you'll begin to see the grand picture. The more faith you have the more you can do because the more responsibility is lifted from your shoulders. Gone is worry and fear because you understand that everything happens for the *right* reason. This is the place that you must strive for, and just the striving brings greater satisfaction and results.

Choices Teach You to Reflect

A choice temporarily stops you by giving you more than one option. The choice puts you in conflict with your desires and forces you to organize them into a hierarchy of importance. Because you believe you can have only one, you stop and ponder which choice will serve or fulfill you more. A choice reverses your thought process and forces you to go back and reexamine your actions, motivation, and position, allowing you to adjust your vision and your dream. When you face the fear of losing or letting go, you suddenly become aware of its value. The fear of not having it in your life and the difficulty you have in moving forward without it changes your perception and interpretation of events. You begin to look below the surface, to go beyond what things appear to be, and you begin to understand true motivation. The more your choices encourage you to reflect, the more your mind gets used to going back and repositioning you in your thoughts and actions. It becomes an automatic process that eventually can be done in a blink of an eye. This process is essential to your ability to interpret your experiences, glean the gifts, and move forward without fear.

If for any reason you are never allowed to think for yourself, make decisions, or make mistakes, you will not develop this process and the world will appear just as it presents itself. There is nothing more dangerous than this. Nothing is exactly as it seems. Life is an iceberg, and you're the *Titanic*—if you don't know how to see what lies under the surface, a simple little pile of snow could take you down.

Have You Made These Important Decisions Yet?

Following are three important decisions you will have to face before you can move forward in your life and in this book. Have you made them yet?

1. Whose dream am I going to live—mine or someone else's?
2. What is important to me?
3. What is my intention?

You need to look at what's important, and what's important will be determined on whose dream you are living. Ask yourself what do you want to create, receive, or accomplish from your quest? What are the expectations you have? Do you want to express yourself, your ideas, and see them live? Do you want recognition, power, money, and acceptance? Do you want to change the establishment, challenge the beliefs of others, or transform the world? The weakest intention is the desire for security and safety. This makes you follow fear, not the courage of your heart.

How Prepared Are You to Make Choices?

Be prepared. If you *know* the problem, it's only a matter of time before it's solved. Your problem now is you. You need to understand who you are and where you're going, or you'll have trouble getting there. Answer the following questions and you may understand what is missing in your awareness.

- Is there someone you cannot leave behind? Are you trying to make someone happy? Do you feel guilty about pursuing your own life?
- Are you afraid of not having enough?
- Are you afraid of being alone or not recognized?
- Do you have a passion?
- Are you afraid of being emotionally or physically abandoned by family and friends?
- Do you have a voice? Can you say no to others?
- Can you separate yourself from the group and do your own thing?
- Do you listen to your instincts? (*This is your inner guide and it is an essential part of the journey.*)
- Do you still need praise or fear rejection?
- Do you have a plan or a strategy for your life?
- Are you actively working on your dream?
- Do you know your values and what your limits are?
- Are you too dependent on the opinions of others?
- Can you support yourself?
- Do you like challenges?
- Can you see yourself successful?
- Does anger frighten you?
- Does disappointment stop you?
- Do you believe you can achieve what you desire?

The more you rely on yourself, the stronger your instincts become. Find a goal and you will find the courage to separate, the confidence to connect, and the faith to pursue your journey—and you will take your leap of faith.

Interpreting Your Experiences

Once you've made a commitment to yourself and your destiny, you need to look at how you interpret the results of your choices. Your ability to accumulate different kinds of opinions from different sources and select what is important is the key ingredient to a smart and clever mind. Here are some points to ponder.

Books

What can you learn from books? A lot! Whatever it is you want to be, someone has done it before, and chances are either someone has written a book on that person or they've written one themselves. Biographies are a wonderful way of helping you experience your dreams. With the Internet, there is no reason to be uninformed. There are oodles of information out there on everything. Remember, information is power.

Role Models

Your role models (such as parents, teachers, and friends) have a great influence on you. It's how you initially learn—through example. If your examples don't have a lot of firsthand knowledge or experience, they may not be able to pass it on to you. Pick a role model, either someone you know, or someone who has accomplished what you would like to do, and observe them, copy them—learn from them. That's the easiest way to learn how to get the job done.

The Negative

Ignorance of the law is no excuse, legally and in life, too. You need experience, and the wisdom that comes from it, to survive in the competitive world. If you still believe in your childhood fantasies of right and wrong, you'll be in trouble. If you have to tell the truth, you'll be lied to constantly. If you have to be right, you'll always be compromised. *Life will balance your beliefs with opposition until you can let go of choice and not choose for yourself or others, but choose to know, to learn, and to grow.*

Some people pay too much attention to what can go wrong, thus discouraging others before they start, but most people overlook the negative, hoping it will go away or never show its face. It always does. Face the negative, put it together with the positive, and look at the whole picture. Don't keep them separate.

Isolation

What isolates you is what you haven't given voice to. The feelings and emotions you hold inside are your source for creativity and the reason for your isolation. Whatever you hold on to becomes a magnet that attracts others. If you are angry and afraid to express it, you attract and are attracted to angry people. If you are afraid to set limits, you attract others without limits. If you do not have a dream, you attract someone with dreams that take over your life. Your best protection is always self-understanding and balance. When you can do it all, you can have it all.

Too Much Information

If you feel as if you have to know everything, you'll know nothing. The people who are really smart know what is important and what isn't. They get the whole picture and add important details, not every step. They can reduce an idea to one sentence—sometimes one word. Smart people know what doesn't belong more than what does.

Instinct

Your instinct is the best guide you can have. You develop it by using it. If you never listen to yourself, you never hear your instincts even when they're screaming at you. The more you pay attention to your needs and your dreams, the more you can hear the voice within. This voice can see beyond appearances; it's your compass that will show you which direction to go, who to trust, and when to go forward or let go.

Self-Denial

Self-denial is nothing more than fear that is willing to hold on to illusion even at the risk of living a lie. You'd rather pretend to be happy than be happy, pretend to create than create, pretend to have courage than admit you are afraid. Be honest with yourself. You can't build a good relationship with you if you never fess up and tell the truth.

Things to Remember When Making a Choice

Every time you make a choice you position yourself for the next one. If you can look at life as a pool game, you will see that your next shot is as important to think about as the present one. If the choice you make leaves you without another choice—how good can it be? Thus, choices become the links in a chain that either weigh you down or pull you toward your goals.

Following are things to keep in mind on your quest to make good and powerful choices. Let these thoughts challenge your present patterns and actions.

- Don't focus on results. When your mind is on the task at hand and not focused on results, you'll get results.
- Separate what you do or don't do correctly and what needs work or improvement.
- Seek council from someone who knows more than you; don't ask friends for advice who just want you to feel good.
- Seek council from someone who is not invested in your results.
- Choose the choice that both fits your rational needs and "feels" the best. Intuition is important.
- Don't lie to yourself. Face the facts.
- Consider whether the choice moves you closer to your goals.
- Know your most selfish position. Ask yourself what you would do if you didn't have anything or anyone else to worry about.
- Consider: What is the best that can happen? What's the worst that can happen? Are you willing and capable of accepting the results?
- Once you have your position, challenge it yourself, and let others challenge you, too. If you can hold your own and still believe in what you want after everyone has had his or her say, you're ready to decide.

Rubber Banding Back

The most dangerous time is immediately after you've made the choice for your dream. A greater fear begins to seep into your consciousness after the joy of having taken a new choice fades. You now feel alone. You begin to question whether or not you can make it all by yourself. If you give in to the fear, you'll turn around and run back, hoping to patch up your differences, afraid to ever make a choice again that leaves you out of your comfort zone and alone. What you need to do is nothing. Hold your position and let it become comfortable. You're in a new environment; it takes time before it is familiar.

Holding Two Conflicting Points of View

When you have been through the struggle for self, you learn that it is all right not to agree. You learn that you don't have to accept or oppose someone else's opinion. You can hold your own point of view and they can, too. In fact, you may learn something from your differences. The gift of tolerance is the beginning of unity.

When you can play with two thoughts, two emotions, and two points of view, you begin to play with manipulating your environment. You need to be able to shift others without having to always confront them.

A Focal Point

You've proven to yourself that your opinion is the most important—you have a position, a focal point on which you can measure everything else. What next? Having this point allows you to change it or move it. Remember, you can't alter a position if you don't have one. So it's not so important what your position is at first, it's more important to take one then improve it.

If you never make choices, you create an environment for others to step in and take over. Following are things you can invite into your life if you avoid choice:

- You serve as a scapegoat for others.
- You give your power away and invite someone in to tell you what to do.
- You keep yourself stuck or paralyzed.
- You're condemned to a life of repetition.
- You avoid responsibility because it always leads to choice.
- You can't make commitments, so you can only go so far in a relationship or in a career.
- You become a great manipulator and liar. You deceive yourself.
- You live in fantasy.
- You choose others who reject you; this way you can blame your lack of advancement or relationships on the world and not on your unworthiness or fear of taking a stand.
- You take on too much responsibility because you can't choose or let go.
- You live in anger and frustration because you are not moving forward and using your talents and your spirit.

- You block change from your life because something new will challenge your position.
- You make your world smaller and smaller and wonder why you feel so insecure and unhappy.
- You become a pleaser.
- You have no desires or passion because these would lead to action and choice.

When you make good choices you open yourself up to new opportunities and you begin to feel strong, confident, and powerful. Through good choices, the following can come into your life:

- You gain knowledge of yourself and others.
- You gain faith in your ability to make choices, because a choice is a risk.
- You eliminate information. You know and understand more what you really need.
- You see yourself as a person of action.
- You turn knowledge into wisdom through experience.
- You can expand your horizons because you know how to commit and let go.
- You begin to see beyond the packaging and the glitter. You learn to trust yourself.
- Others can rely on you to add your opinion.
- You connect to your inner voice and inner guide.
- You learn from your mistakes.
- You are open to opportunity and so you see it.
- You change your image.
- You invite the universe to surprise you. This is how you attract luck.
- You shape and create your world. It gives you creative power.

The Father Teaches You How to Choose

Your father is where you learn the power of choice. Did your father believe enough in himself to reach out and take a risk? Did he succeed when he did? If your father never took risks for his dreams, he has taught you to be afraid and not to believe in your spirit. If your father took risks all the time and they brought your family down and into debt, you may be afraid to take risks because he took all the wrong ones. If your father took risks and succeeded, how-ever, you will be given one of the greatest gifts of all: the ability to take a chance for what lies in your heart. (See Figure 7.1 for the Gemini Star.)

The First Level of Consciousness

The first level of consciousness divides the eleventh house and first step, and the third house and fifth step. It challenges the soul to not be afraid to de-stroy someone else's truth through their new and creative vision. If you pro-tect others you will limit yourself. You must create what lies in your heart. Others need to have their truth challenged if they are going to grow; they need to let go of the old and move into new and better ideas. Fear pushes you to seek a vision in the future and ignore your own path now. When your ego is strong enough to let go of its need for praise and approval, you'll be ready for a vision that will lead you to your destiny.

Step One: The Eleventh House

Aries: I'm Everything to Everyone

I used to believe that it was better to be loved by many hearts than by one. Why choose when there are so many delightful possibilities. After years of seeking, play-ing, and trying to live up to everyone's expectations, however, I realize that there is something wonderful about being special to just one person. They know you without you having to prove yourself; they understand you without you having to explain; they love you in spite of the extra pounds or the jokes that just don't come as easily or quickly as they did once long ago. You are loved for being you.

The Gemini is afraid to choose what or who will inspire it, what or who will represent its truth in its perfect world. As long as you need to be the hero, the image of perfection, you cannot make a commitment to one path, one purpose, or one person. Without a commitment you don't get the big reward; you get the quick fixes, the fun moments, the jokes, the tricks, the laughter, and the fun. This is the icing of life, but if you eat a tin of icing without a cake, you know it can make you sick in no time. Life needs a bit of struggle to highlight the joy; it needs hard work to bring a different kind of satisfaction into the picture. When you work hard for something you feel good about it

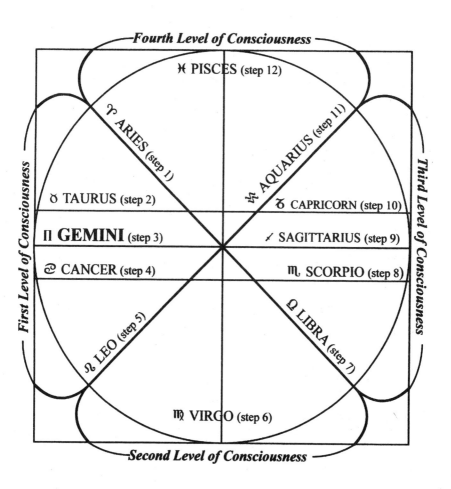

Figure 7.1. The Gemini Star

and yourself. When it comes easy it goes easy. Mix them up, that's what you're good at. Life is about variety but it's got to have a core. You need a vision to grow your apple around.

> You are in level one if you need to be everyone's hero.
> You are in level two if you have a vision you want to pursue.
> (Levels three and four are listed at the end of step one in the fourth level of consciousness.)

Step Two: The Twelfth House

Taurus: Everyone Loves Me

Love is a tricky thing: I need it in my life, but it takes too much from me. I want everyone to see me as perfect, so I give up much more than I should to make sure I'm loved. Finally I had to let go, and when I did I found out that I didn't have to do all that. The people who really loved me were there. The people who were using me left. I'd say that's not bad results.

The Gemini struggles with seeing itself as worthy of love. The souls that have been able to challenge others with their voice will be in a better position. If you haven't learned to say no, or oppose others yet, then being a Gemini will not be fun. Here is where you get caught in the grip of choice. You can't move forward or go back until you either surrender your whole truth and become someone else's slave or you let go and risk it all—risk love and protection, your ego, and your illusions all for the illusive promise of something called truth and a dream.

> You are in level one when you want to be loved by everyone.
> You are in level two when you want to be free of dependent love.
> You are in level three when you have faith in yourself.
> You are in level four when you love yourself unconditionally.

Step Three: The First House

Gemini: I Seek Knowledge and Wisdom to Make My Choices

In the past I would give up my choice to someone who seemed to know more than me. If I went to a professional or anyone with more knowledge, I gave in to them—

not anymore. I've learned that my instincts, my inner voice, are wiser than truth or knowledge, and that when I feel something strongly I need to listen to it and choose what it tells me, even when the "professional" is saying differently.

If you are not connected to your inner voice and it is not what is guiding you, you resort to manipulation and the power of your charisma. The more you listen to you and not to your ego, the more you are not afraid to reveal your ambition and desire to be taken seriously. This allows you to feel satisfied with yourself, instead of worried about approval. The problem is your feelings of unworthiness: You are overcompensating for them by not taking yourself seriously and by hoping someone else will see your value and your worth without you pointing it out. You need to own your power through commitment and perseverance, then others will respect you and give you what you deserve.

If you take on too much responsibility for others, and hope that they will reward you automatically, you will be sadly disappointed. You want to believe that the reward is not important, that it is selfless love that really matters, so you allow yourself to be used by others who see your desire and use it for their own end. When you can ask for what's coming to you, you won't have to.

You are in level one if your choices are made to gain acceptance and approval.
You are in level two if your choices challenge the truth of others.
You are in level three if you believe you deserve the big reward.
You are in level four if you make choices for your dream.

Step Four: The Second House

Cancer: I Protect My Fears and Weaknesses

I used to hold in everything that might create controversy, because it was so important to me to be accepted or recognized. But now I don't get upset if someone criticizes me; I know that they're afraid and that if I believe in myself, they can't control me.

You value compassion and protection and it gets you in trouble. Chances are you were not protected emotionally as a child and you're still looking for someone to take care of you. Not a wise move. If you are the caretaker, you enter a relationship by doing everything and wondering why, later on, none of your needs get met. You set yourself up to be deprived. You must slow down and allow others to participate in fulfilling the needs of the moment. Everyone can do something, no matter how small—it all counts. Stop protecting yourself and begin to make the tough choices. Risk your ego being hurt for the truth. If you can't look at the truth, you're headed for disaster. The sooner you know the truth the easier it is to adjust.

> You are in level one if you give or receive too much protection.
> You are in level two when you go beyond your fears for others and take a risk.
> You are in level three when you have faith in you and your dream.
> You are in level four when you have faith in each moment.

Step Five: The Third House

Leo: I'm Strong If I'm Free

I used to feel that if I was free, I was strong, confident, and charismatic and if I wasn't free, I lost my power. This means no commitments and a lot of pressure. I couldn't keep doing it and besides, those who make commitments actually do less work. I had to change my ways—it was a matter of survival.

Your ego is your asset and the problem. Don't let it get in the way of making the right choices. It wants to be free to be it all. That's fine when you're a teenager trying to discover who you are and where you're going, but it doesn't work when you want to create a life. You've got to commit and learn how to commit in stages. Not everyone deserves all of your loyalty or your perfectionism. You will not decrease your value if you let go, if you make a mistake, or if you just don't show up. You're human. Don't try to be the hero all of the time. Be attentive where attention is needed, and let go of the rest. When you give the same to everything, something's got to give.

> You are in level one if you feel that strength is dominance or pleasing others.
> You are in level two if strength is standing up to the authority.
> (Levels three and four are listed at the end of step five in the second level of consciousness.)

The Second Level of Consciousness

The second level of consciousness divides the third house and fifth step, and the fifth house and seventh step. It asks that you let go of supporting the truth of others and accept your own uniqueness and vision. Until you feel the inner necessity to express your differences in spite of what others say and do, you cannot pursue your dreams. When the ego lets go of seeking praise and begins to pursue the truth, you become strong and feel good about yourself and your destiny.

Step Five: The Third House (Second Level)

Leo: I Must Choose for My Truth

Most of my life I tried to avoid making important decisions, because they were important and I never felt prepared or smart enough to step up to the plate. Experience has taught me that you never feel smart or good enough and the best way to choose is by listening to your instincts and by letting go of the small stuff—yes, it's all small stuff.

D day has arrived. No more excuses. You've got to take charge of your ego and let it feel sad, disappointed, or depressed—it'll get over it. Life is passing you by because you won't make the important choices; you're afraid to decide what has priority in your life and what doesn't. If you choose to discover your own truth, you're on your way to becoming a creator; if you don't, you will still keep auditioning for the part. There's no escape, so surrender.

> You are in level three if strength is faith.
> You are in level four if strength is turning your problems over to a higher power.

Step Six: The Fourth House

Virgo: Faith for Truth

I know that my desire to protect myself from the judgments of others has prevented me from finding my truth; I want others to see me as perfect and good and so I've held on to pleasing and doing the "right" thing. I now know that I need my truth to feel strong and that I must stand up for what I want or I'll never get it.

The moment you choose for what you want right now and stop waiting for the perfect moment is when you take your power and become a creator. Don't wait, act now. There is no better time than right now.

> You are in level one if you are holding on to a future reward.
> You are in level two if you can commit to your dream right now.
> You are in level three if you have faith in your own wisdom and are not afraid to ask for what you want.
> You are in level four if you have faith in your dream.

Step Seven: The Fifth House

Libra: My Strength Is My Truth

I've always been afraid of getting in touch with my passion because I'd be forced to follow it and face my fears. The truth is that I want, more than anything else, to do only what I love, but I've been too worried about what others think and what inspires them than what lifts my spirit and soul. Life is about my vision and what it inspires in me. I must choose to listen to that and nothing else.

When you see your truth as your strength, you are inspired by it and that makes you strong. Inspiration gives the spirit strength and when the spirit has strength the impossible gets done. Spirit does not know the word "no." It only knows how to lead and choose for unity and healing. When you are strong enough to believe in your truth you find that you become a leader because you have the ability to inspire others. Now you've got a true responsibility—to stay committed to your path so that others can follow you and gain strength from your choices.

> You are in level one when you listen to what others tell you.
> You are in level two when you challenge what others tell you.
> (Levels three and four are listed at the end of step seven in the third level of consciousness.)

The Third Level of Consciousness

The third level of consciousness divides the fifth house and seventh step, and the ninth house and eleventh step. It demands you take nothing personally and start seeing everything that happens around you as a message, not an attack. It's time to see that the universe wants to help you and that you have guides inside through your voice and outside through circumstances that give a message. When you accept that you are loved and guided you will open up to real faith and the third level of consciousness.

Step Seven: The Fifth House (Third Level)

Libra: I Can Face Criticism When I Have a Truth and a Dream

I find that the more I know who I am and where I am going the easier it is to face the judgments and criticism of others. This makes me strong and I begin to accept more of myself. Not everyone's opinion should shape or define me. I must decide what needs improving and what does not.

The more you listen to yourself the stronger you will become. Too many opinions can be confusing. You can't please everyone. And when you please yourself and do what's right for you, everyone pays attention; it doesn't matter if you are doing what they think best, they respect and admire you.

> You are in level three when you listen to what inspires you.
> You are in level four when everything has inspiration because it has love.

Step Eight: The Sixth House

Scorpio: I Want Others to Face Their Fears

I find that I am attracted to fixing the problems of others and great at helping them to face their fears. I can see immediately what's missing or wrong, and what needs to be added to make things work. It took me a while to realize that this was helping me see what I have been missing, but afraid to admit to myself. I'm missing new ideas and choices to making my dream real. I've let myself get stuck, trying to do it one way—the right way—there are so many other choices and paths, and some of them are shorter and easier.

You've been learning about choice to get yourself unstuck—you're stuck trying to get yourself into the future the right way, the perfect way, to a perfect image. That's got to go. You know I'm right because you know how to fix everyone else's problems, but you can't fix the hero's problems—yours—you have to be above it all, away from the negative stuff. You are not the Wicked Witch of the West in *The Wizard of Oz*; you won't melt when a bucket of water is thrown on you. Criticism hurts only when you believe it. It'll get to you, until you commit to you and find your own truth.

> You are in level one if the judgments of others stop you.
> You are in level two if you are challenging those judgments.
> You are in level three if you accept the negative and the positive in you.
> You are in level four when it is your intention that makes you good or bad.

Step Nine: The Seventh House

Sagittarius: I Let My Inner Voice Choose for Me

Wisdom changes as I do. I used to think smart people had all the answers, or at least the most information. That couldn't be more wrong. The best decisions are often made not from a logical position or what seems right, but from the heart or with one's instincts. You know you are right when it feels right and when you have that feeling no one can take it from you. You just know.

When you listen and trust your inner voice it grows strong. You are beginning to see that those who are considered wise are those who listen to themselves, not just the rules. They find their own way of getting things done; they are not afraid of being original. You must trust your own originality. It is what will make you great.

> You are in level one if you are listening to others and their truth.
> You are in level two if you challenge their truth.
> You are in level three if you have faith in your inner voice.
> You are in level four when you can seek wisdom in the unknown.

Step Ten: The Eighth House

Capricorn: I Want My Reward

I love to appear uninterested or uninvolved, but of course I am. I'm afraid to appear as if I'm serious about life because I am very serious about life. I'm still waiting for others to recognize my worth, before I show them what I can do. Now time is running out and I realize that others are just too self-consumed to worry about me. I must take charge of my life and ask for what I want. If I stay in fear, I live in fear—and that's my reward.

As the Gemini you hide your desire for the big reward because you don't believe you're worthy or smart enough to have it. You keep it in the future with your vision of yourself. When you hang around enough people who get big rewards you begin to understand that they are not worthy, either. In fact, many of them aren't as good or as smart as you are. You begin to see that worthiness has nothing to do with reward; it has to do with how you play the game. You begin to expect more from your effort; you ask for more and you get more. Isn't that amazing?

> You are in level one if your reward is what others give you.
> You are in level two if you want the reward of your dream.
> You are in level three when you don't care about rewards.
> You are in level four when your life is your reward.

Step Eleven: The Ninth House

Aquarius: I Am Free When I Can Let Go

I used to believe that freedom came from not making a commitment, but now I know it comes from my ability to remove my ego from the picture. So long as I'm seeking praise, I'll never go for the bigger rewards. I'll stay stuck looking to be validated or discover who I am.

As soon as you realize that it is your ego that is in the way of your freedom, not commitments, you are on your way to letting go and success. You will feel stuck so long as you are afraid to own one truth and not be associated with all truths. You must define you, then you can change you. But start somewhere.

> You are in level one if you believe that freedom can only be had if you
>   are alone.
> You are in level two when you can be alone and enjoy it.
> (Levels three and four are listed at the end of step eleven in the fourth
>   level of consciousness.)

The Fourth Level of Consciousness

The fourth level of consciousness divides the ninth house and eleventh step. It demands that you let go of your desire to be perfect and join the real players in the world, the ones that make the tough decisions, the ones that inspire others, the ones that lead us to new ideas, inventions, and discoveries. You are unique and that uniqueness wants you to participate in the world. It will not come out until you know how to manage others and not get swept into their dreams or lives. After you learn to set boundaries through self-discipline and learn the ability to make the right choices for you, you will be ready to own your dream and to experience the freedom that comes when you become the hero in your own drama.

Step Eleven: The Ninth House (Fourth Level)

Aquarius: I Am Free to Have My Vision My Way

The freedom I feel from not worrying about what I say and who I offend, because it doesn't agree with them, is incredible. A weight is lifted and I realize that I could never create before because there were too many restrictions. The most amazing part of it all is that others are not as sensitive as I thought they would be. They listen to what I say, instead of fighting me.

Freedom has come to you through your courage to choose for truth rather than freedom. When you can give it up you can have it. What you try to control always stays just outside your grasp. You were able to choose for truth because you found the courage to remove your ego from the situation and look at it honestly and without expectations. Your reward is the freedom to pursue your dream as your truth. Others are beginning to notice that you are a person of inspiration and power.

> You are in level three when you see that freedom comes when you choose for truth not for freedom.
> You are in level four when you feel free no matter what is going on in your life.

Step Twelve: The Tenth House

Pisces: My Dream Is My Reward

My dream is what got me through difficult times; yet I didn't have faith in it and I let it go. But it didn't let me go. Whenever I wanted it back, it was there just as strong as ever. What you love is always in your heart.

The Gemini has learned the lesson of letting go. To do this it had to remove its ego from the picture and let inspiration lift it up and carry it forward. Once motivation comes from within instead of without, you don't need others to get going, all you need is yourself.

> You are in level one when the dream is your escape.
> You are in level two when you challenge others to pursue your dream.
> You are in level three when you have faith in your dream and are not afraid of criticism.
> You are in level four when your dream sets you free.

Step One: The Eleventh House (Fourth Level)

Aries: I'm the Hero of My Own Dream

I placed my vision in the future because it interfered with my need for praise. Once my ego committed to my dream, my vision joined in and showed me exactly where I want to be and what I want to do.

When you're not afraid of the truth it comes to you. Protect the truth. Run from it and you find that you have to face your fear anyway and you've lost some valuable time. Now you know how important it is to ask for truth and wisdom, rather than a certain result. When you know the truth you can always make the right decision.

> You are in level three when your vision shows you the way to your dream.
> You are in level four when you are the hero of your life.

The Cross

The cross is composed of the eleventh, fifth, ninth, and third houses and is where change must occur. (See Figure 7.1 on page 161.) The two fixed houses represented by Aries and Libra challenge each other to see a greater truth:

Aries (eleventh house): *My vision is lost so long as I can't commit to a truth. I will not be able to see myself in the future so long as I avoid defining myself and my dreams.*

Libra (fifth house): *I look up to others who know their truth and stand up for it. I must find the courage to do the same.*

The two mutable houses represented by Aquarius and Leo must anchor themselves in this new truth by taking a stand:

Aquarius (ninth house): *I am free when I begin to take myself seriously and stop worrying about what others think. When I do I learn that I have an inner wisdom that I can count on. Counting on me is empowering. The more I commit to my own needs, the more powerful I feel and the easier it is to express what I truly want. Faith is the key factor here, when I have faith in me I make choices that lead to my dreams and their rewards.*

Leo (third house): *My ego, and its need for praise and acceptance, has kept me from making the choices I need to make. I must risk love and see what lies beyond and in the future.*

8

CANCER:
Protection/Enlightenment
(June 22 through July 22)

Cancer is the wound you hide
The pain and anger you keep inside.
If you continue with compassion
If you ignore your truth and passion
Then change will be a thing to fear
New ideas, you won't hear
Others will start to pass you by
You'll fill your loneliness with a lie
Safety is not what your spirit needs.
It's yearning for risk and daring deeds
Wake up, get going—time is dear
Life is love, not worry and fear.

Question Four

About Your Parents: How did your mother express her love and prepare you for the world? Did she make you feel protected? Did she know the secrets of your heart?

About Yourself: How much do you protect yourself and others from your truths and desires? Do you take on too much responsibility in one area and, in so doing, avoid it in other areas?

The warm veil of illusion has thinned and the stark boldness of truth is trying to break through. The pain of betrayal threatens to destroy your dreams.

As you lose faith in the promise and in love, you are forced to look at the darkness and the possibility that sadness is all there is. Don't be afraid, the child in you is dying so that the new and stronger you can emerge. The child can no longer support or protect you; the past must be let go of. You need more than a hero's heart to manifest a dream. Cancer and the Sixth Step will help you add perseverance, containment, loyalty, toughness, and faith to your talents.

As the world becomes "real," the warm blanket of your childhood seems tattered and torn. Can you face a future that is cold and compassionless? Can you spiritually survive a world without the promise of *perfect* love? You hold on to your dreams with a vengeance and you weave greater fantasies to cover the holes where *the truth* threatens to break through. They will not take these things from you.

A Whole New World

The universe is about to become your partner on your journey, and the faith you have expressed in your life will become a warm bubble of protection. It sends you experiences through outer events and messages through your inner voice or instincts to help keep you balanced and on your path. But it can't do its magic until you pay attention and open yourself up to a world where you are the star and everything that happens to you, happens for you and because of you. Without faith and a sense of wonder, this attitude could be seen as megalomania, and at the very least eccentric, but that's what brings out uniqueness and genius. When you begin to feel connected to everything around you, it opens you up to all the little links that before went unnoticed. For example, the traffic jam on the way to work caused you to be late, but allowed you to run into the exact person you needed to see in the lobby before you went to your meeting. If you had arrived minutes earlier or later, the encounter would never have happened—and it gave you the information you needed to close the deal! This incident is only one of a hundred that happens to you when you begin to see the synchronicity of life. The beauty of it is that it creates a feeling of being loved and supported—panic diminishes when things don't go right and you learn how to accept what is happening as part of the bigger picture. Thus what happens to you from without is connected to your instincts within; the circle is completed through faith. You can now feel safe no matter where you are or what you do because you are protected and guided. You are seldom surprised, deceived, or depressed because you have been forewarned and prepared for the events that are coming your way. If you listen to only one part of the package, inner or outer, you will find that you misinterpret the message; instead of being forewarned or prepared you can easily be deceived. Your information is distorted by your fear, past experiences, and old patterns that do not allow the new information to come to you and support and guide you. Without the circle of faith around you, your life is doomed to repetition and falls—your world comes apart in the same places over and over again. For example, the image in the stone had to speak to the artist Michelangelo before he could release it from its bondage. The universe has to speak to you before you can see your destiny and shape your environment around this image. The vision you receive from within drives you forward with faith, not panic or vengeance over others who get in your way. To proceed from this point on you need your inner voice and instincts. You cannot move forward on your journey without the circle of faith being completed. Without it you will fall, and nothing will work, support will be gone, and betrayal will be your middle name. If this is your reality, you must realize that you have abandoned yourself by not looking to you and God for the love and direction you are seeking. It's time to give up seeking answers and desires outside and through relationships and allow your own inner faith and powers do the job.

Your environment plays an important role in your journey. It can shape you by creating resistance, by inspiring you, by leading you, and by challenging your ideas to be bigger and greater than you ever thought possible. When you're not connected to you, you feel stuck. The key is your ability to listen—can you hear what the universe is saying? There is a message in every moment of every day if you are wise enough to see it or pluck it from its disguise. Life is shaping you to reach for it with the full power of your creative genius. Run from its strong opinions, criticism, and demands, and you'll hide from your self. Challenge it with your vision; challenge it to surrender to you. When you do you bring what's inside out and you reveal the jewel that lies within your heart.

Resistance is essential. You need pressure from above, you need others to tell you no, that you can't do this or be that. And if you can't fight back, you don't believe. Why put time and energy in what you have no faith in. Others are not going to pay attention until you pay attention. No faith, no gain. Take the risk; you'll get the reward if you have patience and don't expect it right away.

Cancer is the sign of the nurturer and the mother who protects her child from the harsh and cruel world. There is a time, however, when the tender mother must become tough and shove the bird from the nest—for to survive it must learn how to fly. If you were born a Cancer, you can either deal with an overprotected childhood that built fear and kept you soft and weak and unable to cope with the tough competitive world, or else you were not protected at all and so you want independence, but are afraid to rely on anyone or anything. Secretly you are hoping to be rescued from the responsibilities that lie before you. When you stop feeling sorry for yourself, or believing that the world betrayed you by not giving you a family that fit the perfect image or the dream, you will be ready to turn the cold reality of truth into a loyal and faithful friend—one you can count on no matter what turns your life takes, or what rewards you are given for your efforts.

Your quest is to move out of illusion and a false sense of safety, and into faith and truth, which will protect you for the rest of your journey. The path that leads away from your home and the known is not an easy one. You must have faith and the spiritual strength to stay on your path and not be seduced by others. Souls are waiting by the side of the road to offer you whatever your heart desires, they have given up on their dreams and so they feed on yours. What will protect you from lies? How do you know when to trust and when to hide? The answer is easy if you've turned within and listened to your inner voice. This is your guide.

To get to your inner world is not easy: You must pass through your fear, anger, and the feelings of unworthiness that you put inside, hoping they would disappear. Instead, they grew stronger, because they've been repressed and denied a voice. These thoughts of lack keep you seeking the wrong reward; they support a needy ego that desires recognition and protection through money and security instead of faith and new ideas that lift you up and show you a greater world. As you slink into your wounds and others reach out to protect you, you feel safe for a moment, until you realize what you had to give up to keep this childish need alive—you've given up your truth, your strength, and the courage to be your own person. To protect yourself from your whole truth you attract other children to take care of you. No truly strong and independent person would keep you small and weak when you are not.

Yes, the world was not what you were told it was: goodness does not bring automatic rewards, and wisdom does not always win the prize. In your eyes the only way to hold on to the dream is to have someone show you how to get there. That's not entirely wrong. Others and their knowledge can be helpful, but you need to use their knowledge, not rely on it. When you can devour truth and spit it out your way, you're ready for the monsters that are waiting by the road.

There is nothing more magical than an experience or idea that has the power to awaken in you something new. The awakener is not always as worthy as the message it brings, and so they must be seen as two separate things. Cancer's favorite role is the awakener. Cancers are great at showing others the path or sharing their knowledge, validating creativity or exciting imagination. Isn't this what your mother did or should have done for you? Mothers are supposed to solve the mysteries and weave the fantasies that first capture your heart. Whoever plays this role in your life will have a hold on your psyche and you will be afraid to let them go.

The Cancer is caught between the world of illusion and fantasy and the world of reality. It has learned to live in one and believe in the other, and so often it lives a life divided. The Cancer's reputation of fluctuating moods and inconsistency is primarily due to lack of commitment to the truth, or real intentions. They still don't trust that they can create the magic, even though they do it all the time. It's easier to see greatness in others than in oneself. Their challenge is to have faith that if they persevere with faith, the universe will surprise them with a miracle.

The Cancer knows that enlightenment lies beyond what you know. Unconsciously the Cancer puts itself in new situations—crossroads of change—and surrounds itself with people who stretch their mind, body, and spirit to get the job done. When they find the courage to trust—the magic starts happening. The danger is when the fantasy is confused with faith. They both are created by your imagination, but one has your beliefs and ideas behind it, the other is a form of escape.

The Cancer is looking to be chosen, not to choose. It has trouble seeing its greatness, so it wants others to validate what it feels inside. God could validate you in a moment if you turned to Him. But most Cancers turn to others, and not everyone has good intentions. You may be put down in order for someone else to feel strong, not because you don't have the talent. You sometimes feel that if a beautiful woman loves you, you must have something to offer; if a famous person chooses to work with you, you must have something to offer—your worth comes from the choices of others, not yourself. The Cancer must risk itself and choose for its own intention, commit to its goals no matter what others do, and persevere beyond its feelings of isolation and loneliness—when it does, the miracles start happening.

When spirit leads instead of the ego, your values change and you see the world in a new light. Beauty is not an outer image, it's a generous soul—one that shares whatever it has, no matter how small. Intelligence is no longer the repetition of facts; it's the wisdom to trust your instincts and the faith to accept even when you don't understand. Strength is not seen as the ability to overpower someone else; it now becomes acts of kindness in the face of adversity—its perseverance, loyalty, humor, and creativity.

The Cancer is selfish at a core level; it knows it must take care of itself or no one else will. It may try to mask its selfishness behind kind words, pleasing actions, and compassion, but deep down it's committed to its own goals. Bravo!

The Power of Vulnerability

There is power in not being first, leading the way, or showing your strength. Race car drivers or runners know that it is easier to let someone else take the lead and exhaust themselves by breaking the force of resistance (in this case the air), while you coast in the vacuum created behind them until you're ready to make your move. It's one way of pacing yourself. Great military strategists know that they must be able to turn their weaknesses into strengths. If the enemy sees you as weak, they often don't prepare the same, letting down their guard, which allows you to take advantage of the situation. If you show your strength you create the need for others to meet your strength with more power. Adding more of anything is a very simplistic way to increase power, it's much more clever to use your opponents' weaknesses against them, and that includes their need to be strong and win. It is easy to get someone with a great ego to over-commit early and leave you an opening.

Thus, it is not always who has the most, or is the best, it's how you use what you have that gets results. To use your so-called weaknesses you must know what they are and how to include them or make them work for you. This happens when you are not afraid to learn from your mistakes, to look at what went wrong, and to accept your limitations. Yes, weaknesses can easily be turned into strengths through acceptance or meaning—give something meaning and the wound gets healed.

Following is a list of things you condemn yourself to by not allowing yourself to be vulnerable:

- You can't fall in love.
- You can't be intimate.
- You can't share your fears.
- You can't ask for help when you need it.
- You can't let others do things for you because you feel vulnerable.
- You can't receive gifts or love.
- You will have all the responsibility.
- You will have very little consideration from others.
- You will have few friends.
- You will be a loner.
- You will feel empty and dissatisfied with whatever you have.
- You will be attracted to very helpless, vulnerable people, or hate them or both.

How to Trust the World Again

You learn how to trust when you switch from trusting others and what they say or promise to trusting yourself and your instincts. You don't have to trust anyone else if you can trust yourself. To trust yourself you must be able to look at the negative and the positive, first in you and then in others. No one is perfect and to see them as such is asking for trouble. Here's a checklist to see if you are ready to trust yourself:

- Can you connect and reach out?
- Can you separate from others when you need to be alone or when they become too critical or abusive?
- Can you see both the negative and the positive? Or do you see what you want to see?
- Can you see beyond appearances and words? Do you believe what others tell you automatically?
- Do you realize that what others do to others will eventually be done to you? (*If your friend can cheat another friend, he can cheat you, too.*)

When you are ready to see yourself, all your intentions and fears, you are ready to see the world as it is, too. *You can only be deceived if something you want is more important than your truth.*

Passive Aggression

Cancer is the sign of passive aggression. It doesn't confront easily, but it also doesn't give in easily; it just outlasts you. It's learned an important lesson: Why waste energy on confrontation? Just don't listen to what others say. It's amazing how many problems just go away if you don't meet them with your truth or anger. Of course, when this is taken to an extreme, life is ignored and not all problems go away. It is so important to be able to choose which problems to confront and which to ignore. Experience, once again, is the best teacher.

You Are Not an Island

When the quest for greatness gets under way one begins to examine what can make a difference in one's performance. You are preparing to compete with thousands of others and thus any edge you have matters. Whenever one turns inward and seeks answers, information is revealed. Now you discover that everything you do is connected to your performance: the food you eat, the exercise you take or don't take, even the thoughts you think influence results. In fact, the power of what you believe seems to be the most important factor. The placebo pill proved that if you believe something is going to make you better, it works. So attitude can directly affect your physical body. Doctors have also learned that prayer or faith makes a difference. It has been proven that prayer can improve a person's health. Thus the mind, body, and spirit are connected, not separate worlds functioning alone.

And this is the enlightenment of Cancer—it is not enough to have your body and mind in great condition, you must also have your spirit in good shape, too. What feeds the spirit is laughter, sharing, prayer, nature, meditation, spontaneity, surprise, and the unknown. The spirit loves to play. Don't ignore your spirit by doing only work and eliminating fun. Your work will improve if you are happy and enjoying life. If you ignore your spirit, it won't matter how much success or money you have, you will feel empty, disconnected, and alone. The spirit needs friendship, sharing, and community; it wants to awaken and enlighten; it wants to help those in need. When you share, what you share is increased in you. Quantity no longer works; less is more. You increase your strength and spirit by letting go or sharing what you have. What you give or share is increased by the universe. Hold on to something and it will shrivel up or become a heavy burden. Thus when you give love, you have more love to give; when you help someone in need, you heal your feelings of lack and self-worth. The road to better health and healing lies in how connected you feel to others and yourself.

The Power of Mystery and the Unknown

God is a mystery, He lives in the unknown and God has power. We associate mystery with power. People are attracted to mystery, to what is hidden, not to what is shown. It is the closed door that everyone wants to open; leave the door open and everyone will pass by without looking inside. What you expose or show becomes real and in so doing, fear and power are diminished. That is why secrets are so powerful, they can contain greater amounts of fear than they deserve, but you'll never know their true power until you expose them and share them with others. You'll never know what you can rely on in yourself until you test yourself and make your talents real. You've got to risk losing some power to gain real power.

The Power of Sharing

The North Coastal Native Americans had a Give Away ceremony. They believe that giving things away brings abundance. When you create space in your life, you allow the universe to give to you, and what the universe gives is so much better than you could ever find yourself. Whatever you are not using takes energy to hold on to. What you are holding on to, you must protect. Freedom comes from holding on to faith, not possessions. When your spirit reaches out and supports someone else, when you share your knowledge, your experiences, your time, and your creativity with another soul, you increase your spirit's power and ability. Those who never share have small spirits. Their spirit has not grown beyond their physical needs, and so every bump and turn throws them off center. Yes, spirit is like a bumper on your car, the more you put it out front and use it to connect with others, the stronger and more protected you feel. Sharing is like a cosmic bank: the more deposits you make, the more faith you have to draw on. Keep your cosmic bank full and life will be an exciting and a wonderful journey.

Choose Your Response

Self-control now becomes something you value. Without it others will control you. The first place to use self-control is with response. Automatic responses give others the control. You gain the strength to choose your path when you choose how you will respond. If someone is angry and strikes out with harsh words, you can return the harsh words or ask them if they've had a rough day. When you don't have to react you get to create. Don't let the fear and doubts of others turn you into what you don't want to be.

The Power of Pain and Suffering

As you become aware of your pain and the emotions that limited you, you may begin to feel as if your life was wasted—that the part of you that suffered was for naught. Almost all great people have suffered, and suffered intensely; there is no other way to gain understanding and true knowledge of yourself or others. If you've never been needy or afraid, you will not be able to create anything with meaning, depth, or power. Those who suffer and find a way to use their suffering are those that are truly empowered. In any walk of life, knowledge of suffering only adds meaning and depth to your existence. It gives you knowledge that others don't have; you can go deeper, which means you can go higher than others who have not experienced it. Learn to give meaning to your pain. Help others through sharing faith and understanding; find a cause that expresses your emotions, turn it into creative expression; or just become a better person. All of these choices are the gifts of having suffered.

Turning Your Life Over to a Higher Power

What is protection? Is it physical strength? Is it cunning, endurance, or is it faith? It is faith when you feel loved and protected by a divine force that doesn't judge or punish for mistakes, evil actions, and thoughts or anything that takes you away from love. To give up control is to gain it. To turn your power over to the universe rather than try to work things out all by yourself is to allow yourself to be led by a higher power. How much of your parents' choices were based on faith? When and where did you feel safe? You'll be surprised to discover that moments of safety come not from having money or winning awards, but from spirits connecting. When you can share yourself with someone else, you can feel safe and protected.

The Mother Creates Emotional Safety

Your mother is the higher power when you are a child. She is the one with the magic to turn pain into joy and make a hurt feel okay. The greatest protection you can have is love. If you felt connected to your mother through love, you were able to open up to her and share your feelings, desires, and dreams. If she listened to them without judgment and encouraged you to follow them, you have received a very empowering gift. If she encouraged you to go beyond your fears and mistakes and helped you to see a greater idea, you will know how to bridge the gaps in life early through faith. (See Figure 8.1 for the Cancer Star.)

The First Level of Consciousness

The first level of consciousness divides the eleventh house and first step, and the third house and fifth step. It demands that you believe in yourself enough to face the judgments of others. Love can no longer be unconditional, or the desire to be protected. You must be able to ask and choose for what you want and let go of what you don't, always looking ahead to the consequences and accepting responsibility for your actions. The truth of others is in the way of your vision. Go beyond your need to please and you will see it.

Step One: The Eleventh House

Taurus: Love Is for Dreams

I never believed in myself, only others. I thought that the only way I could have what I wanted was to attach myself to someone who had what I wanted. Of course, that didn't work, because I ended up doing the work and never being the center of attention. All this changed when I began to feel that I could do what they were doing. The more faith I have in myself, the more connected I feel to others and the more I want to help. The more I help, the more faith and love I receive, and now I know that I can love and be loved. If I can give it to others, I'll find it in myself.

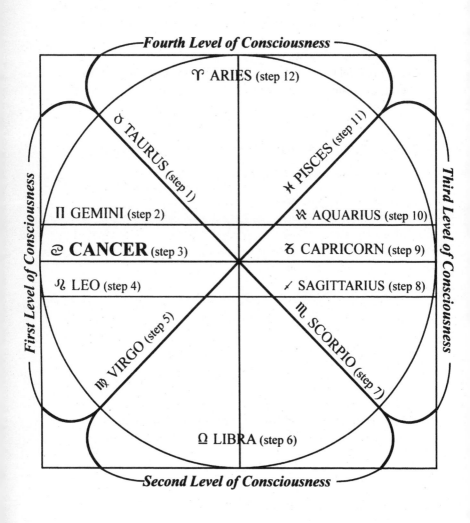

Figure 8.1. The Cancer Star

The Cancer needs to feel that it is worthy of love before it can make its life happen. If you come in feeling worthy, you will be able to skip the first part of this story—you'll be able to support others and in so doing discover your strength, that is, the power of love to make you strong. You have a great deal of love in your heart; that love is meant to be used for your own dreams, too.

> You are in level one when love is perfect.
> You are in level two if you are seeking truth over love and protection.
> (Levels three and four are listed at the end of step one in the fourth level of consciousness.)

Step Two: The Twelfth House

Gemini: My Choices Must Inspire Me

I was told that wisdom came from those who had knowledge or experience. However, knowledge doesn't have all the answers and neither does wisdom. I feel there's something missing. As soon as I gained faith in myself, loved myself, I began to realize that love has its own kind of wisdom and when I could let love direct my choices, they seemed to work out just fine.

Love inspires, and it is inspiration that lifts you out of pain and sorrow. Without love even wisdom falls short and nothing seems to work. Love is the thread that connects our choices and gives them meaning. Without love your choices remain isolated islands unable to help you move toward your goals.

> You are in level one if you make your choices for freedom.
> You are in level two if you are challenging the judgments of others.
> You are in level three if you are making your choices for a reward.
> You are in level four when your choices are made for your dream.

Step Three: The First House

Cancer: My Reward Is to Be Me Without Fear

My need to feel safe and secure has made me seek support from others rather than freedom and love. Of course, it's seldom there the way I want it. It wasn't until I began to depend on me that things turned around. I saw that I also gave mixed messages. I was either there for others or I wasn't. There was no logical reason for my choices; they were all based on my needs, not theirs. Until I learned to show up for me, I couldn't show up for anyone else. When I did I felt free.

As the Cancer, you must learn to stop depending on others for support and begin to give it to yourself. Until you do, you will feel insecure, full of anxiety and worry, because you know that you can't rely on others the way you want to. You can do it. You can give to yourself whatever you need. This is the beginning of true freedom.

> You are in level one when you depend on others for protection.
> You are in level two when you are ready to let go of protection.
> You are in level three when you have faith and depend on your dream.
> You are in level four when you are not afraid of breaking through the illusions that protect others.

Step Four: The Second House

Leo: My Ego Feels Lost Without a Dream

I can no longer depend on wisdom, or praise; neither matters when you are doing work that doesn't inspire you. I was the one who gave up on my dream. Without a dream my ego has nothing to do but look for freedom and ways to break out of the box I've built around me.

The Cancer is forced to hide its strength and its ego because it has given up the motivation and inspiration it needs to reach for something wonderful in life. Without a goal or a dream you will seek escape, and the number one escape is moments of freedom. The problem with this choice is it doesn't change your world, when you return you feel imprisoned again. Once you connect to your passion, or something you love, everything comes together.

> You are in level one if you feel strength is found in control and knowledge.
> You are in level two if you feel strength is facing your fears and the judgments of others.
> You are in level three if you feel strength is the reward of your truth.
> You are in level four if you feel strength is the ability to see beyond your fears and problems to a greater idea.

Step Five: The Third House

Virgo: When I Let Go, I Find My Faith

I gave my choices over to others once I let go of pursuing my dreams. That was a mistake. I hate taking orders from others, and yet I have trouble saying how I feel. I either get angry or I leave. What I started to do is help others follow their dreams. I could see where they needed help, because it wasn't my fear. Maybe others can see what I can't see in myself?

Once you open yourself up to help and helping others your life changes. Cancer is about sharing and faith. When you give faith you get it back. So don't be stingy with your support, but allow yourself to receive it too. If you don't, you are blocking love from your life. The door has to work both ways for you to find balance and happiness.

> You are in level one when you give up because you are afraid.
> You are in level two when you give up the truth of others in order to see your own.
> (Levels three and four are listed at the end of step five in the second level of consciousness.)

The Second Level of Consciousness

The second level of consciousness divides the third house and fifth step, and the fifth house and seventh step. It wants you to let go of holding on to a truth that no longer protects or inspires you. No truth is real until you can stand up for it and now you are asked to risk love and face judgment in order to move forward. The confrontation is not easy, because you either have a strong dominating figure to oppose, or no one is there at all. It's hard to confront a ghost. However, if you can just take a stand where you think you belong and meet the challenges that it attracts, you can gain the strength you need to move forward.

Step Five: The Third House (Second Level)

Virgo: Letting Go Gives You Your Vision and Your Dream

I was afraid to face those who have strength and power because I always saw myself as having less. But the truth is I'm strong, and their dominating nature comes from fear. Once I really believed in what I was doing, their power over me dwindled and I found even more strength in myself, because I found my truth and that led me to my dream.

The more you stand up to your fear and the authority in your life, the more love you feel for yourself and the more of your truth you will discover. You can only count on what you're willing to fight for. This is your truth.

> You are in level three when every day gives you a reward.
> You are in level four when you are never afraid because you can create a vision that overcomes fear.

Step Six: The Fourth House

Libra: My Truth Is My Intention

I didn't have a truth or a dream because I was too worried about safety and security. Once I found the courage to stand up to others and believe in me, I began to see my truth take shape. I finally have an identity—I know who I am. I can feel what I'm all about and I can see where I'm going and what I really want to accomplish.

You cannot find your truth until you challenge the authority of others. If you can't stand up for your dreams how can you follow them? Without courage you cannot find a truth or feel strong. You've been protecting others from your opinions and accepting their negativity—that weakens you and empowers them. Stop working for others and put yourself first.

> You are in level one when your truth is what others want it to be.
> You are in level two when you challenge their truth and your own.
> You are in level three when you have faith in your ability to get the rewards you want from life.
> You are in level four when following your dream brings you love.

Step Seven: The Fifth House

Scorpio: I Let Others Control Me for Love

I could never trust love, because it always tried to control me, but now I know that that wasn't love: it was fear. I can surrender to love and not the behavior of control; I can separate the heart from fear. When I can do this, I can love almost anyone.

When you can begin to separate fear from love by separating one's behavior from their heart, you enter the realm of understanding and forgiveness and you are able to connect with someone and disconnect at the same time. You've just solved your problem of holding on and letting go. You hold on to the heart and let go of the fear or negative behavior. When the heart is present, you are present. When it's not, you're entitled to disappear.

> You are in level one when you believe you are good or bad.
> You are in level two when you can hide your truth from those who are
>   negative.
> (Levels three and four are listed at the end of step seven in the third
>   level of consciousness.)

The Third Level of Consciousness

The third level of consciousness divides the fifth house and seventh step, and the ninth house and eleventh step. It asks the soul to have faith that the reward will be there when the time is right. It's time to commit to the work and not the reward. Let it be whatever it is. Until you can let go of the reward, it won't come to you the way it should. Follow your truth and let it cut the path to your destiny. Your truth is what inspires you; have faith in what inspires you and you'll find your destiny and your purpose.

Step Seven: The Fifth House (Third Level)

Scorpio: I Let Go of Love and Seek Wisdom

I used to believe that love was everything, but my pursuit of it has only brought me pain and disappointment. I am now seeking wisdom. I need to understand what life is all about and what is important.

Once you begin to let go you begin to experience love in a new way. You cannot have anything in your life with strength and power until you let go of it. As you gain understanding you realize that it is the reward you seek that is getting in the way. You want things to fit into certain images and fantasies, and they must go for you to find true intimacy.

> You are in level three when you know that you are both good and bad. You are in level four when you know that it is your intention that makes you good.

Step Eight: The Sixth House

Sagittarius: Wisdom Is Surrendering to Your Inner Voice

I had given up on wisdom, and instead held on to security and what I thought would make me safe. In so doing I realized that those with wisdom did the opposite: they let go of security and took risks for their dreams. I could see that they were listening to themselves, not fear or others. I tried it myself. It works.

Wisdom is the knowledge to choose for faith, change, and the unknown. When you want to keep control you limit your possibilities and your power. You can't control God's world, He's in charge. The world is constantly moving and changing and the more you can align yourself with its rhythm, the happier and healthier you will be.

> You are in level one if you believe everything you are told.
> You are in level two if you confront what others tell you.
> You are in level three if you listen to your inner voice.
> You are in level four when you turn your questions over to a higher power.

Step Nine: The Seventh House

Capricorn: I Need to Know the Way

I used to want money and praise, but now I want to know where I'm going and how to get there. I am attracted to people who know who they are and where they're going. They have faith in themselves and faith that the path will appear.

You may have thought that a path was a straight line. Well, the path of spirit zigzags a great deal. It takes you to the best opportunity, which means that sometimes it even goes back before it goes forward. You need faith to follow your path; it will not take you on a straight road. That's why your inner voice is so important, without it it's just too easy to get lost.

> You are in level one if your goals are to escape the moment or to find pleasure.
> You are in level two if your goals are to be independent.
> You are in level three when you let go of reward and follow your dream no matter what.
> You are in level four when your reward is your life.

Step Ten: The Eighth House

Aquarius: Freedom Comes When I Surrender with Love

If I do the work without love, work is work. If I can find a way to give it meaning or make it a challenge, I enjoy it. I am free when I surrender with love to what I have to do.

When you work with love it is not work; it's a creative act that is inspiring and exciting. Everyone deserves to work with inspiration and love. Remember, it's not the work you do, but the attitude you bring to that work. Do what you have to do and surrender to it with your heart, and you'll find that you have the power to change work into joy.

> You are in level one when freedom is an escape.
> You are in level two when you stand up for your differences.
> You are in level three when you believe in what makes you unique.
> You are in level four when there are no differences—only spirit expressing itself.

Step Eleven: The Ninth House

Pisces: I Accept My Dream

My dream used to be a burden, because life was a burden. My dream was nothing but a path of hard work for a promise in the future that may or may not happen.

When I learned how to turn work into joy, my dream was no longer a burden—but pure joy.

Once you can accept your dream you begin to see the dreams in others and if you can support each other, you can both grow strong. Dreams don't like to live in isolation—they love to be the center of attention. So share your dream, let others give you ideas and support, let them save you time and effort and help you turn work into pleasure. When you can, dreams become a source of strength and power.

> You are in level one when your dream is an escape.
> You are in level two when you face authority in the pursuit of your truth.
> (Levels three and four are listed at the end of step eleven in the fourth level of consciousness.)

The Fourth Level of Consciousness

The fourth level of consciousness divides the ninth house and eleventh step. You are asked to have enough self-worth to step into the role of hero of your life. It is time to become the center of your own drama. You now have the magic to turn work into joy—add faith to fear and turn it into love—and with that kind of power there will be no evil to fight. When you can turn things around you are free to love and be whatever your heart desires.

Step Eleven: The Ninth House (Fourth Level)

Pisces: My Dream Has Magic

I see that my dream is a gift from the universe and that when I accept it, I accept His love. When I accept His love, I accept my divine powers, the ones with the magic to bring about change. My dream has my love and so it has the power to change my life and the lives of others.

Once you have the power of love, you have the secret to life. You are now attracted to mystery rather than facts. You are drawn to the inexplicable rather than what's been done. Your experience has taught you that love leads to mystery and greater truths. There are many more things to discover. Life is exciting and full of wonders to be known.

> You are in level three when you have faith that you deserve the rewards you desire.
> You are in level four when the world is one big dream.

Step Twelve: The Tenth House

Aries: I Am a Hero

I have found my path but it doesn't reveal itself to me all at once, only one step at a time. It's teaching me how to have faith and just do what I can right now, and the next step always appears. It's amazing how much gets done when I do that. I have faith in my path and I am the hero of my own life. I am pursuing a dream I love.

Life unfolds with faith. The more faith you have the more it unfolds. Trust that you will be guided to where you need to be; stay connected to your inner voice and you'll be shown the way.

> You are in level one when you are the hero for others and follow their vision.
> You are in level two when you are the hero for your dream and confront others.
> You are in level three when you have faith in your dream and you as the hero in it.
> You are in level four when you know there is always another greater vision and challenge to meet.

Step One: The Eleventh House (Fourth Level)

Taurus: Love Is Eternal

I used to seek love and couldn't find it anywhere. Now I accept life and love wherever it is and I find it everywhere and in everything I do.

The lesson of acceptance is the hardest lesson of all, but every time you understand it a little bit better, you learn and grow. Stop resisting life and accept it. When you do you will find that everything you need is right before you.

> You are in level three when love is the reward you are seeking.
> You are in level four when love is your dream and the world is one big dream.

The Cross

The cross is composed of the eleventh, fifth, ninth, and third houses and is where change must occur. (See Figure 8.1 on page 184.) The two fixed houses represented by Taurus and Scorpio challenge each other to see a greater truth:

Taurus (eleventh house): *When I get enough experience I begin to see that I am as worthy as anyone. I begin to have faith in myself and this gives me faith in my dream. I'm now ready to confront the authority.*

Scorpio (fifth house): *I oppose the authority and stand up to them, instead of protecting them from the fact that they are unfair, unkind, and controlling. When I find the courage through love to face my fear, I begin to see my truth, and from my truth my vision emerges. My ability to confront my fear has freed me from the need to protect myself and others and to be able to receive the rewards of life I deserve.*

The two mutable houses represented by Pisces and Virgo must anchor themselves in this new truth by taking a stand:

Pisces (ninth house): *I give up my dream and see it in others; when I honor it in them, it comes back to me stronger than ever. I can't lose my dream, so I surrender to it.*

Virgo (third house): *I am stopped by the authority of the fifth, which is judgment. I am afraid of others hurting me, but when I find my dream I get tougher and have more courage and so I stand up to the opinions I disagree with. Now I know that when I used to let go it was out of fear, not love.*

9

LEO: Strength
(July 23 through August 23)

Leo seeks great strength and might.
It wields the sword of wrong and right.
Its mission is to find the source.
The eternal power of The Force.
Its challenge is to let things go.
To find its faith in friends and foe.
Go to the light and you will see.
Fear turn to love that sets you free.
Do not forget that from above.
Is where you find eternal love.

Question Five

About Your Parents: What were your father's strengths and talents? Did you see him as successful?

About Yourself: How successful are you socially and professionally? Do you isolate yourself? Do others enjoy your company?

Leos have witnessed the greatness of their soul; they don't need others to tell them they are special. Their crowning achievement is self-love. They no longer waste their time seeking praise or validation because their focus is on their goals and their desire to understand life's mysteries. Once the Leo turns inward and seeks the deeper rewards of spirit—faith, adventure, change, loyalty, generosity, and of course love—it begins to bring forth its spiritual strength.

Spiritual strength has the power to resist seduction, temptation, and the lies that lead one away from destiny and greatness. Without spirit it is too easy to get stuck on the treadmill of desire—an exhausting endless road of discontent. With self-love comes self-acceptance, and now the magic and miracles of the world lie within your grasp. Love, you discover, has amazing powers. If you shine it on fear, it transforms it into love; shine it on your own fears and you have the power to heal your own wounds. Yes, it's the beginning of invincibility, the first taste of divine powers that lie within us all. As the Leo begins to overcome the obstacles that once paralyzed it and filled it with shame and fear, within it emerges the question—why? What is life all about? Who am I and where am I going? Yes, a philosopher is about to be born.

Leos have not picked easy lives; they love a challenge because they know it makes them strong. The inner and outer circles of faith that were connected in Cancer must now shift their balance. Faith and the inner world must become stronger than fear. When this happens the ego surrenders to the inner journey and unites with spirit. You are now able to commit to hard work, so real confidence can be built. If you struggle, you gain faith in your skills and your ability to perform. Repetition and resistance are no longer enemies; they are tools to help you overcome. The greater the resistance, the stronger the unity between mind, body, and spirit and the more self-discipline you develop. You will need self-discipline to be the best and overcome the competition. Once the focus is inward, it works in many ways: you are no longer worried about measuring your worth through the achievements of your adversaries—you are competing with you and your last score.

As you begin to feel isolated from others, the need to please others diminishes—after all they are not taking care of your needs. You see the value of being different; it's what makes you strong. As you accept your differences, they get acknowledged: You get the job because you can do what others can't; you get the girl because you stand out in the crowd. Those who love their differences give them magnetism; those who hate their differences feel isolated and worthless. You began to *use* unity and your ability to please others—they help you get through the door or win someone over to your position.

Your ability to see inside your own heart allows you to reach the hearts of others—not a small gift. When you open your heart, no one can say no. You now have charisma. As your path begins to take its own direction you realize that you need a new set of values, something that can change and grow with you—yet something that never changes. You see the difference between per-

sonal judgments and universal justice. Only eternal truths can sustain a real
hero.

The New Rebel

The Leo is wiser and more experienced than the idealistic Aries who re-
sponded immediately to any call for help. You are willing to slow down and
eliminate any room for failure by doing the work and learning every step well.
You discover your greatest challenge is removing your ego from the issue. You
will not become truly strong until you can see the choices before you without
worrying about the reward. If you can take this lesson one step further and see
the choices of your adversary without your ego, you'll be able to understand
what they want from you, what is motivating them, and what they really
need. This knowledge can make the difference between winning and losing.

As you gain wisdom from experience you realize that strength is not what
you thought it was. It has nothing to do with dominating others physically or
mentally, it is about facing your fear and being able to find the self-discipline
to stay on your path. Without a commitment to your heart, without a burning
passion, you will never be able to avoid temptation and the seductive powers
that come your way. What you need is spiritual strength. The way you get
stronger spiritually is through helping others. When you can help others, you
help yourself. What you teach, you learn. Pass on your knowledge, and you
will rise. Reach out to others, and you will grow. This is how you gain the
inner strength to win and stay on top.

The Choice of Joy

Joy is a choice, not a rite of passage. If you don't choose to have it in your
life, it won't be there. There is too much suffering, fear, and tragedy in life to
allow joy to exist without a commitment to it. You have to seize it and hold
on to it in spite of what is going on around you. This is where you must be selfish; this is where you ignore others. They have no right to take your joy, but
they will if you let them. With joy comes freedom and happiness. To hold on
to joy you've got to get rid of guilt, which means your lack of self-worth has to
go, too. You're entitled to be happy. You're entitled to want more than your

mother or father or your friends do. Don't feel guilty because you have more than they do and it's not enough. Why should their fears be your boundaries? Why should their limited values deprive you of happiness? Have the courage to be happy, not just successful.

Love and joy cannot be sought; they are the gifts of your intentions and your actions. You must know how to ferret out love in moments of fear, to hold on to love when others are invested in destroying it. Joy cannot be given to others, but it can be shared. If you feel joy, others will be drawn to it. Joy is what you believe is possible; it is your interpretation of the experiences in your life. Leo is where you reap the "light" of your life. By light I mean faith, joy, purpose—the love you choose to experience in your greatest moments and your saddest or most difficult times. Joy is what the world needs more than compassion for pain. Choose joy and protect it, share it and make others reach for you and your joy. Raise the consciousness of the world; don't lower yours to feel less left out.

Intimacy

Intimacy is probably the most difficult thing you will face in your life. Most Leos have no trouble solving problems, changing the world, or doing the impossible, but they freeze when it comes to opening up their inner worlds and allowing themselves to be vulnerable enough to be intimate. When you look at their past, it is easy to see why. However, it doesn't matter what you were given in life, it's what you do with it that matters. Because you have suffered, experienced betrayal, been controlled, or abandoned you know what love is, because it was missing. We never know something well until it is taken away. The absence of it allows you to see it and understand how important it is in your life. When something becomes important to you, you begin to choose for it—that is, try to bring it into the moment. Leos want their childhood back and the ability to be spontaneous and playful. With Scorpio ruling the fourth house of the home, you know how to survive without love, but you must now teach yourself how to live with love.

The danger lies in overprotecting yourself from pain or trying to keep others from controlling you. If you take this route you will feel isolated and alone. If your parents were weak, you may be overcompensating for that weakness by swearing you will not be seen as weak or vulnerable. Unfortunately, most of us associate the expression of feelings as weakness and the ability to act without feelings as strength. True power comes when you can blend the two—when heart and mind support each other instead of battling it out to the end. You are not your parents unless you either repeat or oppose their behavior. Find your own position and you'll begin to feel your true power.

The first step to intimacy is to tell yourself that you're no longer a child and you're capable of taking care of yourself. If you're a Leo who has chosen to remain a child because you're trying to recapture your past, you will stay stuck and your relationships will probably not last. Dependent relationships are usually imbalanced and maintained by a single need. When that need gets fulfilled, the balance changes and the relationship is over. What are you trying to get away from? A weak mother or father? A tyrant who ruled your life without love, abandonment, or perhaps abuse? If you have found yourself in the same situation because you have picked a person that seemed different from your family, but then turned out to be a clone, your first challenge is to recognize the issues and take care of them. Don't expect to be rescued. You must be independent and self-sufficient to be able to be truly intimate. This way you can surrender without need, and come back to yourself. You give because you have, you share because you want to, and you love because you recognize a loving heart.

Intimacy can be achieved only if you can leave or separate easily. If you can't leave a room, you won't enter it. You must learn how to face your issues of abandonment and let go when the time is right. If you hang on out of desperation you will not only chase others away, but you will also drive yourself crazy. You cannot relax and be comfortable in a relationship if you feel every independent choice is a desire to leave you.

Need is the virus of intimacy. It latches on to the heart and destroys what is real and strong. When you want your needs met by others, it makes you weaker, not stronger. Yes, others can help and encourage you, but you've got to accomplish the need yourself. Don't seek to protect yourself from what happened to you; seek to become strong and independent so that it will never happen to you again. Overprotecting yourself keeps love at a distance and love can change your life. You become independent in a relationship by getting a job and saving your money, by taking a class and learning a skill, by reaching out and connecting to support groups that help you find yourself and the strength to leave what is not healthy. You have to make room for what you want in your life—you must make room for self-love, for your desires, and for your heart. Let go of the reward, of safety that imprisons, and of your fear of abandonment or being alone. To have intimacy you must not be afraid of being hurt. There is always another choice, a new path, another relationship, and something better and more rewarding waiting for you. You have to have faith to be intimate—faith in yourself. When you can learn from whatever you do, and you have faith in your future, you will find the courage to open up and expose yourself to another heart.

Isolation

Isolation comes when you don't have the skills to cope and so you escape life instead of confront it. Instead of giving up on life, give up on everyone else's life, and take back your own. You are meant to do something wonderful and unique; don't toss that away for approval that doesn't last. Within your heart is where you were meant to be; follow it and the path will unfold.

To get out of the pattern of hero and workaholic, which leads to emotional isolation, you need to acknowledge that you have emotions, feelings, and needs. This does not make you weak; it makes you human. You will be stronger when you can let go and take some time to nurture yourself. Without alone time, you don't get to know yourself, and you feel disconnected because you're disconnected from you. If you don't make yourself a priority, no one else will.

If you're not a workaholic and still feel isolated, chances are you have someone with a strong ego as the center of your life. Leos who are not comfortable with being the center of attention are attracted to those who are. Instead of getting your needs met, you perpetuate the problem by serving someone else's needs—someone who is never going to pay attention to what you want unless you learn to stand up and ask for it and are not afraid of being rejected. If this is you, go back and review the past few steps.

Abuse is not a stranger to Leos. If you were abused, you don't have to stay isolated and alone. You are meant to use your suffering to help you open your heart by helping others. What you have within you is great compassion, understanding, and knowledge of how pain and wounds can keep you paralyzed. If you can find a way to use this knowledge in your everyday life, you will give the experience meaning. Whatever you give meaning to empowers you—give meaning to your wounds and they will not make you a victim, they will make you strong.

Adding Love to Fear

No pain, no gain is definitely your motto. If you had too much pain in your childhood you may run from the slightest sense of sorrow, but this will keep you isolated and alone. You need to add love to fear and change it. You need to learn from your pain and change it. You need to understand your pain and avoid the same mistakes in the future. To do this you must go beyond it and embrace the wisdom and knowledge you gleaned from the experience. To go beyond the experience you must go through it. Those who can face their fears and look beyond them will heal themselves and be strong. If you can write a better novel, be a better mother or friend, find a greater purpose than protecting your pain, you won't become a slave to your pain. You must see that there was a gift in your darkest moment, if you can just take your focus off what you lost and begin to see where it took you and why. Life is not a straight path; it has twists and turns in the road. Look back and you'll see the meaning of a wrong turn, a mistake, and what looked like a disaster. Half of your experiences show you where you should not go so that you can see what you need to see. Learn to let go of expectations, let go of reward; follow your heart and you'll find your way.

Separate Dependence from Love

Most love relationships run into trouble because the soul is still seeking someone to protect it and take care of it. If you are looking for protection, chances are you won't find love, you'll find control. If you are looking for freedom, you won't find love—you'll find someone unable to commit or be loyal. If you are looking for recognition, you won't find love—you'll find a person without an ego who depends on you for his or her strength. If you are looking for your spirit to feel free and someone to share it with, you *will* find new experiences and love. You will create an atmosphere where love can grow, not where it will be destroyed. Love should be shared, not sought as if it were an object or seen as only possible in one person. Be responsible for your emotional happiness and you'll find what you are looking for.

202 ★ THE STAR WITHIN

The Hero

All fire signs (Aries, Leo, and Sagittarius) have a hero issue. They all want to play the leading part. Aries desires to save those in distress; its vision is to be pure and perfect and work against evil by protecting beauty, love, and innocence. Leos need to take the hero of Aries and become the hero in their own life. They need to place themselves at the center of their world and fight for their truth, their beliefs, and their dreams. It's time to use your energy to create your vision, not to protect it. Cut the umbilical cord that keeps you more in the lives of others than on your own path. Within you is your own uniqueness, something special to offer the world. The hero of Sagittarius will take what makes you different and special and offer it to the world.

Division Is Over

The Leo is not afraid to face its fear and mix it with joy. Fear and pain don't diminish joy—they empower it. Thus we began the blending of light and shadow, the sweet with the sour. The Leo has experienced enough of life to know that it doesn't work when you keep things divided into compartments such as good and bad, right and wrong, me and you. Yes, good people do bad things and bad people do good things. Doing something right often leads to creating everything wrong, and following the wrong path often leads you to the pot of gold at the end of the rainbow. How do you make sense of the world? Is there any way to know what is real and what isn't?

The only way to know if you are on the right path is by listening to your inner guide and your heart. If you do not pay attention to your intuition or your inner voice, you find it hard to know just what to do. The right choice can leave you feeling empty and alone. You've got to learn how to make the choice that *feels right*. When you rely on your feelings rather than just your mind, you can't go wrong. To do this you've got to go beyond logic and your need to feel in control. You have to have faith in the universe or a higher power—one that is guiding you and leading you to happiness and your destiny.

Where Is Love?

Love is everywhere if it is within you and nowhere if you don't have it in your heart. It won't matter if you are on an island in the South Seas, in the mountains of Tibet, or in the middle of New York City, when you have love in your heart—not fear—you will attract love to you.

Love is not the desire to be loved. When you're looking for love you live in fear of not finding it. The relationships you attract are desperate, not happy. If no one is ever enough, you will never find enough. If you are always measuring love against an image or an ideal, it can never be right or fulfilling. Tell yourself you don't know what love is, that you're willing to experience it in a new way. You have a right to have love your way, but not out of judgment, out of choice. Know what makes you smile, happy, delighted, and challenged. Know that you need to be challenged. Love should not be locked into one image—it should amuse and excite you. When love has only one expression, you are cutting it off from the passion that ignited it and it will go stale and die.

High Principles

One of the ways Leos escape pain and sorrow is by having strong beliefs and lofty principles. This lifts you above your grief, but it keeps you stuck by making you feel isolated and alone. High principles give you strength or something to rely on when you lack faith in yourself—they are substitutes to inner knowing and love. When you hold on to one truth and don't allow it to change with the needs of the moment, you become a tyrant or a dictator. Yes, your intentions are to help others and show them the best way, but they have the right to find their own way. Your way may not be the best way for them. There is no such thing as *the best way*. Truth is a very individual experience and although we can strive to be honest and respectful to others and ourselves, all the rest is up for grabs. There is no best job, no best way to handle Aunt Mary, no best way to earn money—we all have our own unique approach. Learn to accept the truth of others—choose for your own truth—and you will stay on your own path and receive what you need from others.

The Checklist

To reach self-love you must be able to:

- Postpone gratification.
- Choose a response instead of react.
- See your needs and feelings as important.
- Disappoint those you love for what's important or essential to you.
- Adjust your values as you change; adjust your priorities to suit the new consciousness that comes with every experience.
- Stand up for your truth or what you believe in.
- Divide your truths into what you value and what serves your goals.
- Gain from mistakes and tragedies. Learn something from what goes wrong and use it to give those moments meaning.
- Go beyond betrayal and rejection and not take it personally. Others reject and let go because they lack faith. Once you have faith you understand this point.
- Let go of the control (fear) and surrender to your heart. Listen to it and let it guide you. The more you trust it, the more it will serve you.
- Be your own best friend. Can you give yourself a pep talk, praise yourself and give yourself a reward?
- Balance work with play—real play—the kind that frees the spirit and allows you to feel free and good about life.

The Father Takes You into the Outer World

It is how your father was received by the world that will determine whether or not you see him as successful and strong. If others respected and loved him, it won't matter if he is the president of his company, or has a big house, because you will feel proud and eager to follow in his footsteps. However, if your father was very successful and no one liked him—including your mother—you may have trouble following your dreams and becoming successful. You will believe that this makes you into a not nice person. If your father loved you and brought you into his world, it won't matter what that world is. You value it because you value him. If your father was the head of the mob, you might have to look at what you value and separate your love for him from the environment in which it was created. Your mission is to see that success can be whatever you want it to be; the choice is yours. You don't have to repeat your parents' mistakes. (See Figure 9.1 for the Leo Star.)

The First Level of Consciousness

The first level of consciousness divides the eleventh house and first step, and the third house and fifth step. You are challenged to accept your strength and choose for your truth no matter how wise or powerful others are. No one knows the secrets of your heart, so no can choose your path. Do not fear that you lose your freedom if you choose to be strong; on the contrary, you gain freedom when you become independent.

Step One: The Eleventh House

Gemini: I Avoid Choices If I Can't Be Perfect

The path to success is hard work and it reveals my weaknesses. If I follow my heart I will have to face up to the fact that I'm not perfect. To own my power is to shatter my illusions and the images that have sustained me. It's easier to let others take charge and accept their truth—or is it?

So long as you don't learn how to add your heart and soul to what you are doing, you will stay removed from your greatness and your power. You need to turn your choices over to a higher power and listen to your inner voice. You will then see that faith is stronger than facts and knowledge. Faith goes beyond the mind, and what it can and can't understand, and it finds the solution to the problem in the unknown. You don't have to be perfect to be great; you just have to believe in yourself.

> You are in level one if your choices rely on knowledge.
> You are in level two when you can challenge what is known.
> (Levels three and four are listed at the end of step one in the fourth
>   level of consciousness.)

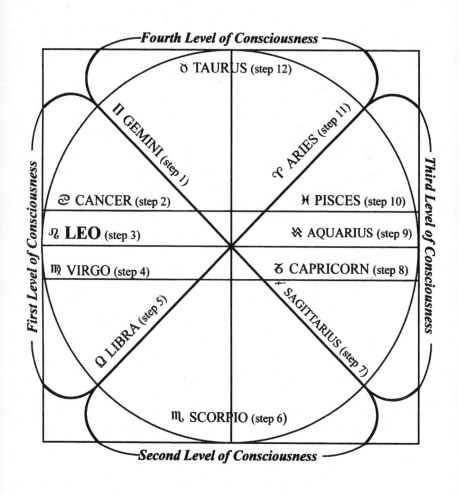

Figure 9.1. The Leo Star

Step Two: The Twelfth House

Cancer: There Are No Guarantees

I work so hard—sure I get compensated, but the sacrifice is a lot and others who do less often get more. Is there no fairness in life? The reward was so important to me that I've forgotten about the work—all I think of is the results. This influences my choices and I make more mistakes. I need to let go and have faith that everything will work out all right.

You are so worried about how things are going to turn out that you've taken yourself out of the moment, and that means you have less power, less instinct, and less joy in your life. Let go of the results and you'll be present and more successful.

> You are in level one when you depend on others for protection.
> You are in level two when you depend on yourself for protection.
> You are in level three when you have faith and depend on your dream.
> You are in level four when you have faith that the moment you're in is
>   where you should be.

Step Three: The First House

Leo: I Have the Strength to Turn Things Around

I used to believe that you turned something around by forcing it to happen, by putting pressure on others to do a better job. What I've learned, however, is that the more love and support I give to others, the more love and support they give me when I need it.

When you can let go of force and add love, you change your environment and the people in it. If you treat others with love (that doesn't mean you become their doormat), you create unity and a feeling of togetherness. Others enjoy giving to you because you have seen them as human beings with a heart, not as a workhorse. This is different from the pleasing love of the early steps; it does not come from need but from a true desire to give. This creates a different result.

You are in level one if you feel strength is found in approval or dominance.

You are in level two if you feel strength is challenging the authority.

You are in level three if you feel strength is faith.

You are in level four if you feel strength is turning your problems over to a higher power.

Step Four: The Second House

Virgo: I Try to Do Everything Perfectly

I am consumed with doing everything perfectly and so I never get everything done, or to my satisfaction. When I can see what is essential and can separate that from everything else, it is easier for me to let go. I must learn how to delegate and believe that what happens is for a reason and that doing things "right" is not always the best way. Everything has its own path to take, even my projects.

The worst thing you can do is try to do it all perfectly. When you need to be perfect you don't have faith in your ability to wing it, or make it work. The more you take a risk and open yourself up to new possibilities, the more faith you have in yourself and the easier it is to see what can be eliminated. Not everything in life should get the same importance. There are times when details are essential to the success of a project and there are times when your health or need to relax is more important than getting everything right. The lesson of letting go is one of the hardest. Keep reflecting and observing that you are the issue and only you can give yourself more love and time.

You are in level one when you give to please others.

You are in level two when you give to strengthen yourself.

You are in level three when you find the freedom you are seeking in your work.

You are in level four when you feel loved by yourself and others.

Step Five: The Third House

Libra: I Choose for Truth and Still Get Rejected and Judged

I thought that choosing for truth would be easy, but I realized that everyone had their own opinion of what truth was. There is always someone smarter than me telling me I'm wrong or judging my choices. When do I listen to myself?

When you listen to others you run into trouble. Go ahead and glean information that you don't have, but you must make the final choice. Only you can choose for you. Everyone has a different definition of truth—just go to the philosophy department in a bookstore. If everyone can't agree, how do you know something is right? It has to be right for only you and only you need to know what is important for the moment. Your wisdom will grow as you do. Listen to the universe, it will send you what you need and help you get your answers. All you have to do is be open and listen.

> You are in level one when your truth is what others want it to be.
> You are in level two when you challenge their truth and your own.
> (Levels three and four are listed at the end of step five in the second level of consciousness.)

The Second Level of Consciousness

The second level of consciousness divides the third house and fifth step, and the fifth house and seventh step. It asks you to look at wisdom as an expression of an experience and not as an irrevocable truth. You cannot depend on pure knowledge to keep rising in consciousness. Instead you must be able to see truth where others are afraid to look, such as in the shadow where anger, fear, and nothingness exist. This has wisdom, too, and if it is ignored it will defeat you.

Step Five: The Third House (Second Level)

Libra: I Listen to the Truth in My Heart

I am no longer confused by whose truth to follow, or who is smart and who isn't; instead, I listen to my instincts and let them guide me. Of course, I study and make myself familiar with what I am doing or where I am going, but I don't need to know everything to get going; I will learn as I go.

Once your truth is based on your inner voice you are able to make a better choice, which gives you the confidence to let go of things having to be perfect. They are what they are. You can now accept the answers you get from the universe even when they don't make sense—you have faith that things will turn out the way they should in the long run. If you didn't get the job it's because there is a better one on the way or a different opportunity that you wouldn't see if you were working. With the power of acceptance you can commit to a path without getting too impatient that things are not working the way you want them to, when you want them to.

> You are in level three when you have faith in your truth and your dream.
> You are in level four when your truth is based on your vision.

Step Six: The Fourth House

Scorpio: I Can't Find Love Because I'm Not Perfect

I can't see myself surrendering to anyone or anything—especially love. All my relationships love me but I find fault with them. I guess it's because I have trouble accepting myself. If I could accept myself and love myself I'd find someone I loved.

You now see how silly it is to believe that love cares whether or not you are perfect. Love goes beyond images to the spirit. When you find someone who shares your spirit you find love, and surrender is easy because you have not lost control—you feel empowered. With love in your life everything is easier. If you are self-critical you attract either that criticism or someone who is oblivious to your faults. This doesn't come from love; it comes from stupidity. And so you don't respect them, but at least you don't get judged. The best way is to begin to praise and love you. See where you can improve, and support that improvement instead of attacking yourself or saying you can't do it. Love is the path you have chosen; it won't appear until you learn to love yourself.

> You are in level one when you believe you are good or bad.
> You are in level two when you can hide your truth from those who are negative.
> You are in level three when you know that you are both good and bad.
> You are in level four when you know that it is your intention that makes you good.

Step Seven: The Fifth House

Sagittarius: I Look Up to Wisdom

Wisdom is a wonderful thing but it doesn't have all the answers. Wisdom has taken me far, but if I had stopped at wisdom I wouldn't have gotten some of my most important answers—I needed faith and my heart for that.

It is important to use wisdom and let it take you as far as it can, but don't stop there. There is a greater truth that lies beyond what makes sense and what can be figured out with logic. To find this knowledge you need to rely on your instincts, passion, and love.

> You are in level one if you believe everything you are told.
> You are in level two when you can challenge what you know.
> (Levels three and four are listed at the end of step seven in the third level of consciousness.)

The Third Level of Consciousness

The third level of consciousness divides the fifth house and seventh step, and the ninth house and eleventh step. It asks that you be able to own your vision and your dream even if it doesn't make sense or seem wise to the majority. It's time to follow your heart—if you let wisdom and rewards dictate your dream, you will never find your passion or fulfill your destiny.

Step Seven: The Fifth House (Third Level)

Sagittarius: The Reward I Want Determines My Wisdom

I used to wonder why some people were just smarter than others. I soon began to notice that those who were not concerned with the reward were able to do and learn more and got ahead. I have to look at my need to achieve and how important it is for me to receive recognition for what I do. I think it gets in the way.

When you let go of the reward you open the door for real advancement. When we focus on anything in the future it takes us away from the moment, the only place where things can change or happen. Stay focused on the moment; do the work and you'll get the reward you want and more.

You are in level three when you have faith in your differences and your
unique ideas.
You are in level four when love gives you all the answers.

Step Eight: The Sixth House

Capricorn: I Let Go of My Fear of Not Being Perfect

*I was driven to do everything and do it myself. Finally I realized that was impos-
sible and to accomplish anything meaningful in life I'd have to get past this feeling
that everything should "look" right. When something "feels" right it's good enough
for me and I let go.*

When you make the shift from outer images to an inner measuring system,
you are on your way to success. Your instincts are going to tell you when something is right or wrong, and when you can rely on this rather than appearances you move to the head of the line. This also allows you to accept steps
and rewards in life that may not feed your ego or fit the image of success, but
it may give you important experience or just plain make you happy. And isn't
that what life is really about—being happy?

You are in level one when you believe that being perfect fits an image.
You are in level two when you value your freedom to express over an
image.
You are in level three if you have let go of the reward and are following
your passion.
You are in level four if you love your life and what you are doing.

Step Nine: The Seventh House

Aquarius: Freedom and Success Are One and the Same

*Freedom is something I have always valued, but no matter how I have pursued it
something always got in the way. When I learned how to accept the moment with
my heart, however, I began to turn my life around. The power of the heart is the
power to change fear into love. It's the power to heal. When you add the heart, you
add the magic.*

You have the secret to success: You love what you're doing and you'll go right to the top. When you love what you're doing, you do it well, and you make it your own. Love brings out your uniqueness and it is your uniqueness that will make you great. Others come to you for what makes you unique and special. Everyone has something special to offer the world.

> You are in level one when freedom is an escape.
> You are in level two when you stand up for your differences.
> You are in level three when you believe in your differences.
> You are in level four when there are no differences—only spirit expressing itself.

Step Ten: The Eighth House

Pisces: I Reveal to the World My Dream

I have protected my dream and held it inside because I was afraid that it would not bring me enough satisfaction or wisdom if I pursued it. I now realize that it is the dream that protects me, and that when I stand up for it and use it in my life, others acknowledge me, listen to me, and think that I am wise. The dream is my source of wisdom when I have the strength to share it with others.

When you dishonor your dream by ignoring it and believing in everyone else but yourself, you undermine your strength, magnetism, truth, and wisdom. When you can stand up for your dreams, they empower you and lead you to where you need to go.

> You are in level one if your dream is an escape.
> You are in level two if you are confronting the dreams that others want you to pursue.
> You are in level three when you have faith in your dream and follow it with your heart.
> You are in level four when the world is one big dream.

Step Eleven: The Ninth House

Aries: I Give Up on the Hero

I wanted to be a hero—someone others could depend on, someone who made a difference in the world. I thought that if I pursued my own dream and vision, others

would see me as selfish and I would never be able to be a hero to anyone but myself.
This brought me the answer: I need to let go of being a hero and just love my dream.

When you let go of being the hero, you let go of the ego and can see your vision more clearly. Yes, now you will be able to expand your vision and accept a greater truth about yourself.

> You are in level one when you are the hero for others and follow their vision.
> You are in level two when you are the hero for your dream and confront others.
> (Levels three and four are listed at the end of step eleven in the fourth level of consciousness.)

The Fourth Level of Consciousness

The fourth level of consciousness divides the ninth house and eleventh step. It asks you to accept your dream as the source of wisdom and truth. When you do, you no longer have difficulty making choices because all your choices come from your dream. The dream resides in the heart and so your reward and your choices are both love—there is no separation—they have merged.

Step Eleven: The Ninth House (Fourth Level)

Aries: I Recognize the Hero in Me

I thought I had lost the hero, but when I let go I saw everyone as a hero and I realized that I was a hero, too.

Never forget that what you let go of you see in others; validate it in others and it will rise within you. Don't give in to jealousy, hate, or anger; honor the best in humanity and it will uplift you. Letting go of heroism allows you to see your real strengths. It is not just the big challenges, but the ability to fill life every day with love, joy, and enthusiasm that makes a true hero.

> You are in level three when you see others as the hero of their dream.
> You are in level four when you see yourself as the hero of your dream.

Step Twelve: The Tenth House

Taurus: The Reward I Want Is Love

I have let go of love, attacked it, sought it with passion, but I finally have found it within me. You cannot seek love; when you become love through loving acts, you will have love in your life.

The love you always wanted is now found within your own heart. You have learned that through acceptance you have the power to change your world and to change it through love.

> You are in level one if you are seeking and giving unconditional love.
> You are in level two if you are confronting the rules of love.
> You are in level three if you have faith in your dream.
> You are in level four if you give yourself unconditional love.

Step One: The Eleventh House (Fourth Level)

Gemini: My Choice and My Truth Are the Same

My fear of making the wrong choice took me on a journey that led to the heart. Now my choices come from love and faith, and so they are not in conflict with my vision of a perfect world—the future and the moment are one.

When you don't judge your fear but give it love and support you change it into love. When there is love there is unity and harmony and a way to solve the problems of the world.

> You are in level three if you are making your choices based on your inner voice.
> You are in level four when love determines your path and your voice.

The Cross

The cross is composed of the eleventh, fifth, ninth, and third houses and is where change must occur. (See Figure 9.1 on page 206.) The two fixed houses represented by Gemini and Sagittarius challenge each other to see a greater truth:

Gemini (eleventh house): *I have given up on choices because I didn't believe I was wise enough to make them. However, once I started believing in myself and my dream I found my truth and that made me wise.*

Sagittarius (fifth house): *I oppose authority and stand up to it; I do not protect myself or anyone else from the truth or my dream. It is better to know than to stay ignorant. The more I accept what I do know, the more I am able to surrender to my heart and it leads me to love. My ability to confront my fear has freed me from the need to use my ego as my source of strength and has enabled me to receive the rewards and the magic of life that I deserve.*

The two mutable houses represented by Aries and Libra must anchor themselves in this new truth by taking a stand:

Aries (eleventh house): *When I get enough experience I begin to see that when I listen to the voice within me my choices are better than those of the experts—the voice knows me and what I need. I begin to have faith in that voice and that gives me the faith to make more choices and to confront those who believe they are better or wiser than me. I find my voice and my vision.*

Libra (third house): *I am stopped by the authority of those that I believe are better or wiser than me. What I have learned is that no one knows better than me when it comes to my life. Others can give me information and advice, but only God and I know my destiny .*

PART FOUR

The Third Level of Consciousness

"Without faith a man can do nothing; with it all
things are possible."

—Sir William Osler

The third level of consciousness is all about faith. The world the way you knew it begins to fall apart as you gain experience and knowledge of how the world really works. Your truth, values, possessions, and friends—whatever you were holding on to up to now—is being challenged, and to grow and go higher you must let them go. If you can't let go you can't move forward and accept what doesn't make sense or what doesn't give answers. Do you believe that you will be given what you need to get the job done? How strong is your faith in yourself and your dream? Only what you truly believe in will work. This is where you learn what is important and what isn't; the only difference is the universe is doing the testing, not you. You may have to go without a job, friends, or money; you may lose what you wanted because of fate. Is it over? Can you rebuild what you lost? Can you keep going when there is nothing to hang on to except what you have in your heart? The Wheel of Fortune has turned, and what was in the light goes into the shadow, and what was in the shadow comes to light. You must have faith that the wheel will turn again, and that what you lost will come back to you. The more you believe the more exciting this period of the journey will be. It's where you learn what is really holding you together— your beliefs and faith.

VIRGO: Faith

(August 24 through September 23)

Where am I going, who am I today?
In how much of my life, do I have a say?
It all seems so useless, hopeless, or wrong.
What ever happened to my soul and my song?
Is there something more, what could there be?
Is this something invisible, that I can't see?
Is joy a choice, that could me mine?
Have I reached the end of sorrow's line?
Within me I hear "Open the door."
Love lives in your heart, it sits at the core
Open up, let go, turn it over to God
Stand up, sit down, lay close to the sod.
Within you are answers, stop seeking outside
Happiness is yours, just give up the pride.

Question Six

About Your Parents: In what did your mother have faith? What did she
believe would give her strength or a feeling of importance?

About Yourself: In what do you have faith? What values work for you in
good times and bad? What do you believe is the one thing that will
change your life?

As a Virgo you are wise and clever enough to know that the world before
you cannot be conquered by hard work, perseverance, and talent, nor can you

be protected by money, fame, and possessions. Too many factors lie beyond your control. But fate or nature's wrath are not your only problems, it's consequences that worry you now. You didn't escape the ignorance of your past, and so now you're afraid to choose—What if you make a mistake? Was luck just a postponement of your punishment? Was the universe just waiting for a more effective time to cause you pain and sorrow? Could God and the world be that cruel? Or is there something you are missing that could change it all and turn this confusing chaotic world into a place of logic and common sense?

It's called faith and when you have it you see that it alone divides the human race, not social boundaries, wealth, race, or color. Those who have it have the advantage, they endure where others give up; they find a way when the path is blocked; they are protected and divinely guided when earth caves in around them; and in a competition, they spring ahead and leap beyond the finish line. Therefore, don't feel superior if you own a great business or take vacations on your yacht—happiness and real power are only possible if you have faith. To have faith requires you to take risks and struggle to keep going when there is no visible sign of support. Laziness is not rewarded in heaven or on earth, and there's a reason for it: it stunts your growth. When you don't have a challenge there is no resistance and without resistance you will stay where you are, accept the answers you are given, avoid fear, and ignore new ideas. Boring people are lazy people, they have removed themselves from life's challenges and they are holding on to exactly what is causing their paralysis— fear. When your life is about fear, it's about walls and limitations, not excitement and adventure—it's about giving up, not letting go.

When you give up, you need a protector; when you take control your ego wants to conquer and be superior; and when you let go you do so out of faith and confidence in yourself and life. Many Virgos have turned their power over to someone else. This happens when you erroneously believe someone else knows your life better than you. What you didn't realize is that without power you serve, you don't share. Someone becomes the ruler and someone the servant. It's not about equality—it's about control. To share you must have something to offer, and you feel that you don't. If you have expressed your feelings of lack by taking the power, you are the tyrant, the leader—or the person everyone goes to—to get a job done. You have all the responsibility and this can make you selfish and angry. Because others don't give to you, you must take care of your own needs, and if there is a lot of anger, you may become insensitive to others, even cruel. Not enough responsibility swings the pendulum in the other direction. We have too much sensitivity or emotional neediness here. When you avoid power, you must get your needs met by using fear to gain an advantage. These souls meet their needs by being the victim or getting ill. Of course the black hole that lives within will not be satisfied by any of your offerings, for it needs faith to diminish its yearnings; your spirit is deprived.

To be happy in life you must acknowledge that you have both spiritual and physical needs. The circle of faith that began in Cancer and empowered through hard work in Leo must now be merged in Virgo. Faith must be used in your choices and brought into the moment. This is done by using others to make you strong. Yes, whatever you acknowledge in others you strengthen in you. Each time you have faith in someone else you increase it in yourself. When you see others as greedy and evil, you strengthen greed in yourself. When you see others as loving and giving, you strengthen love in you. What you truly value you will see in the world around you. And how you honor what you value determines how it will treat you. Letting go is how the process begins. Let's take love as an example. You must first let go of your need for love and have faith that you will find it. When you see others as loving and share their love, you increase the power of love within you. If you continue to do this you will become love, a symbol of it, a magnet for it, and you will have it in your life.

The following three steps will help you learn how to let go and strengthen something in you:

1. *Take what you want and turn it over to your higher power, the universe or God.* You are not ready to receive until you have the faith to let go. Have faith that it will return.

2. *Look around.* As soon as you let go, your environment will be filled with what you feel is gone. If you want to be pregnant, and you let go of it, everyone you know will be pregnant.

3. *Take the challenge.* Can you be happy for others when they have what you want? Can you honor what is missing whenever you see it and be happy that it is in your life, even if it is not with you? Validate it and you bring it forth in you. Be jealous or condemn it because others have it and you don't, and you cut yourself off from what you desire. Once you increase its power within you through faith you become a magnet for it in life.

The ability to bring something to you through faith gives you the confidence you need to go out in life and accomplish your goals. If you know how to use symbols, the process will be easier.

The Power of Symbols

To gain the faith you need to let go, you must be able to rise above particulars and see the bigger picture—you need to look at life in symbols. If you love art and want it in your life you can have it, but if you want a particular piece of art, you might run into trouble. The universe can fulfill your love of art, but it can't necessarily give you one piece, because this may require the consent of someone else (we all have free will). It's the same with love. If you want love, marriage, and children, you can have it; if you want this particular person, you may not get him or her. The other person has to agree. Turn the objects of your desires into symbols and you will have abundance. Letting go is just moving up the ladder to a greater vision of the world. If you can't let go of the small things, you can't see the bigger picture. If you must stay attached to particulars, you won't get the gift of understanding or be able to forgive. Without these two incredible gifts, healing will be difficult. Without healing you will stay in anger and desire and never reach your greatness.

If you had faith in yourself and your dreams you wouldn't need protection, just a helping hand. Your goal would be new and greater ideas, not the limitations and protection of old ones. If you've shut down or tuned out life, you have tuned out yourself and you've stopped listening to your inner voice. Without this inner link to the greater wisdom you are totally dependent on others and your environment. Instead of the universe speaking to you through resistance and events, you see the pressure as an attack, challenges as another problem to be solved, and the quest as a fearful, dark path to be avoided.

You are seeking power—outer power and divine love—and in so doing you have split yourself in half. One part of you has judged sensitivity and compassion as useless and so you avoid vulnerability at all cost. The part of you that yearns for love is unhappy with the luxury, power, and fame that you have chosen to protect you. Deep down you're looking for eternal truths and love. Because you don't know how to integrate power and love, you see them as separate and in opposition. When you gain the consciousness to reevaluate strength, you become confused by what and where you find it. You know that the essence of love is not pride, that truth is not a mask, that strength of spirit is stronger than control, and that the only people who reveal these qualities are the downtrodden victims of the world. Stripped of their desires, devoid of dreams and thoughts of freedom, the victims of life are the true heroes—they keep on living without the promise of a reward. They move forward without protection, masks, or pretenses, without pride or even truth to sustain them. They do what they have to do and many find meaning in each moment. Their joy is always embraced by pain or sorrow; yet they hold on to it with laughter and play, creating and propagating, always accepting and hoping that tomorrow will bring a new and better day. Their life depends on God, fate, and a higher power. They follow the path presented to them. Is this not a hero? Is this not you? Does faith mean you have to be impoverished and poor? Is this what you are afraid of? Is this why you seek to distance yourself from poverty and victims by having money, success, and security?

If you are a Virgo who has begun to soul search, you are connected with the emptiness you feel inside. This emptiness makes you resonate more closely with victims than those who are victorious. You see that those who are in power take the spoils of their battles and indulge, use, and waste the resources of life, seldom sharing it with the less fortunate. You choose a winner to protect you and at the same time you loathe his or her values. You despise how they create solutions by creating more problems, how they hide their feelings and emotions and never listen to any one or stay present in any moment that does not have them at the center. This is the world of the ego, and you've got one foot still there and one foot raised to reach a new awareness where spirit is at the helm. Do you hide your spirituality and fear that someone will recognize the bareness and loneliness of your soul? Don't fear this place of honor, for it indicates that your soul is ready to accept the higher realms of its existence. It is the lessening of your attachment to the world of luxury and success that gives you strength and spiritual power. You are pitting your spirit against values that you don't believe in and you wonder why nothing works. Who are you anyway? A mask for the world to see? Or a spirit ready to uplift others and the world through the power of its being?

The world will not change through force. To turn life into the promise—a wonderful place where competition does not exist, where justice prevails and love and harmony always wins over fear and anger—you've got to change you and let go of others. When you can see yourself in a new light, you can see others in a new light, too. For example, your angry boss will be just a weak and fragile man no one listens to. In your vulnerable father you will see the strength of spirit, the ability to put others first, the sensitivity to care, even if it means more sadness and pain. He refused to live with walls, and it cost him dearly. How does one balance the ego and spirit? How do we give and receive and keep the flow of life going?

You need to compromise or let go to balance the scales of extremes. The best way is by turning your problem over to your higher power. When you do you free yourself to see the issue in a whole new light. Faith allows you to let go of it, and when you can let go you can take the position that needs to be taken to get the issue resolved.

Turning your problems over helps you forgive others. Once you can forgive you have the power to heal. The ego loves to imitate forgiveness and use it as a source of power. It rises above others and says "I forgive you" as if it were God. That is not forgiveness and it's not healing, it's annoying. You are seeking to be in control, not letting go. In fact, it is because you can't let go that you pretend that you can forgive. When you pretend you have forgiven you get even as soon as you get the chance. And you do it in a way that allows you to remain unconscious and innocent. This is not empowering; it is manipulating, and sooner or later it will turn around and bite you in the tail.

The more self-control you have the less control over the world you need. It's time to choose a response instead of just respond. Don't return in kind what you are given, choose your actions and you will become the creator of your world. When the waitress at the diner doesn't say good morning, don't get angry—ask her if she's had a bad day. Use the power of your inner joy to reach out to others and turn their unhappiness into love, even if it's for a moment. Have you ever thought of how contagious a smile is? When someone is happy everyone wants to be around them. That person can be you, but to be truly happy you have to choose it; you must reach for joy and hold on to it.

Joy

Joy is a choice. If you never reach for joy, it will be a traveler passing through your life. When it's there you will not enjoy it, but when the moment passes you will let it go. Joy is not capable of choosing you, it's a magnet and what it is attracted to is love. So if you look at it with envy, anger, or need, it will turn away and seek an open heart. To choose joy you've got to believe you deserve it. You must be able to see it around you and open yourself up to receive it. It takes strength to hold on to joy, because you must push suffering and sadness aside, and we all know how heavy they are. If you're reluctant because you're afraid of being disappointed, hear this. Joy does not promise you anything, it offers you itself right now, in the moment. You don't have to wait for joy, you can have it whenever you choose, or you can let it go and go back to your pain and sorrow. It's up to you.

Fear and Love

Since you can't divide the world between good and bad any longer, try separating fear from love and the experiences you associate with them. The experiences of fear are black-listed in your psyche, while those with love get all the attention. Some of them may be judged wrongly; perhaps the judged object just happened to be around and had very little to do with what happened. It doesn't matter; every time you see it, it brings up fear. If your first bus ride to school was a nightmare you may avoid buses. If your first love was a foreigner and he jilted you, you may hate foreigners. You get the picture. Go back over your fears and free your associations.

The Power of Choice

Experience has taught you that those who can make the tough choices are the leaders of the world. They are the ones who get the rewards. You begin to admire those who take charge—those who are not afraid of making others angry by taking a stand that needs to be taken. Decisions—strong ones—backed by belief and confidence make you feel safe, protected. You see that those who can express their truth directly, quickly, and without trying to protect anyone actually do less harm. Protection and too much compassion prolong the pain. You want the bad news first; this way once you accept it everything else is a piece of cake. You are attracted to those who judge quickly and harshly. They don't sugarcoat life, but they deal with it head-on. You are tired of illusions and empty promises; you don't mind being let down, just get it over with fast.

What you are learning is that you are not really in control. It is only when you can be in uncertainty that you will discover a greater truth. To choose uncertainty you must be able to turn things over to Him.

Acceptance of the Ego

The strongest position is one where both the ego and your spirit are leaders; they share the position of power depending on the demands of the moment. Sometimes being nice just doesn't do it. For example, if your boss is trying to coerce you into sleeping with him, being nice won't protect you. You may have to threaten him, and mean it. When someone is trying to hurt you, you must protect yourself before you think about forgiveness. The ego is there to provide a buffer zone so that you don't have to fight for every little battle, because your ego's got an attitude that keeps the bullies away. When your ego is seeking attention, instead of working with you toward a goal, it works against you; it wants its fix or instant reward. Once you can give your ego faith, however, and get it to work with you toward a greater reward, then you'll have increased your magnetism and decreased your inner conflict.

Values and Self-Discipline

Once you have broken a few rules you realize why they were there—they give you boundaries and limits to protect you. Values are inner limits that protect you from desire—yours and others. Values and rules should be strong for children and useful for adults. If your values don't work, they don't serve you and you need to replace them with what does. It is hoped that by now you have tested the values of your parents and put your own twist to them. Values give self-discipline because you know what you would and wouldn't do under any situation. The more discipline you have, the more focused you are on your goals.

The Virgo soul knows how to either deprive itself or surrender to self—indulgence. There is no middle ground in the beginning. Either you are coming into Virgo afraid to let yourself go, or you are running at full speed toward your desires. Both choices lead to disillusionment and disaster. When you deprive yourself, you gain strength over your desires, but as soon as you let go of deprivation they return in full force—or stronger. Just ask anyone who has been on a diet. It works only as long as you are saying no. As soon as you give in to your desires, your desires once again go out of control. Acceptance and letting go is the key factor. You must accept the moment and yourself to break the grip of your desires on your psyche.

Your Inner Core

Truth—everyone's got a truth and a belief that's all their own. Each of us redefines the Ten Commandments—we make them work for us. Thou shall not steal becomes thou shall not steal from my family, but it's all right to cheat the telephone company or the government. Humans make their truths work for them, at least the strong ones do. The danger is that you'll lose touch with the essence of truth and end up violating what you truly believe in. Your challenge in Virgo is to hold on to your truth and still be friends with the truth of others. It's important to be able to accept differences without feeling the need to eradicate or conquer what doesn't agree with you. The only motivation for that is fear. If you don't believe enough in your faith, the faith of others will threaten you. And instead of looking at your beliefs, you try to destroy the messenger of new ideas. Not a positive way to grow, but a popular choice through the centuries. When you reach a level of awareness that others are important to your own survival, that differences are what make you strong, you will reach out to your fellow man and help him become strong, knowing that by so doing you also have strengthened yourself. When you go to a foreign country you are asked to do this all the time. You know your rules, you respect theirs, and you return to yours when you are back home. Throughout life, others will challenge and test your values. Do not give them up for temptations, adventure, or a lack of courage. Respect them, change them, but don't dismiss them; they are the core of your beliefs and they are there to serve you.

If you still don't know how to let go, pray for guidance. Hold the two conflicting thoughts together and let them battle each other. Tell yourself you want to learn how to let go, and ask for help. I guarantee you will either find yourself in a situation where you have to let go so that you can learn the lesson, or you will experience the magic through someone else. The universe is the best teacher if you can just open your eyes and let it take you to where you need to go.

Who's in Control?

Who has the real power? This is the question that concerns the Virgo. For those who divide love and fear, the answer is different. Fear's authority is possessions, money, and fame; spirit's authority is love, unity, and peace. The highest authority is God, the second best is a blend of worldly success with spiritual strength. When you use your mind and spirit together and direct them to support your goals, you have the best of both worlds at your disposal. People in the business world look upon you with respect, and spiritual souls will recognize your goodness and your willingness to make a difference. When this happens, money and power don't interfere with your spiritual life—they are used to bring comfort and empowerment to all. If you are in the public eye and you use your influence to direct either youth or the population toward a better world, then you are doing the world a service and you are using your success to do it.

Criticism and Judgment

If you're a Virgo, the words criticism and judgment are not strangers—you live by these two words too much. Let's look at why. Part of your mission is to see what's missing and see what's wrong with a situation, *so that you can make it right*. If you can't implement change, it's better to keep your mouth shut. You also hate being in uncertainty and the unknown, which means you dislike it when others hesitate and do not make quick decisions. This fills you with anxiety, so you often jump in and make decisions for them. Of course, this cements their dependency on you and continues to disempower them and assures you that they won't take charge of their life. You want the control and that's what has to be let go of. Not everyone wants to know what you think is wrong with their life, and if you offer this too often, you may lose a friend. Your inquiring mind should be used to serve you, not to correct the lives of others. If you don't make your own mistakes, you won't learn. Let your children make their own choices and give them the consequences to those choices, and they will learn and grow strong.

The Quest for Balance

Balance—is it possible for a Virgo? Of course it is, but only when you shift your focus from trying to create order in your environment and start creating inner harmony through faith. The biggest problem to balance is responsibility—most Virgos take on too much in one area and not enough in another. You probably gained approval as a child for doing the chores, helping out, being smart, and getting things done. If your parents started to expect these things from you, you may find that all your relationships are a burden. You choose people who let you do it all. It gives you the control you want, but not the love. Give up the control and accept help; let things get done a little less perfectly and you'll be happy instead of right.

When you fall in love, love overrides the negative and everything seems rosy and wonderful. Your state of mind has the power to overcome the mind's problems because the heart is happy. Keep your outer world perfect and your inner world will be confused and you will live in chaos. Take the time to sort out yourself. Rely on wisdom and the desire for truth no matter where it takes you, and you will find the peace and balance you were seeking.

The Mother Gives You Faith and Your Working Values

It is through your mother that you will learn the values that work and the ones that don't. What did she have faith in? Did her faith serve her well or did it keep her a victim and helpless? If your mother gave up on her dreams, she may value security, money, or a good image. There is nothing that will serve you less than these things, and if they were her values, her life was not about joy and the creative force. You must replace her values with those that work for you. Do not repeat her mistakes; instead, dare to risk to live by the rules that serve you. (See Figure 10.1 for the Virgo Star.)

The First Level of Consciousness

The first level of consciousness divides the eleventh house and first step, and the third house and fifth step. The soul finds itself caught between love and judgment and the need to protect itself from the pain of feeling unworthy or imperfect. As long as love and negativity or judgment remain separate and opposing issues in your life, you will not achieve the wisdom you will need to meet your goals. When you can let go and accept all of yourself you will discover a deeper and greater truth.

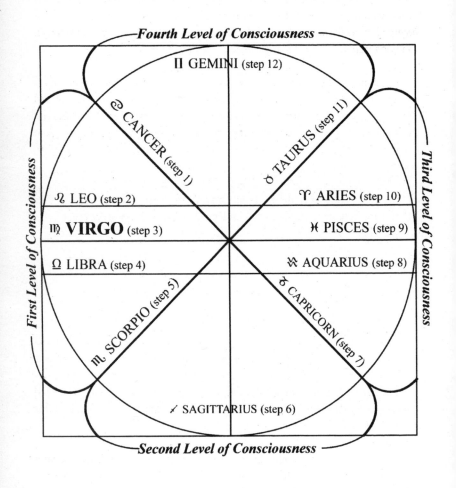

Figure 10.1. The Virgo Star

Step One: The First House

Cancer: Protection or Love?

The more successful I am, the more knowledge I have, the more I want to be protected. It doesn't make sense. It's as if I'm seeking the wrong rewards, so the accumulations of beautiful objects, homes, money, and glittery people only emphasize my own emptiness, not abundance. There has to be more, but I'm afraid to search for it because I know the answer lies with the needy, the lost, and the victims of the world. I'm not a victim. I will not look for myself in the forgotten.

You don't have to look for yourself in the forgotten, but you do have to remember what you let go of. You have lost your connection to your dream and with it your faith and spirit. Now you see it everywhere, in everyone else. And until you support their spirit, and help them reconnect to their dreams, your own spirit won't find the faith to push you beyond your ego's need for comfort, pleasure, and reward.

You are in level one when you depend on others for protection.
You are in level two when you challenge your need for protection.
(Levels three and four are listed at the end of step one in the fourth
level of consciousness.)

Step Two: The Eleventh House

Leo: Can I Be Strong if I Look at What Lies Inside?

I'm only as strong as my truth and my dreams and these things were just a mask, so I have no strength at all. I try to compensate for my lack of strength by removing myself from those who are sensitive and weak. I can serve the homeless or the ill because it is looked upon as an act of strength, and strangely enough it makes me feel stronger and more connected to me. I find that helping others is the only thing that makes me feel good about me.

You have reached the fork in the road; you can no longer continue your journey without your spirit and remain strong and invincible. You can make all the money you want, collect all the gold and jewels your heart desires, but love—real love—can't be bought, faith can't be bartered for, and truth cannot be hidden behind a mask forever. Your truth, the truth that says you are a divine being with a destiny, a purpose, and a uniqueness to share with the world, can no longer be hidden from you—others have known this for a while. Now it's time for you to shatter the mirror and look inside.

> You are in level one if you feel strength is found in approval or dominance.
> You are in level two if you feel strength is challenging the wisdom of your need to be perfect.
> You are in level three if you feel strength is faith in your dream.
> You are in level four if you feel strength is turning your problems over to a higher power.

Step Three: The First House

Virgo: What Is Holding on and Letting Go?

Haven't I let go enough? I've given up everything I want to do to please everyone else. My life revolves around others or keeping busy, what else do I need to do? I need to face the sadness in my soul. I'm lost and I don't want to admit it. I'm tired of doing, working, and striving just to hide. I need my dreams back and my goals. I need to choose without guilt and shame and own my own destiny.

Once you reach the point of desire, you're ready to find a greater truth. The search is on. You must hold on to your faith and let go of all the rest. What is really yours will come back to you, what is not important will be cleared from your path.

> You are in level one when you give to please others.
> You are in level two when you give to strengthen yourself.
> You are in level three when you see what you want everywhere around you.
> You are in level four when you have what you want all the time because it is within you.

Step Four: The Second House

Libra: Can I Have Truth Without Freedom of Choice?

Truth is such a big issue for everyone. I pretend that I have it by making strong, decisive and wise decisions, so much so that others come to me for advice. But I'm just playing with truth and pretending to be strong. I feel so empty and lost because I'm not doing what I love; I've chosen to be taken care of rather than to fulfill my dreams. I know now that will never make me happy.

You know better than anyone else that truth is not possible when you accept someone else's values, dreams, rewards, and wisdom. To live the protected life you've got to give up your inner yearnings and find happiness in what others are happy with. This works for a while; in fact, it's the reason you've become disconnected, but your giving heart has led you back to your own. To keep giving makes you want your own path more; to stop giving makes you feel weak and empty. You are divinely stuck.

> You are in level one when your truth is what others want it to be.
> You are in level two when you challenge their truth and your own.
> You are in level three when you have faith in your truth and your dream.
> You are in level four when you see truth in every moment.

Step Five: The Third House

Scorpio: If I Let Go of Love, Can I Choose Again?

Love—I thought it wasn't as important as money and security, but I'm beginning to wonder. Only when something is missing do you really see its value. The more I surrender and do things the "right" way or the "boss's" way, the emptier I feel. The emptier I feel the more my inner voice speaks to me and tells me to choose again. Maybe I will.

You have reached the point of choice again, and you are pondering how to choose this time. Why not learn from your mistakes and try something new? You don't need protection, you need love. When you have love you have protection and security—the kind that makes your heart sing.

> You are in level one when you believe that you are either good or bad.
> You are in level two when you can hide your truth when it's necessary.
> (Levels three and four are listed at the end of step five in the second level of consciousness.)

The Second Level of Consciousness

The second level of consciousness divides the third house and fifth step, and the fifth house and seventh step. You are asked to challenge the wisdom of the rewards you are seeking. Is this really what you want? If you are listening to your inner wisdom you still have your dreams and chances are you have love in your life. If you have taken the path of protection, you will question everything you have and everything you do. The key ingredient to your truth lies in satisfaction. How filled are you with divine discontent? How satisfied are you with your life?

Step Five: The Third House (Second Level)

Scorpio: Love Is the Only Reward Worth Surrendering To

There is no question in my mind that what I want is love; love is the most precious thing in life. I feel love everywhere: in nature, in children, in work, and in the people around me. It brings me joy and happiness and it makes me want to help others find this love and joy in their life.

You have reached a place of great wisdom and truth; you realize the necessity of love and its power. When you have it, it doesn't matter what you have; when you don't have it, it makes you want everything to excess. The more you pursue desires, the more obsessive and excessive you become; the more faith and love you have in your choices, the more you can accept and let go and find happiness with what you have.

> You are in level three when you know that you are both good and bad. You are in level four when you know that it is your intention that makes you good.

Step Six: The Fourth House

Sagittarius: Real Wisdom Comes When I Let Go

I let go of listening to myself a long time ago and then this voice came back so strong it frightened me. It was never gone; I had just ignored it and when I thought it was lost forever, it came back wiser and stronger than ever. How could I not have listened to its wisdom? Perhaps I needed more experience before I paid attention.

Anyway, I listen now and it's guiding me back to my heart, to my faith, and to an exciting world.

You are stronger than you think you are. You are a survivor and you don't give in just because you are afraid. There is nothing wrong with fear if you don't let it paralyze you or stop you from hearing your own inner voice. Once you know that fear can be faced without dying, you will face it again and again and feel victorious each time. You now have a secret of the universe— facing your fears makes you stronger, running from them undermines your strength and what you believe in.

> You are in level one if you believe everything you are told.
> You are in level two if you confront your beliefs.
> You are in level three if you listen to your inner voice.
> You are in level four if you turn your questions over to a higher power.

Step Seven: The Fifth House

Capricorn: I Want a Reward That Expresses My Truth

If only I knew what I really valued, choosing a reward would not be difficult. But I'm changing. What I thought I believed in does not make me happy. Is it me? Do I repeat it and try to improve on the process, or do I try something else? What should that something else be? Could it not have to do with worldly rewards? Do I need more spirit in my life—more faith and love?

You have reached the point where nothing makes you happy. It doesn't matter how much you have, how many parties you go to, or what your pay-check reads, you're not happy. You are fighting your need to feel free, to give and to share, and the need to hold on and be miserly. Fear has made you inse-cure and so it doesn't matter what you have—it's not enough.

> You are in level one if your goals are to escape the moment or to find pleasure.
> You are in level two if your goals are to follow your dream.
> (Levels three and four are listed at the end of step seven in the third level of consciousness.)

The Third Level of Consciousness

The third level of consciousness divides the fifth house and seventh step, and the ninth house and eleventh step. The third level is always about faith. You are asked to have faith enough to be free again, to risk yourself for the heart and let go of judgment and what others think, or feel. You are as much spirit as you are anything else, but you have controlled and contained your spirit until it won't listen to you anymore and it has vowed to create one crisis after another in your life until you learn to listen to it.

Step Seven: The Fifth House (Third Level)

Capricorn: I Choose for Faith

I have learned through choice that trying to be safe only makes me more anxious and when I take a risk for my heart I feel strong and alive. There is no choice; there is only a path to love through fear.

You are experienced enough to know that there is no escape. The only way to rid yourself of anxiety and fear is to face them and go through them, and in so doing acquire faith. When you have faith you can deal with whatever life offers you and find meaning and sustenance in it.

> You are in level three when you let go of reward.
> You are in level four when your reward is life.

Step Eight: The Sixth House

Aquarius: When I Hold On to My Uniqueness, I am Free

I have had to hide my differences in order to find acceptance and approval, but now I truly know that what makes me different is what makes me special and where my real talents lie. When I hold on to my differences and uniqueness I feel free and I am happy.

It is a wonderful feeling to know that you do not have to hide who you are. When you can let go of worrying about hurting others because your truth is different from theirs you are truly free. Until then, your life is limited by the pain and sensitivity of others, and you know how much pain there is in the world to limit you.

> You are in level one if freedom is something you can't have now.
> You are in level two if freedom is your ability to seek the rewards you want.
> You are in level three when freedom is the ability to express yourself.
> You are in level four when freedom is love.

Step Nine: The Seventh House

Pisces: Lost Dreams Are Not Lost

Dreams—they catch your heart and then they demand so much of you that you have to let them go. If you do let them go, they don't leave—they just show up in everyone else. What I've learned is to support in others what I want to have for myself. So instead of ignoring dreams, attacking them, or keeping others from pursuing them, I help everyone reach for the clouds. The clouds are where I want to live.

You know that nothing is lost in the universe. Whatever you let go of just becomes removed from your vision, but it can be found in your heart and in the hearts of others. When you see the world as connected, it presents itself to you as unified and strong. If you see everything separate and compartmentalized, you will feel lost and alone. Open you heart to the synchronicity of life and it will carry you through your sadness, problems, and temporary setbacks, always showing you a way out by offering you a greater idea than the one that led you down a dead-end road.

> You are in level one when you fulfill the dreams of others for approval.
> You are in level two when you challenge the dreams that imprison you.
> You are in level three when you have faith in your dream.
> You are in level four when life is a dream.

Step Ten: The Eighth House

Aries: There Are Heroes Among Us

I'm hiding the hero in me, or I let go of it completely. I really feel that it is not the successful people in life that are the heroes; it's the poor who keep going with nothing to live on but faith. I have so many things to be grateful for and still I'm not happy; I'm ashamed of myself. I judge myself. I reach out to the poor and offer my support. I want to make a difference and I commit to doing that. In so doing the hero in me returns.

You have learned once again that judgment does not serve anyone. All you need in order to find love and support is to give it to others. There is no other way.

> You are in level one when your ego hides its heroic nature.
> You are in level two when you fight for those who have nothing.
> You are in level three when you support those with love who have nothing.
> You are in level four when you see life as an endless series of greater visions.

Step Eleven: The Ninth House

Taurus: I Let Go of Love

It seemed to me that I had to choose between love and protection, love and reward—the reward being the luxuries of life. If I chose love I lost comfort; if I chose comfort I lost love. Then I realized that they were divided in me, and so I saw them as divided. Love is comfort, love is luxury, luxury is love. They are connected and can come in one package—if you so choose. See them together and they will be one.

When you begin to realize that the world gets divided by your thoughts, not because it is divided, you can begin to seek higher thoughts that create unity and not division. Your attitudes shape you. Use your ideals to help you reach higher.

> You are in level one when you are seeking and giving unconditional love.
> You are in level two when love is sought through power and rewards.
> (Levels three and four are listed at the end of step eleven in the fourth level of consciousness.)

The Fourth Level of Consciousness

The fourth level of consciousness divides the ninth house and eleventh step. You are challenged to let go of protection and turn your choices over to a higher power. When you do you unite mind, body, and spirit behind one voice and one path and you gain strength and faith for the journey.

Step Eleven: The Ninth House (Fourth Level)

Taurus: I Accept the Love of God

If I live in God's love everything is taken care of. I accept God's love as my protection.

When you reach the place of faith you realize that there is nothing to fear and you allow love into your life. When you become dependent on God's love you will never be let down, but you must not let Him down. That means when the world seems to turn into what you don't want it to be, keep your faith and persevere. There must be shadow in life to enjoy the light. So accept it all and you'll transcend it all.

> You are in level three when you have faith in love and let go.
> You are in level four when love is everywhere and in everything.

Step Twelve: The Tenth House

Gemini: I Turn My Choices Over to God

Control—when you're young and foolish you think you can control others, life, or just the simple things around you. What you learn is how foolish that is. You have choice through intention. God knows what you really want, and when you align your will with His you get it.

The burdens of life get lifted when you learn how to turn what you don't know over to Him. Do your share; don't get lazy. God does not like to help those who don't help themselves. Do everything you can do and then ask for help. It will come.

You are in level one when you let others choose.
You are in level two when you give up choice and seek truth.
You are in level three when you let your inner voice choose.
You are in level four when God chooses—you turn it over.

Step One: The Eleventh House (Fourth Level)

Cancer: Faith Is My Shield

I have learned faith through letting it go. I now know that I am protected, that abundance is mine if I can see abundance and bring it out in others, that love is everywhere, and that God loves me just the way I am. He wants me to be happy and have my dreams come true. I'm going to let Him help me get there.

True wisdom is the knowledge that through faith everything is ours. It is important to believe that you deserve love and that the universe wants you to be happy. Once you make friends with your environment it starts supporting you instead of attacking you. You move out of survival mode and into a world of belief, a world where dreams and fantasies do come true.

You are in level three when you see a new idea.
You are in level four when you open yourself up to faith.

The Cross

The cross is composed of the eleventh, fifth, ninth, and third houses and is where change must occur. (See Figure 10.1 on page 230.) The two fixed houses represented by Cancer and Capricorn challenge each other to see a greater truth:

Cancer (eleventh house): *When I get tired of protecting myself and feeling insecure I begin to challenge my world and my choices. Do I really need all of these things to make me happy? Wouldn't love make me happy? I begin to choose for love and it appears in my life. The more faith I have in love, the stronger it makes me until I realize that my possessions don't define me, love does. The greatest love of all is God's love. I choose Him.*

Capricorn (fifth house): *I oppose the authority and those who have it all. I no longer seek things or their approval; I seek to find my heart and my passion. When I do I attract others with heart and begin to feel more supported and loved than ever before. It allows me to listen to my inner voice and that leads me to realize that I don't need to worry about choice if I turn my path over to God. My ability to let go has allowed me to reconnect to my dream by helping others find or reconnect with theirs.*

The two mutable houses represented by Taurus and Scorpio must anchor themselves in this new truth by taking a stand:

Taurus (eleventh house): *I give up on love because I believe I need money, safety, and luxury more. When I give up love, I discover that it is always with me. To bring it closer, I must value it, and I learn to value it through letting go.*

Scorpio (third house): *I am stopped by the authority of the fifth; I am intimidated by those who have more than me and their judgments of me. If I dare to confront them, I will see that it is only fear that makes them attack me and that if I have faith and stick to my intentions, I can go beyond their resistance.*

LIBRA: Truth
(September 24 through October 23)

I have a mask I always wear
It makes me feel not quite so bare
I tell the world that it's my truth
No one cares or asks for proof
I keep what's real deep inside
What keeps it there is my pride
It takes a hero to leave the pack
It takes great strength to turn your back
On all that others want and hold
Without these things can I be bold
To free me from my ego's grasp
I must let go of my sad past
Attachments keep me on the ground
Ideas take me round and round
They lift me up and keep me there
They ignite my fire and fill the air
I am different, I see my fate
I'll be a hero, if I can wait.

Question Seven

About Your Parents: What inspired your father in life?

About Yourself: What inspires you? What lifts your spirit and gives you joy? Is this a part of your life? If not, why not?

Truth inspired and guided you through the darkness, giving you comfort when your world was falling apart. As long as you could hold on to truth you could weather the storms of life, knowing that somehow things would turn around. Well, they did and you survived, but it wasn't truth that was holding your hand, it was faith. In the harsh light of day you see that even truth is an illusion and one you must let go of. As you reflect on your journey you see that the wars and battles you have fought trying to bring certainty and honesty to your life have left you empty, depleted, and feeling isolated or alone. And now, once again life has lost its meaning. This loss can leave you depressed and confused, or you can sit back and see that the universe has an incredible sense of humor—it takes whatever you have become attached to and turns it into a comedy. If you don't laugh, others will. You see, from this point on nothing is sacred and anything goes.

Truth the way you saw it let you down. It kept your inner world strong, but others didn't honor or respect it. Instead of being looked up to for having high ideals, you were seen as a snob; your quest to always do the right thing gave you an aura of judgment. Could you have given truth greater meaning than it deserved? Truth or high ideals are a trap, just like the images of Aries that set you forth on your journey. These perfect pictures gave you an escape from the emptiness and pettiness of life. Truth is nothing more than a facilitator, the vehicle you chose to help you go beyond the obstacles and temptations that try to lure you or stop you from your goals. If you succeeded to stay focused, truth served you well and you should honor it, not hold on to it. Truth is a means to an end, not the end. Now it's time to face the pettiness and turn it into something great. If you're ready for this step, you won't need your truth anymore.

You have learned that the more you try to make others hear your truth the less they listen. Even truth can become an obstacle of love when it is seen as the redeemer, or *the only way*. Does it really matter who's right or wrong? Isn't intention more important than truth? When two people want the same things they will find a way to connect; when they want different things it doesn't matter how much they have in common, it's never going to be enough. The Libra must reach a point where it is tired of being controlled, denied, chosen, and abandoned for its truth. You must experience its limitations and ineffec-tualness before you will begin to seek something beyond truth, and by the way, there is something more.

The sign of Libra is where you reach the end of the line. Everything you were told about life and the world has been proven to be untrue. You have given with all your heart; you have championed the lost and lonely; you have tried to do the "right" thing; you have striven to be perfect, strong, and humble; you have both followed and led, and nothing has brought you satisfaction and peace. Little by little your consciousness has grown and with it your divine discontent. The world the way you see it is a terrible place. As you try to pull together the bits and pieces of a new truth, you struggle to find a place to take a stand. You've learned that the world is not just about you. We are all connected and no one can take their journey alone. Sooner or later even the most independent person will need help, and if you have never reached out and helped someone else, then you may find helping hands are scarce indeed. The way out of ignorance is humbleness; ask for help from above. If you've helped others in order to fill a need in you to be in control, others may rise up and dishonor your gifts, laugh at them, or toss them away. Helping others only brings balance when it comes from the heart and love, not from need and fear. Without real love, life is a fluctuating pendulum that swings between abundance and loss, a teeter-totter that goes up and down, or a merry-go-round that swirls and swirls keeping you out of focus and balance.

Once you come to terms with yourself and know that there is no place to hide, no place to run, no way to escape the next step or the next lesson, then and only then will you surrender. The ability to let go, to turn things over and be guided, is the first step on the new journey. The ego must surrender to its higher self; it must ask for surprise, the unknown, the unexpected; it must see what it needs, not what it wants. When choice is finally accepted as coming from love and above, instead of from desire and feelings of lack, wisdom and faith will be a part of each of your choices, and what you will build will be built on faith, that divine cement that holds your house up even when the structure falls apart.

Like the fall season it represents, Librans must learn how to hold on to the core of their being and let go of all the rest. It's time to connect to your dream, claim it, own it, and let whatever doesn't support it fall. Your faith is being tested. In order to move forward you must believe in where you are going and what you want to do. As you take a step for your own path others will become cold and turn away. To be great, you must winter the abandonment that comes from separating your truth and dreams from those of others. Most dreams are created out of the need to escape or have more. If you keep your dream in the same environment that created it, it will not receive the nourishment it needs to manifest. Old wounds will trigger old patterns of dependence and fear. Take your dream into your heart and do not be afraid of what others think or do. Your mission is to stay committed, no matter what obstacles arise, or what troubles come your way. Each time you clear the debris from your path through hard work or ingenuity, you become stronger, build faith and confidence, and separate yourself from those who have less faith. Yes, faith will be the ultimate divider in life—not race, opportunity, or wealth. Those who believe in themselves and their dreams will climb the ladder of success, no matter what the obstacles; those who don't will be left behind to blame life, circumstances, and injustice for their failures. The choice is yours: blamer or creator.

Can you create what you want from nothing? You've made it this far because you've learned many lessons and you've tasted success. Can you combine your knowledge, talent, and what you have right now and begin to build your dream? Can you take an idea from start to finish, and not wait for things to be perfect? The results are not as important as your ability to complete the process from beginning to end. Once you have done it all, you can refine it.

It's important to see yourself as the successful person you are striving to be. Don't wait for the future. Find that greatness in you now and project it into your attitude. When you do, you will have brought the future into the moment. If you keep struggling in business and act like a novice, others will treat you as such. Take an attitude that allows others to know you believe and know what you're doing, and they'll believe too. When you love what you do, you enjoy what you do, and others are always attracted to love and joy. This attracts support from others and helps you to keep going. To find your purpose takes time—please don't be in a rush—you can't make it happen; it must unfold. Don't hold on to what wants to go; let it go. Life is taking you someplace you need to be. Stop fighting the process and surrender to your path. See everything as a gift and a chance to get stronger. Fear is nothing but a place you feel there is no love. Go there and bring love with you. You are the torch that brings the light.

Libra challenges the ego to believe in the spirit and the journey. It is tested to hold on through faith and not give up when reward or recognition are not around. Without the ego's cooperation with spirit, victory cannot be accomplished. You give up when others turn their back, when things go wrong, and when the world doesn't know you exist. Do you have enough love for yourself to keep going? Have you prepared yourself for the big test? If you're wondering how you're doing, answer the following questions:

- Are you independent physically and emotionally?
- Can you stand up for yourself and say no to others—oppose their truth or position?
- Can you protect yourself and your dream by hiding it? Can you risk yourself and your dream by exposing it to the right people?
- Can your ego take a backseat? Can you learn from others or support someone else who is doing what you want to do?
- Can you let go of your desire for perfection and accept wherever you are and do whatever needs to be done to keep going?
- Do you know what you believe in and what you want to accomplish in life?
- Are you able to face your fears, express your anger, and reveal your true intentions in spite of what others may think?
- Can you choose for truth, that is, to know what is really going on, instead of what you want to hear or see?
- Can you accept any reward for what you're doing because you're doing what you love?
- Can you seize the moment and risk yourself and take a chance, even when you feel you're not ready?
- Can you support the dreams of others without being jealous? Can you help others achieve what you want to achieve?

When you can create your dream in the dark, not just the light, when you can put it together with what you have, instead of the perfect parts, you will be a master creator. To be a master of anything you must be able to do it with the bare essentials, anyone can do it when everything is there, perfect and abundant. You must be able to keep going when things don't fall into place, when you get criticized for what you believe in, or when the world doesn't recognize your talent or your truth. Are you there for you? Do you support yourself? These are the souls who are ready for more. If you're not, go back and do the work.

Wisdom

As you reach higher you see the little things in life that really matter. You value loyalty, honesty, spirit, and those who can lead and inspire. You begin to believe that if justice could just enter one moment, it would grow and spread and be acknowledged by others and perhaps even change the world. You try to live by your truth in spite of the world and in so doing you become swallowed up by those committed to injustice. Little by little you feel depleted of energy or devoid of the will to keep going. You discover how useless it is to give to those who don't understand—souls who are so needy they just keep sucking your energy without offering you anything back. Everywhere you turn there is a new battle to fight, a new wrong to right, a new yearning to fulfill—there has to be another way. There has to be something more.

It's time to get out of the light and accept your other half (or get out of the darkness and accept your light), the part of you that refuses to acknowledge your pain and sorrow. Don't you know that pain is love, love that hasn't been heard; sorrow is love, love that doesn't have faith? You have separated from these emotions because you've judged them as meaningless and unworthy to be in your presence; yet you did not get rid of them, they are all around you. Surrender to them and you'll go beyond them. Hear their voice and give them love. What happened to you has meaning; you didn't suffer for nothing. Use your pain and it won't use you. Include it in your life and it won't dominate your being. Let it be a part of who you are. The dark moments of your life have made you strong—you are a survivor. Once you accept your fear you'll hear your inner voice and know you are connected to the world and others.

The Libra needs a new and greater wisdom to lead it into the unknown. It now sees that wisdom was a form of protection, keeping you feeling safe and separate from the unknown. Now that you want to see what lies in the mystery of life, you must let go of wisdom and truth. To be where your instincts tell you to go may not seem wise. To give up a career and dedicate yourself to your passion may not appear to be the smart thing to do, but if you follow your instincts, wisdom will come from it, reward will come, and everything will fall together. What you are beginning to realize is that the process that has taught you about life must go, and a new process must replace it. Ground zero is your heart.

The Unknown

The Libra knows that the greater truth, one that is eternal, lies in the unknown. Where else will you find what can't be destroyed, unwavering loyalty, pureness of heart, greatness of spirit and courage, and unlimited love? It must lie in the mystery or secrets of the world. You are attracted to the primordial chaos of life, to ideas on the cutting edge, and to the strong ideals that support them. When you become the facilitator of a new idea, you become the magician, and it is your truth and beliefs that bring this new thing to life. You are your truth. There is no gap or division. What you choose, say, and do creates you and your truth. It is no longer separate from you. When you see your life as your truth you see the truth of others in their lives. You have gone beyond promises, images, and perfect pictures—truth is evolving with you; it is not a static thing. When you surrender your heart to any moment, you are surrendering your truth to that moment and you have just made it yours. You have changed it by adding to it the love that was in your heart. Stay outside the moment; judge it, circle it, try to take just part of it instead of the whole thing, and it will fight you, resist you, and become your enemy. When you learn to turn yourself over and take yourself back, that is, remove your ego long enough to see the truth of someone else, and bring it back to your truth, you will not create opposition—you will create love. Give judgment and you'll get anger and separation. Each time you surrender you become the midwife of a greater truth, never totally certain what you will give birth to. That's the excitement of life. Power lies at the edge of life not in its belly. Opportunity lies at turning points—fallen dreams or their birth.

The New Hero

You feel like a fallen hero because you failed at your initial quest—you wanted to save those you loved and instead you fell yourself. When you look closer you realize that it was your ego that couldn't go the distance, not your spirit. It believed that you and only you could make things better—you left out God and the universe. God knows not to interfere if you don't want Him to. You wanted to do it alone and so He let you. For a while it seemed to work—you helped others, but then they became dependent. Their faith was in you, not within themselves. They didn't grow stronger, you just became overburdened. The hero must learn to support the strength in others, not protect their weaknesses. Your heartfelt efforts may be judged as your need to be superior, and so they won't even get recognized. If you always know better, you must think you are better. All you have to do is make one little mistake, one slip of the tongue, one moment when you choose for yourself and not them, and instead of support you get their vengeance and poison. Stop setting yourself up by helping without an invitation, and even with one, you must have the wisdom to see what someone is really asking you for. You give too much knowledge because you want to know all the details; every nuance is important to the mind that seeks perfection. Others, however, just want to know yes or no—whether you approve or not. Until the seed within them takes root and sprouts a desire to *know*, the soul will not want any more wisdom than what it needs to do the task at hand. Only those awakened to their destiny will search for truth and push beyond answers, knowing that beyond the answer is a greater question, one that will lead to a greater truth.

It's time to put yourself at the center of your world—be the hero of your own story. To do that you must be willing to separate from others, to accept your differences and what makes you unique. Your uniqueness needs you to facilitate its birth. It's time to shed the mask you wear to look good, the one you fashioned in order to survive. You do not need to please the world any longer; you need to please you and your God. The world needs your uniqueness, not what makes you like everyone else. New ideas will bring the new consciousness to the world. Those who seek that new consciousness within them will lead others forward and show the way. To do this you must commit to your true intention and get rid of any *truth* that stands in the way.

Share the Burden

The battle before you is not clear. Who is the enemy—those you love? The opposition has taken a stand and on the other side is everyone who has less faith than you, and to your surprise that includes many of the people you love. If you love them, shouldn't you stand with them? If your family doesn't believe in you, don't lean on them for support—they'll hold you back. It's time to grow up and find your own way. Their way didn't work, do you want to repeat their mistakes just to please them and make them happy? I know you don't have a role model to emulate because you are breaking new ground here, so you must look to myths and the gods to shape your soul. You need someone invincible to hold you in faith, not a mere mortal. The key is to see your strength, but not to show it. You will avoid a lot of unnecessary battles when you can take your ego out of the picture and hide it behind your good nature. Strength creates opposition, faith inspires support, and faith in others guarantees support. Let others profit from your efforts by allowing them to help and you will find your strength become stronger.

Listen to your environment and don't try to conquer it; become its partner.

Synchronicity, or the lining up of events beyond probability, will begin to happen. You will magically arrive at your destination by failing, falling, or just taking the wrong turn in the road. Before long you will begin to see that there are no wrong turns, just different paths. The world will become a world of symbols, not separate pieces of information. Everything that happens will have many levels of interpretation and will speak to your mind, body, and spirit together as one. Nothing is without meaning. When your consciousness becomes aware of symbols rather than details, you are ready to make big leaps in your journey.

The Quest for Power

Power is unleashed at the moment you create or destroy. We all want to seize that power and hold on to it, but this is where self-control becomes essential. If you hold on to power, it will bring you down because it is not a force that can be contained, it is meant to flow. Those who can let go can become a channel of power and wisdom because things flow through them. Power creates opposition when it becomes static. When a soul cannot move forward and open itself up to a new and greater idea, it may seek to destroy in order to release the power it feels it has inside. If you are a sniper seeking power through destroying the lives of others, this feeling of power will be short-lived because it is based on others and not you (your ability to destroy others). To reach for power through destruction requires a lack of faith, a belief that you are not entitled to the force of light. Of course, ultimately you destroy yourself. Gandhi chose to stand in faith and call forth his greater idea, one of change through nonviolence. He helped India reclaim its power by taking it back from the British. When you hold on to images you must remove the impediments of your vision through destruction. Hitler held on to an image of a perfect race. To keep it perfect he had to eliminate the handicapped, the Jews, the Gypsies, or anyone that didn't fit his image of beauty and greatness. That is your choice: Move forward and seek the greater truth by creating and opening yourself up to new thoughts and ideas, do nothing and be manipulated by others, or go back and destroy the obstacles that kept you from becoming great and in so doing destroy part of your strength and your heritage.

Inspiration

The Libra has the tough position of looking at life and realizing that every-thing you learn or depend upon will eventually fade and die. Loss is not your fault. Loss or letting go is a part of life. What is missing has meaning; what comes easy is ignored. What you struggle for is what you value. God stays mys-terious so you will want to know Him. If he walked alongside you, you wouldn't see Him or value His words. Every time you give birth, something in you also dies—an old idea, a fear, a belief, or a limitation. Creating—bringing forth and giving birth—begins the process of dying. Don't hold on—reach instead for inspiration, the eternal truth of God. What inspires you brings you close to Him, close to your destiny and purpose. Follow your passion and what uplifts your spirit and you won't go wrong.

The Father Has the Gift of Inspiration

Inspiration is the gift of love. You should be inspired by your father and his quest to express his truth and his uniqueness. If your father believed in life this is where his creativity will be expressed and this is where he will lift you up and take you beyond the problems and pettiness of life. If nothing inspired your father, if he sat in front of the TV and never moved, you must find your own inspiration. You need it as much as food and water. Without something to inspire your spirit and your heart you will emotionally die, feel depressed, and give up on life too. (See Figure 11.1 for the Libra Star.)

The First Level of Consciousness

The first level of consciousness divides the eleventh house and first step, and the third house and fifth step. It brings the Libra into conflict by forcing it to choose between its own desires and its need to save and protect those it loves. It is drawn to cutting-edge ideas and dreams that will take it away from its family and the safety they have provided. By pursuing what is in its soul, it feels it is invalidating everything that it has been given or that its truth repre-sents. If it chooses to be the protector instead of the seeker, it will disconnect from its inner wisdom and in so doing lose the inner guidance so necessary for its success and happiness. Once it realizes that it cannot save anyone, not

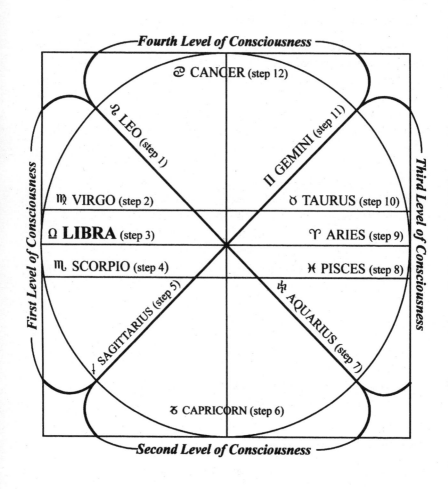

Figure 11.1. The Libra Star

even itself without faith, it will begin to accept its humanness, and in so doing see its divinity and invincibility. When you are humble enough to acknowledge your limitations, others will give to you the love you have so desired.

Step One: The Eleventh House

Leo: I'm Strong Enough to Do It All

I saw that others could not make good decisions, nor find the strength to solve their problems, so I stepped in and took over. To do that, I gave up my freedom and independence; I gave up my dreams and I did it all for love. That was a big mistake. No one appreciates a sacrifice; they don't like to be taken care of, even if they need it. What everyone really wants is to be seen as strong. When I stepped back and helped them face their fears instead of protecting them, they felt good about themselves and I found the love I sought through doing it all.

The Libra must learn to remove its ego from the situation and let others make their own choices. It needs to learn to accept that others have their own process. Not everyone is ready to make the "right" choice. Some of us have to run into the wall a few more times before we want to see the better path or greater truth. If you take choice away from others, they will resent you and work against you, even if your intention is based on love. Let go of saving others and you'll help them through your example.

> You are in level one when your ego believes that it is the only person capable of saving the situation.
> You are in level two when you seek freedom rather than the role of hero.
> (Levels three and four are listed at the end of step one in the fourth level of consciousness.)

Step Two: The Twelfth House

Virgo: I Am Holding On to the Light and Goodness

I want so much for the world to be a good and safe place. I do what I can to make it better, but in so doing I feel that it has taken away my freedom and my dreams. I realize now that I am hiding from the shadow, I'm afraid to let the sadness and darkness in, because I'm afraid I'll lose the light. I can't lose the light if I have faith in it.

You will feel divided between right and wrong, the light and the shadow, as long as you don't have faith. Once you begin to believe that there is a force stronger than you, you will not be afraid to face your feelings and express your anger and sadness. All Libras have anger because they were not protected as a child. They had to be strong early in life, because the adults around them were either weak, struggling, or not there emotionally. With nothing to depend on except themselves, they have learned to rely on their strength, but they don't realize that that strength came from faith. Accept that you are divinely protected and let go.

> You are in level one when you give up your freedom and dreams for others.
> You are in level two when you accept your anger and take back your freedom.
> You are in level three when you hold on to your dreams and let everything else go.
> You are in level four when there is only surrender and no holding on or letting go.

Step Three: The First House

Libra: I Want to Be the Hero in My Dream

I have this voice inside that is calling me to greatness, but I don't know what I'm supposed to do. I think at first I'm meant to save those I love, so I sacrifice myself for them. That doesn't work—I become weaker and they become stronger—but their strength is dependent on me. It is not until I take my own life back and begin thinking of my own dreams that I realize this is my mission. When I let go saving others, I have to face my anger at them for letting me do it. Of course, I'm really angry at myself for letting my ego believe that it could be so heroic. I need to be the hero of my own dreams.

You now realize that the only way to effect change in others is by becoming independent and strong yourself. You are ready to become the hero in your dream. When you do you bring new strength and power to your life. Suddenly you can do things that once seemed impossible. All the energy that was lost serving the hopelessness of others is now at your service and you feel recharged.

You are in level one when you protect others from their truth.
You are in level two when you are ready to discover your own truth.
You are in level three when you see your truth as a part of a greater purpose.
You are in the level four when your truth is faith and an idea that you have yet to discover.

Step Four: The Second House

Scorpio: I Am Angry

I used to feel that it wasn't good to pay attention to your anger; if you ignored it, it would go away. What I learned is that I can't hold it in; it comes out in other ways. I need to be able to accept my feelings even when I don't understand them or even if I don't see their value right away. Anger is a great motivation and it always shows me a truth I'm overlooking. If you avoid your anger you are easily controlled by those who don't.

You avoided anger in your quest for peace and what that did was render you powerless. Your need to protect yourself from anger—yours and theirs—only made the matter worse; everyone became angrier. What you need to do is look at what makes you upset and realize that being aware is almost as good as solving the problem. You can't heal it, fix it, or share it with others to get their ideas if you don't acknowledge that an issue exists. Have the courage to go into your negativity and give it a voice.

You are in level one when you avoid your anger and shadow feelings.
You are in level two when you stop trying to free yourself from negativity and seek a greater idea as the solution.
You are in level three when you have faith that the problem is there to teach you a greater truth.
You are in level four when you accept your anger at God for not making a perfect world.

Step Five: The Third House

Sagittarius: If I Use My Wisdom for Others, It Doesn't Work

I believed so much in truth and wisdom that I thought I could make a difference in the lives of others. What I learned is that everyone has their own inner truth and all mine does is interfere with theirs. I've got to learn to let go and trust that they will find their way just like I did.

Wisdom serves those who seek it, not those who need it. If you are not ready for wisdom you won't pay attention to its magic. If you are ready for wisdom you'll find it in everything you do. So open yourself up to wisdom for yourself and realize that others will find it when they are ready.

> You are in level one if you believe everything you are told.
> You are in level two if you confront your own beliefs.
> (Levels three and four are listed at the end of step five in the second level of consciousness.)

The Second Level of Consciousness

The second level of consciousness divides the third house and fifth step, and the fifth house and seventh step. It challenges you to seek freedom from having to make the wise choice. Wisdom depends on the moment and your ability to receive the greater idea. Your mission is to set yourself free of the limitations that come from wanting to do the right thing so that you can pay attention to your real guide, your own voice.

Step Five: The Third House (Second Level)

Sagittarius: I Choose the Magic

Truth and wisdom were in the way of the magic. When I let go of having to make the right choice I began to see that I had the power to change my world by giving it love and by offering my uniqueness. The more I concentrate on my own passion the more I help others do the same. The power to change yourself and others lies in owning your own path.

The wisdom to use your power for self-enlightenment comes from trial and error and many a disillusionment. You have learned a valuable lesson: You only help others when you can show them the way, not by getting off your path to hold them up. When you pay attention to yourself and your destiny, you teach others how to do the same.

You are in level three if you listen to your inner voice.
You are in level four if you turn your questions over to a higher power.

Step Six: The Fourth House

Capricorn: Freedom Is the Ability to Pursue My Own Reward

I used to try to protect others, but I became their caretaker and I had all the responsibility. As soon as I let go and supported their strength and helped them face their fears, they respected and supported me, and I was free to look at what I wanted from life.

As soon as you give up on saving the world and seek your own reward, it doesn't make you selfish, it makes you great. When you get beyond the guilt of living your life for you, you begin to really help others through your example. You are free and your freedom sets them free.

You are in level one when you pursue rewards for others.
You are in level two when you seek your own rewards.
You are in level three when you accept the rewards that come from doing what you love.
You are in level four when life is the reward.

Step Seven: The Fifth House

Aquarius: I Am Free to Be Me

Freedom has always been important to me, so I tried to make others free and in so doing imprisoned myself. I found the courage to let go and do my own thing—follow my own heart—and everyone has gotten stronger and more independent because of it. If only I had known this earlier.

You now have the key to freedom—find your own freedom through facing your fear that if you let go of others they won't make it without you. This is your ego speaking, not your faith and your heart. Everyone in God's world is protected and if they ask for help they will receive it. They will never find their own strength and freedom if you are there taking care of them.

You are in level one when you see freedom as an escape.
You are in level two when you see freedom as the path to a greater idea.
(Levels three and four are listed at the end of step seven in the third
level of consciousness.)

The Third Level of Consciousness

The third level of consciousness divides the fifth house and seventh step, and the ninth house and eleventh step. It challenges the Libra to have faith that there is a new vision waiting for it, one that will take it toward its destiny and real love. To move toward this destiny you must have gained your freedom from others and let go of being their hero. You will not find the love you want so long as you save instead of share. You need an equal, not a dependent.

Step Seven: The Fifth House (Third Level)

Aquarius: I am Free to Seek My Dream

I used to seek the freedom to pursue my goals until I realized that I didn't need permission—all I needed to do was take responsibility for myself. When I did, life changed. With that change came my childhood dream and I knew that I could have this, too. I was able to become my own authority by taking responsibility for myself. If I took responsibility for my dream, I could have that too.

You are at a point where you realize that life is what you put into it. If you wait around for others to either give you permission or see your talents and worth, you'll be waiting forever. What you want needs you to support it and take responsibility for it.

You are in level three when you discover a new vision of yourself based
on your uniqueness.
You are in level four when you see freedom as the path to a new and
greater idea.

Step Eight: The Sixth House

Pisces: My Freedom Connects Me to the Force

I am free to follow my heart and that heart brings me to the edge of life. I find myself attracted to danger, the wilderness, to wherever civilized man has not yet tamed. The primal force in me feels reawakened and now I feel connected to the primal force in nature and new ideas. There is power in chaos and the unformed; there is excitement in pursuing a new idea. Life is wonderful when I open myself up to the moment and my passion.

You have tasted freedom and now you want to surround yourself with it. You love environments that are free, and nature is the perfect choice. When you are around the power and magic of nature you get revitalized. When your spirit is too isolated or wrapped up in civilization, your spirit begins to feel deprived.

You are in level one if you believe in dreams to escape your feelings.
You are in level two when dreams show you the way to freedom.
You are in level three when your freedom comes from facing your fears and having faith.
You are in level four when you are free wherever you are.

Step Nine: The Seventh House

Aries: I Accept That I Am My Truth

I am my truth, not a package of rules or laws that I must abide by. I now know that every choice I make defines my truth, and the more choices I make based on faith, the stronger my truth is and the more I influence others.

You have reached the place of understanding that you do have a mission and that mission is to create your dream your way. You do this by having faith in yourself and your path. When you do you find love, and you are inspired by your work and life.

You are in level one if your vision is to save others.
You are in level two if your vision is to be free.
You are in level three if your vision is your dream.
You are in level four when your vision is a new and better idea.

Step Ten: The Eighth House

Taurus: My Intention Is to Become Love

I used to believe that loving others meant that I had to either sacrifice myself for them and their dreams, or I had to take on their problems. Now I know that when you love someone you have to let them go and allow them to see you as a whole person and not just as their protector. If I become love, others will feel that I love them.

You have accepted that love sometimes brings sadness and separation. It can't always be joyful and in the light. You know you can't fix every problem, but you can bring to it love. Love doesn't interfere; it shows its presence and shares its heart. From love others take strength.

> You are in level one when all you want to do is make others happy.
> You are in level two when all you want to do is make yourself happy.
> You are in level three when you choose for the truth regardless of who it makes happy.
> You are in level four when you see that happiness is a choice.

Step Eleven: The Ninth House

Gemini: I Accept Choice as a Source of Power

I first saw power as taking charge, so I made decisions for everyone thinking that that would make them happy. Wisdom, gleaned through experience, has taught me that the only way to make a wise choice is by doing my share and then turning it over and having faith that what is meant to be will be.

Choice has power when it is backed by faith. It doesn't have power when you use force or try to make things work. The more faith you have in what you do, the wiser the world will see you. Listen to your inner voice and choose what's right for you. Don't worry about everyone else—they need to choose for themselves.

> You are in level one when you listen to what others tell you to do.
> You are in level two when your choices are made to set you free.
> (Levels three and four are listed at the end of step eleven in the fourth level of consciousness.)

The Fourth Level of Consciousness

The fourth level of consciousness divides the ninth house and eleventh step. It brings the ego and choice together—the ego must surrender to the greater idea, the higher power, then it will find the wisdom it is seeking to be free. When you can rely on faith to make your choices, when you are interested in the truth and not the reward, you will always be uplifted and shown a better way.

Step Eleven: The Ninth House (Fourth Level)

Gemini: I Let Faith Make My Choices

I know that I cannot see the whole picture, so if I am wise, I can let go of the part of me that wants to make my choice and accept what the universe has given me to work with. When I do, what I want is brought into the picture in a way I never could have imagined. It's so much fun to see how things twist and turn and work out if I can stay connected to the path of spirit through faith.

You have reached a point in your journey where you recognize your human limitations and you've learned how to bring your divine self into the picture—all you have to do is ask for help and accept what is given to you with love. Open yourself up to receive and you will receive what you need.

> You are in level three when you listen to your inner voice and follow its wisdom.
> You are in level four when you don't think about choice; you just respond with your instincts and love.

Step Twelve: The Tenth House

Cancer: I Am Protected by My Faith and the Next Great Truth

I used to worry about being protected or protecting others. Now I know that if you live in faith and listen to your inner voice, you will be protected.

When you are connected to your instincts you will be protected. You will be guided to do this or that, and when you don't worry about whether or not it makes sense you will find the greater wisdom in your actions. A few of the survivors of September 11, 2001, found that out the hard way. Some did crazy things that saved their lives, but they listened to themselves. The firemen who refused to leave behind an injured woman when it seemed they would all die were saved because of where they stopped. If they had used common sense, they'd be dead.

> You are in level one if you feel *others* need to be protected.
> You are in level two if *you* feel you need to be protected.
> You are in level three when you have faith that God will protect you and those you love.
> You are in level four when you don't worry about protection, just finding the greater truth.

Step One: The Eleventh House (Fourth Level)

Leo: My Strength Comes from Faith

I am able to remove my ego from a situation and see it for what it is, and because of this I can play with life and feel free to be me. Strength is nothing more than the faith to express who you are in the moment. This is true freedom.

When you have the power and wisdom to be yourself, you are ready for greatness and a purpose.

> You are in level three if you have faith that you and others will be shown the way.
> You are in level four when wherever you are is the way to freedom and truth.

The Cross

The cross is composed of the eleventh, fifth, ninth, and third houses and is where change must occur. (See Figure 11.1 on page 252.) The two fixed houses represented by Leo and Aquarius challenge each other to see a greater truth:

Leo (eleventh house): *Eventually my ego gets tired of protecting others—the more I help them the more enslaved I become—so I let go and listen to my* own inner voice and that sets me free. I realize that I have not helped them by overprotecting them.

Aquarius (fifth house): *I accept my own freedom and help others do the same. This frees me to follow my own path. Others no longer resent me because they don't see me as superior, they see me as an example they want to emulate. I am protected through faith and this brings me support and love from those I love. I accept myself as the center of my dream and this allows me to see myself as my truth. When I become the symbol of my truth, I have the magic to effect change in others and the world because my truth came from faith and faith now resides in me.*

The two mutable houses represented by Gemini and Sagittarius must anchor themselves in this new truth by taking a stand:

Gemini (ninth house): *I give up my freedom to choose because I believe that others need me to make their choices for them and to protect them. When I turn my choices over to God, everyone is happy.*

Sagittarius (third house): *No one sees me as good or helpful when I try to help them feel free and strong. True wisdom is the ability to pursue your own goals without guilt and share your knowledge and experience when asked.*

SCORPIO: Surrender/Rejection
(October 24 through November 22)

Scorpios use power to divide the pie
Who has faith; whose ego will die?
Masters of change; they live on the edge
They know that power is found on the ledge
The force that unites all things into one
This force grows inside when they listen to none.
For a higher purpose they reach for change
They seek a life unfettered by blame
The hero of greatness must accept its anger
Yes, follow the tension right into the danger
It's time to go further than truth and the wise
It's time to accept the shadow, the lies
When all is acknowledged, then you will be free
You'll see your perfection; you'll see you in me

Question Eight

About Your Parents: Was your mother able to express anger and separate emotionally from you when you misbehaved or stood up to her rules?

About Yourself: Can you separate yourself from friends and family members who hurt you or take advantage of you? Are you able to speak out when someone does something wrong to you? Or, do you protect other people from themselves?

The messenger of God, the revolutionary, the dangerous genius that is not afraid of change, death, or radical reform—who are you? others ask. Why, you're everything and nothing—you are whatever you need to be and that is the goal of the mission, to be it all. Now my mission is to help you own this wealth of power. For most Scorpios this power is something they fear, avoid, or get criticized for using. We all want leaders, but we strike anyone down who dares to try to separate from the mass consciousness. We want change and reform, but new ideas are condemned as evil and they bring up fear rather than excitement and joy. Is it any wonder that so few great leaders make it to the top? We, the collective voice, will crucify anyone who tries to take us away from our pain, our overspending, and our problems.

Most Scorpios are small, delicate beings—nature's way of masking the power within. By now you should be able to go beyond appearances and not judge a book by its cover. Nature has mastered the act of camouflage; it knows how to hide poison and sharp edges behind beauty, intrigue, and mystery— and so has the Scorpio. It is oozing with charm when it wants something. Just don't get caught in their seductive dance or you may be surprised—the sweetness goes when you step on their toes. Scorpios don't show the anger that drives them. This anger comes from their past and the many betrayals they have endured. Some come into the world without the promise: the love and devotion that every child deserves. The choice now is simple: You can look back and yearn for what you didn't get, or you can be grateful that you have less baggage to hold you back. You have a destiny, and worrying about others only gets in the way.

Scorpios know that *being nice* does not help you get the genius in you out and expressed. It's a competitive environment, and you are faced with a serious choice: Do you want success, freedom, or love? If you want all three you'll have to learn how to surrender to your own vision and stop living the dreams of others to make them happy. If your life was a void, you may have trouble breaking free. Every Scorpio needs a struggle, an obstacle, strong rejection, or the impossible to bring forth their will and break the psychological chains that keep them a prisoner. If your family smothered you with love, you'll want to break free of that love so that you can find your own voice. If you had little or no love, you know what love is and you can see it in the world around you. It's up to you to add love to your life by validating it wherever you find it.

Life for the Scorpio is a double-edged sword. There is resistance to your truth, so you are afraid to own it. Stand up for your beliefs; give up on approval and you'll be free. Never getting validated could take away your confidence instead of building up your motivation and desire to prove to the world that you have something wonderful to offer. If you still get your self-worth from others, being a Scorpio is a nightmare: either you create hostility in others or you hold it in and present a charming façade. Neither choice is acceptable. What you need to change all this is a dream or a goal.

With a dream a Scorpio can remove the attention from itself and place it on the goal. Criticism shifts from you to your project. This gives you distance from others, which allows you to see more clearly what makes them tick. Yes, you're a natural psychologist because you're able to see through masks and go right to the motivation and intention. It's not enough to see into people's hearts, you've got to connect with them. You must risk your feelings and bring out the essence of your being. That's why crises fill the lives of most Scorpios. Death is something that surrounds them; it's there to remind them how short life is and that protecting yourself too long is not wise. When you give your all, however, you get what you want, or close to it. It is almost impossible to stop anyone who has surrendered their total being to an idea, or mission. This can't be faked; you must want and believe in what you're doing; when you do, the sea parts. This is how you are meant to tackle the world: not by hiding and protecting yourself, but through surrendering to your passion.

The spirit of Scorpio is in a hurry; she has struggled so long to express what lies inside you that there is a feeling of urgency to all that she does. If this means you must be viewed as selfish, then selfish you will be. Selfishness is the Scorpio's teacher, and this teacher often comes in the form of its mother. Scorpios either feel smothered or abandoned by their mothers. Often both feelings are present in the same moment. It's not entirely their fault; the truth is no one can give you what you want but you.

Your enemies are anyone without a dream—the souls who can't commit and who will resent your passion and your drive. They will try to stop you by shattering any leftover images that still cling to the illusions of your ego—the ones that see you as perfect. Let them go. When you are called tough, cruel, and even dangerous; when you are labeled evil, angry, and thoughtless, can you still choose for you and your art and keep going?

Wisdom is your source of strength, a wisdom born from firsthand experience. Why expose yourself before it's necessary? Hide your truth until it is ready to take a stand. The Scorpio keeps things to itself because it knows if others are not aware of its decisions or opinions they can't judge them. Let others expose themselves; it gives you the advantage. The problem here is if you carry this attitude into your intimate life, you won't have one. Your spirit needs to share and take risks for love as well as art. If you shut yourself off from all love, instead of getting strong, you will feel weak and the inspiration that upheld you will wane.

The Skills Needed for Greatness

You have the skills essential for greatness, but these skills are threatening to others if success is not attached to them. In fact, your possessing them makes others angry. You are condemned for desiring to separate from the illusion of power and actually grasping it. To do this you must go beyond compassion and feelings and be able to cut out people and things that are holding you back. You must expose the truth, even when it inflicts pain and suffering. You must think of yourself and your needs if your talents are going to grow strong and emerge. You must shut out advice and the wisdom of others and seek your own counsel. How arrogant to believe that within you is all that you need to be great, all that you need to succeed, and all that you need to be loved. You are called ambitious and driven, as if these words should make you flinch with shame. You see through the false cries and rage of others; you know who has talent, who is full of bull, and who will be your rival.

You have the gift of vision and when you cast your eyes toward the hearts of others you can see beyond their mask and into their true intentions. No one's going to fool you again. Your insight reveals that the virus is fear. This is what keeps others from looking at the truth; they're afraid that the illusions of their childhood are not real and that the world is really a hard and cold place. Most will do anything to keep from facing this possibility—unaware that this coldness would turn to warmth if they could just accept it and make it their friend. Once you know someone's fears you have the control. Place a choice in their fear and they'll avoid it; become the ideal that hides their fear and they'll love you. How will you use your information—to serve you, to serve you both?

What Lies Beyond Pain?

When the ego is strong, it seems invincible. Leo rules the top of the chart and what the soul will strive for is the chance to be the best, to change the world through the magnificence of its mind or being. When the ego has been tamed through pain and sorrow, it lets go and the spirit takes the lead. Spirit knows how to be in charge. She takes you to your sadness so you can integrate it into your life. Pain and sorrow can enrich or give depth and complexity to your art. Your painting of children playing in the light will invoke the hidden sadness that lurks around their innocent spirits. And those who felt this way will recognize the message and praise you for it, for it has brought this hidden sadness to their consciousness and in so doing freed them. When something gets expressed emotionally, it is released. It has less power over you. Secrets hold you down; they control you. Do something nasty and keep it a secret and your shame will grow.

When your spirit takes you beyond pain and lets you taste the world of genius, imagination, and universal truths, you will never be stopped by it again. All the soul needs is a taste of these flavors and the pleasures of the world diminish. You now know that there is a force greater than yourself. With this awareness comes the consciousness that we are all connected and that what happens to another affects your life, or the lives of your children. It's time to readjust the goal and add a purpose. Why not *use* your personal success and share your knowledge. Giving back is the greatest joy of all. You are assuring that what you've learned and gleaned from life will not be lost; instead it will be passed on.

Why Is There Suffering?

The wisdom in pain comes when you realize that your spirit never suffers, it's your ego that feels pain. Once the soul can accept suffering as a part of life, it is able to accept its emotions. When you own your emotions you no longer are afraid of being vulnerable or falling in love. You now have true power and the ability to receive. Suffering has taught you to look deeper within yourself; it turned your ego's attention away from your desire to measure itself against others and it showed you the richness of your inner world. Suffering helped you become self-disciplined and aware of consequences. Without awareness you ignored the rules and rushed ahead without caution. Perseverance beyond pain and rejection opened your soul to a new level—one where the competition is less. Few have the strength or the stomach to accept the negative or endure tragedy and loss on the way to their goals. Now the path to success is an open road.

When you become aware of the enormous benefits of perseverance and facing fear, you are not afraid to be tough on others, and you let go of protecting them from life. A few hard knocks do the trick a lot more than endless lectures. With your new vision you are able to see farther and make adjustments to your goals. The unknown is no longer a scary place, because fear and pain are not your limits—the quest is for new ideas and truths that will lift the world beyond its pettiness and suffering.

Your Higher Purpose

Your higher purpose wants to emerge, but it will have to do battle with your ego. A higher purpose does not mean high principles; in fact, high principles are limitations when they become rigid or images that restrict. Remember, highs and lows are connected and if you can't fall into the shadow, you won't be able to soar. Part of you believes that the greatness you feel won't happen unless you are pure and perfect. To be great doesn't mean you must look great. It means you are wise enough to choose faith when you don't know. When you commit to good intentions you may find yourself in bad places. The path of spirit is not linear; it goes up and down. You are greater than your morals and within you is a deep sense of right and wrong—listen to your inner truth. Respect yourself and you will respect others; that is the only moral code you need to survive and stay true to yourself and your God.

Eternal Truths Guide You

The battle for truth and wisdom comes to a crisis in Scorpio: You cannot fulfill your destiny and stay committed to the truth of your past. You need universal or eternal truths as your guide. Truth for most is a mask; the face you show others, the face you want people to see and believe, is you. It represents both who you are or have become through your choices and actions and who you would like others to believe you are in spite of your choices and actions. This dual identity is a source of problems. The easy path will be to allow the illusion to protect you from yourself. Don't let half of the mask become your whole truth. When it does, you enter self-denial big time, and you consciously use the limitations of others to perpetuate your indiscretions. When you force others to relate to only your mask, you can be perfect no matter what you do.

It succeeds because most people don't trust their own feelings and interpretation of what's going on and because few souls have passed the Taurus test of confrontation. For example, if someone is angry and hurts you unnecessarily, and you don't call them for weeks, they may call you and demand a reason why they haven't heard from you. This puts you in the tough spot of having to say a negative "you hurt my feelings—you were rude." If you can't do that (and you'd be surprised at how many can't), this person will make you feel responsible for the lack of communication and you may end up trying to placate them and apologize for something they did wrong. What you have done is protect them from their actions and allowed them to keep their illusions.

Building a Persona

There is a positive way to use your mask: Merge who you are, and who you believe you will be, through belief and create an image of greatness. Your potential will be seen by others right now because you see it. There is no doubt in your mind that you can be who you want to be and so you begin to convince others just through your presence. The ego is often capable of doing this, up to a point. A strong ego that believes it is the best, and projects that to the world, receives attention and some success. Most people don't believe in themselves, so it is easy to push your way into their psyches through the power of your ego or beliefs. When the ego thinks it's wonderful, however, it creates competition, resentment, or servants to the ego, not equality or support. When spirit speaks she does so with love and respect and you get these emotions back.

Love and Surrender

Love is what you are seeking, the unconditional love of the Taurus child. You believed there is a magic path to love, all you have to do is find it. What you will discover is that nothing changes in your life unless you change. The change comes through surrender. Scorpios feel compelled to surrender, but to who and what? When you surrender to loving your parents, they don't protect you and take care of your needs; when you love friends they betray you; lovers leave you. Who then deserves the gift of one's whole heart and soul? Only your higher self and God deserve such total surrender. When you surrender to your higher self you are surrendering to you, your humanness, and your divinity. You feel more whole and loving, you feel strong and powerful. Surrender to another, and they will hold you, either too close or hold you down. It takes great self-discipline, experience, and wisdom to love and let go. Do not take prisoners of the heart or you will find yourself in jail.

When you surrender to others and stay there you become a burden, not a joy. You see yourself through them, and they become your eyes, your heart, your way of relating to others. This oneness is wonderful and frightening at the same time. You are not ready for true independence until you realize how damaging a symbiotic relationship can be. One person will want to separate or break free before the other is ready or willing to let go. Each looks for the weakness in the other to use that to gain an advantage. Instead of unity and love it becomes a battle to survive, and one person always feels more wronged, more betrayed—the other more depressed and worthless.

Anger

Anger is something that is close to a Scorpio's heart. They are almost born angry because the world is not perfect or the way it should be. The difference between the Taurus and the Scorpio is that the Scorpio knows it and sees it everywhere it turns. It is not seeking to hold on to love because it doesn't believe it exists. Yet, there is a thread of hope beyond its despair, for despite its lack of faith, it still surrenders to love above all other things.

Where is God? If there was a God why would He let us all suffer so much? The anger grows, for the world will never be the place you want it to be. Change it. Shape it. Do something to make it different. As you try you gain faith and belief in the creative process. You connect to your spirit and your power to make a difference. When your anger gets work to do, it can participate in your purpose. It has meaning; it's not left to attack you and others just out of idleness and lack of things to do.

Scorpios sometimes seem as if they are avoiding anger because they try to stop you from getting angry at them. If you get angry they might have to look at themselves and see the truth. The Scorpio with courage is the Scorpio who looks for your anger, because it knows that that is where your truth and your spirit lie. There is the danger of becoming attached to the power of anger—remember most people can't deal with it, so it is easy to use and misuse.

The Mother Helps You Emotionally Separate

Your mother is where you will learn to separate emotionally from others so that you can live your own life. If she had trouble expressing her anger, she probably held it in and chances are she endured abuse or disrespect from those around her. When you can't stand up for yourself, you get attacked. If your mother was angry all the time, or her rage was dangerous, you may be afraid to confront others or deal with anger. This will place you in angry situations all the time. Your environment is trying to get you to take a stand and go beyond rage to your rage and the peace that lies beyond them both. It is essential that you be able to stand up to your mother and take a stand for your truth, get angry, or rebel. This can only happen if your mother is healthy. If she is too weak you will protect her, even if you don't love her, and if she is too strong you will fear her. Without the ability to emotionally disconnect it will be difficult to develop intimacy with others. You will either take too much responsibility for them or not enough. If you can see why your position and fear was created, you can change it. (See Figure 12.1 for the Scorpio Star.)

The First Level of Consciousness

The first level of consciousness divides the eleventh house and first step, and the third house and fifth step. It challenges you to let go of protection, the dream, and the reward and let your spirit and creative force carry you to where you need to go. To do this you must not be afraid of pain and sorrow or be stopped by truths that must be logical and wise. Your heart is leading with conscious awareness of consequences and danger, but it keeps you safe by staying close to your destiny and dream.

Step One: The First House

Virgo: I Hold On and Let Go at the Same Time

I have finally learned how to hold on and let go at the same time. If I hold on to love and let go of fear, I will call forth goodness and receive the reward I deserve.

You have reached a point where your faith has the power to cut through illusions. Others like the fact that you can see through them; it's attractive as well as frightening. And there's nothing that anyone loves more than truth

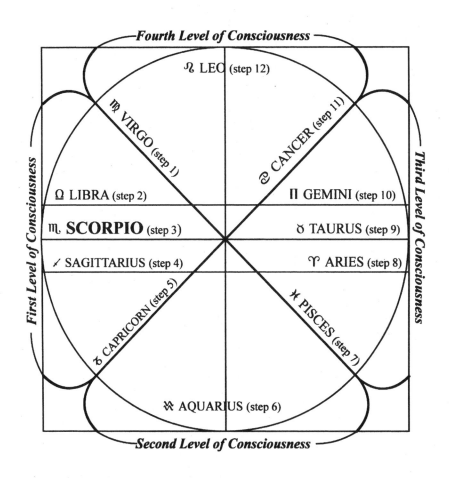

Figure 12.1. The Scorpio Star

and danger. This gives you power and others surrender to you and your voice. You are able to hold out for what you really want because you believe in your power to let go and be tough. This gives you the advantage.

> You are in level one when you hold on to the reward.
> You are in level two when you hold on to your freedom.
> (Levels three and four are listed at the end of step one in the fourth level of consciousness.)

Step Two: The Twelfth House

Libra: My Truth Is Only as Strong as My Shadow

I used to believe that my truth was based on the light and that I needed to ignore my negativity and feelings of unworthiness. However, that just cut me off from a big part of me. As soon as I started to pay attention to all my feelings, even the ones that got others annoyed, I became stronger, my voice was there, and my truth had power.

You have reached the point where you can't go anywhere if you can't say no, set boundaries, or stand up for yourself. Your creative spirit will get knocked around by others, and you will give up your dream—or worse yet rationalize to yourself that it wasn't real. Own your own negativity and use it to keep others in their place. When they know you can get angry or say what's on your mind, they will be careful how they treat you.

> You are in level one when truth is totally idealistic.
> You are in level two when truth is the authority.
> You are in level three when truth is the greater idea.
> You are in level four when truth is whatever the moment tells you it is.

Step Three: The First House

Scorpio: When I Own My Shadow, I See the Light

The shadow is a fearful place when you don't have faith. When I faced my fears, however, and learned to express what others didn't want to hear, I began to see that the light of truth is everywhere, including inside of me. The courage I found to express myself, even when I was risking support and love, allowed me to free myself of my fear of abandonment. There is no need to keep others in illusion—illusion blocks the light.

Making the tough choice, that is, taking a stand on an unpopular topic makes others realize that you can be trusted. When you go beyond your fear that the truth will create abandonment, you begin to find love. You were willing to be alone, so now you don't have to be.

> You are in level one when only others are allowed to get angry or be negative.
> You are in level two when you are the only one that's angry or negative.
> You are in level three when anger and negativity show you the path to the greater purpose.
> You are in level four when you accept it all because it's part of the creative process.

Step Four: The Second House

Sagittarius: I Use My Wisdom to See Where I Am Going

Wisdom and insight are no longer the problem, but how I use them is. I have knowledge and understanding—more than most—now I must decide if I should use these things to get ahead or to serve a common goal. Do I still need to be the best all by myself, or do I believe that I have my own uniqueness and no one can copy it? If I'm truly unique, no one can take that from me or truly imitate me. I have nothing to fear.

You have reached the level of consciousness where you have gifts and now you must use them wisely. It's important to remember that if you cut yourself off from others, you can only go so far. Don't forget you increase spiritual gifts by honoring them in others. If you are always trying to lead others astray or control them, you hold yourself back from your true genius. You must see that you are unique and be freed by this awareness.

> You are in level one when you rely on facts and information for knowledge.
> You are in level two when you rely on your own experiences for knowledge.

You are in level three when you rely on your inner voice for knowledge.
You are in level four when you rely on the unknown for knowledge, the
truth you haven't yet discovered.

Step Five: The Third House

Capricorn: Is Success Enough?

*I wanted to be successful and I achieved my goals; I am the best at what I do, but
it is not enough to make me happy. My spirit wants to be successful, too. It needs a
challenge and wants to find a meaning for everything that has happened in my life. I
seek my higher purpose.*

You have reached a point where success does not bring satisfaction. Praise
seems empty. Satisfaction comes from sharing, giving, and turning the light
on for others, and bringing them a new idea, faith, or a purpose, not a pat on
the back. Don't stop at achieving your goal. You are only halfway home.

You are in level one if you want what everyone else wants.
You are in level two when you want the best you can have from following your dream.
(Levels three and four are listed at the end of step five in the second
level of consciousness.)

The Second Level of Consciousness

The second level of consciousness divides the third house and fifth step,
and the fifth house and seventh step. You are now asked to challenge the
dreams that have imprisoned you and to free your soul and your heart to lead
you to your path and your greatness. You cannot be held down by weakness or
lack of faith any longer. You must leave depression behind and know that the
strength you gain will influence those you love and if it doesn't, they're not
ready to be strong. You must follow the path of freedom to your dream, not
the rewards they promise, these are two different paths.

Step Five: The Third House (Second Level)

Capricorn: My Reward Is My Originality

I have finally learned not to worry about the dreams of others and what they want from them because it only distracts me from my own path and goals. We are all here to accomplish something very personal. There is no need to compete; there's room for everyone's dream. I am unique and want to show the world my truth.

You have achieved the wisdom of accepting your originality. If you stay focused on what you do, love it, and let go, it will take you to where you need to be.

> You are in level three when love leads you to your reward.
> You are in level four when the reward is life.

Step Six: The Fourth House

Aquarius: I Am a Catalyst

I once thought that freedom was the ability to be me, but once I accepted me I got in touch with this magic—I can change things! I stir people up and get them looking for new answers. I change the energy in a room when I enter. It doesn't matter what I look like, I get attention. I'm different and I love being different. It gives me an edge and I put people on edge. Most of the time they love it.

You have the power to bring change through new ideas and perceptions. This is a great talent when you are peaceful inside. If your ego is still seeking recognition, you could be outrageous in your need for attention. If you are a seeker of truth, however, you will have an exciting mind and an exciting life.

> You are in level one when freedom is a place in the future.
> You are in level two when freedom is the freedom to choose.
> You are in level three when your freedom is the ability to face your fears.
> You are in level four when freedom is being you.

Step Seven: The Fifth House

Pisces: I Must Let Go of the Dream of Others

> *It is difficult to be selfish for what you want when you love others. However, I finally realized that trying to support them didn't help them or me. It's time for me to let go and accept my own path and follow my own dreams.*

When you can get out of the dreams that were given you, or the ones you feel obligated to pursue, you are ready to find your destiny. It is a difficult step because it makes one feel lonely and abandoned. Stay connected to your dream and you will build a whole new world around your quest. Have faith and keep going.

> You are in level one when you see your dreams as a way to feel loved.
> You are in level two when you use your dreams to run away from the
>   moment.
> (Levels three and four are listed at the end of step seven in the third
>   level of consciousness.)

The Third Level of Consciousness

The third level of consciousness divides the fifth house and seventh step, and the ninth house and eleventh step. It asks you to have faith in love and follow it through pain, sorrow, and disappointment. If you hold on to it, it will hold on to you and you will gain a new and greater idea of love. Gone will be the unfulfilling illusions of romantic love and in its place is strength, loyalty, and the ability to endure life's changes.

Step Seven: The Fifth House (Third Level)

Pisces: My Dream Gives Me My Voice

> *I love my dream because it allows me to voice an opinion and not have the attention entirely on me—it's on what I want to create and do. This allows others to offer their opinion without offending me. They share their experiences and I can pick and choose which make sense to me. A dream gives you a voice.*

You are right. It is so much easier to deal with others when you're not the focus of attention. Of course, your ego is in your dreams and your creation, but the more you can remove it from what you create, the more truth you will receive in your interactions.

> You are in level three when your dream teaches you how to love yourself.
> You are in level four when success is love and your dream.

Step Eight: The Sixth House

Aries: I Bring Out the Hero in Others

I used to want to be the hero and now I know that it is more important to help others find the hero in them. If I can show them where they have been strong, and how they have survived rather than be defeated, I can help them own their truth and their greatness. There is no greater reward.

You have reached a wonderful point in understanding. You know that your gifts are there so that you can pass them on and help others not have to struggle the same way you did. Make them strong and they will be wise. Help others find their power, and power will not be abused in the world and you will be strong.

> You are in level one when your vision is to rescue others.
> You are in level two when your vision is to follow your dream.
> You are in level three if you see you are the hero in the lives of others.
> You are in level four when you see everyone as the hero of their dreams.

Step Nine: The Seventh House

Taurus: I Love Myself When I'm Good and When I'm Bad

I used to see love as a reward: I had to be good to be loved. The truth is now I know I have to be me to be loved. I have to be able to do what others don't like and be true to myself for me to love me. When I love all of me, others love me, too. It's all so simple.

You know that you get more respect and love when you can own your negativity and when you're not worried about what others think. If you are always concerned about the impression you are making, you will hide your true self and you will attract someone who doesn't see you clearly. Then when you show the real you, they will feel deceived and you will, too—why couldn't they love you for who you are? Why couldn't you show them who you are? When you can find the courage to be you, you will find true love.

> You are in level one if you believe in unconditional love.
> You are in level two if you feel betrayed by love.
> You are in level three if you are giving love.
> You are in level four if you are giving unconditional love to yourself.

Step Ten: The Eighth House

Gemini: I Choose When to Reveal Myself

Choice was something I valued because I saw how poorly most people used it. I knew that if I could make the tough choices, it would give me an advantage. I was right, but it also got me disliked. I began dividing my choices between pleasing others and being tough. It gave a mixed message and to tell you the truth, I felt divided, too. I've learned that instead of pretending to be something I'm not, it's better to just keep silent and not share with others what I don't think they want to hear, unless I'm ready and willing to deal with the consequences.

The Scorpio has reached a point in the journey where it knows that battles are made mostly to convince ourselves that we are strong or better. If you know you are all these things, a battle is wasted. What you need to do is stay on your path and move toward your goals. To do this without creating opposition may require one to hide their choices and not share. The ability to contain and know what and when to reveal is a challenge of the higher self. When you trust your instincts this is not a problem. If you don't, you'll never get it right.

> You are in level one if you make your choices to please either yourself or others.
> You are in level two if you are challenging the choices of others and yourself.

You are in level three if you turn your choices over to your instincts.
You are in level four when you let faith make your choices.

Step Eleven: The Ninth House

Cancer: I Let Go of Protecting My Reward

It used to be so important to me to get recognized and have others validate my worth. I learned along the way that only I can determine my value, and the best way to do that is to not put a label or a limit on it. Leave it up to the universe and you'll do better than you think.

You are ready to free yourself of desiring a certain reward and now you've freed your creativity and your path to take you where you need to be to express your genius and find the next great idea.

You are in level one when you seek protection or to protect.
Your are in level two when you want freedom from protection.
(Levels three and four are listed at the end of step eleven in the fourth
   level of consciousness.)

The Fourth Level of Consciousness

The fourth level of consciousness divides the ninth house and eleventh step. It challenges you to let go and be in uncertainty, the place where creativity is born. This is where geniuses rest. Accept that holding on holds you back. Free-float through life because your anchor is your heart and your instincts, and you will then have the most exciting and successful life—the one you choose for your destiny.

Step Eleven: The Ninth House (Fourth Level)

Cancer: I Accept the Reward That I Have Yet to Discover

I am so aware of the power of choice that now I know and believe that the next one is the best. The greatest reward is the one I haven't had or experienced.

Life is exciting when you are always looking to the new and unborn. It doesn't mean that you don't value and enjoy what is; it means you don't hold on to it for your pleasure. You know that a new experience has the power to bring new insight and greater awareness, and you can see your world more clearly and enjoy it all more deeply.

> You are in level three when you want freedom to love.
> You are in level four when you want what you have earned.

Step Twelve: The Tenth House

Leo: My Originality Is My Strength and My Reward

My view of strength has really been challenged. I used to believe that it was the ability to be successful or hold your own with others, but now I know that that's my ego's way of feeling powerful. Spirit has a whole other opinion. She sees strength as the ability to let go of what is and trust that what is coming in is just as good as or better than what is leaving. Strength is faith.

Your ego is finally cornered and it must surrender. It has no power when you seek the new and the unknown. Fear does not do well in uncertainty, so it must rely on the faith of spirit. When it does it learns to have faith that it will get its chance for recognition and not be left out. If you let your ego constantly seek approval, you weaken your faith, lose your confidence, and find it difficult to go for what your heart desires.

> You are in level one if you feel strength is found in approval or dominance.
> You are in level two if you feel strength is challenging the authority.
> You are in level three if you feel strength is faith.
> You are in level four if you feel strength is turning your problems over to a higher power.

Step One: The Eleventh House (Fourth Level)

Virgo: I Let Go of My Concept of Faith and Accept a New Experience

It's amazing to me how magical life is when you know how it works. I have faith in myself and my dreams and now I don't need my concept of faith, I just reach out to others and support in them what I want to highlight in me.

Wouldn't it be wonderful if everyone in the world had a dream? If they did there would not be terrorism or war. When you have a dream you feel loved and protected. Dreams give meaning to life and they show you the way. Give the gift of dreams by helping others believe in themselves.

> You are in level three when you can let go of your dream and know it will be there when you want it.
> You are in level four when you don't worry about reward, you just choose for what you want and help others get what they want.

The Cross

The cross is composed of the eleventh, fifth, ninth, and third houses and is where change must occur. (See Figure 12.1 on page 273.) The two fixed houses represented by Virgo and Pisces challenge each other to see a greater truth:

Virgo (eleventh house): *I have learned that if I try to deny others their dream I actually impede my own progress. If I can help others have faith, it doesn't mean I lose my power, on the contrary, I increase it—it gives me more faith in myself and my uniqueness.*

Pisces (fifth house): *My ego is my only challenge now. If I see the dreams of others as competition, they will be competition. If I help others I empower myself. When I do this, I am no longer afraid of being judged, because I listen only to my inner voice, which brings me love. I think this is because I now love myself.*

The two mutable houses represented by Cancer and Capricorn must anchor themselves in this new truth by taking a stand:

Cancer (ninth house): *I give up my need for protection and I risk my creative voice in the world.*

Capricorn (third house): *The only thing that stops me from achieving my goals is my need to still get approval and have some comfort in my life. The more I expect instead of accept, the more unhappy I am. When I can accept, I can transcend.*

PART FIVE

The Fourth Level of Consciousness

"The only limit to our realization of tomorrow will be our doubts of today. Let us move forward with strong and active faith."

—Franklin Delano Roosevelt

The fourth level of consciousness brings the soul to a feeling of oneness and peace. When you begin to see that it is your attitudes that separate and divide, not people, you begin the process of change. Change leads to faith and faith gives love and confidence to anyone willing to take the risk. When you risk yourself for your beliefs you turn on the light. The light brings love and a natural unfolding to life. You now want to share. When you want to share you increase love in your heart, and the domino effect that once kept you in fear is now working to increase faith and peace in you.

It has taken the collective consciousness centuries to reach the opportunity we have before us to change the way we think. It takes only a few strong voices with great faith to impact a world that is spiritually starving. If each and every one of you desires to have a great leader, the collective force will churn, and from the shadow of Aquarius these souls will emerge. Your mission is to recognize them when they arrive; try not to stone them if they don't fit your image of greatness, or they don't look wise. You must recognize truth in all its masks, or we will stay condemned to be led by illusions, pettiness, and anger instead of the real thing. You can do your share for world peace by trying to improve your consciousness—that is, by allowing yourself to be you and by supporting the free expression of every other soul you meet.

SAGITTARIUS: Wisdom

(November 23 through December 21)

I am wise when I do not know
I've seen the high, I've done the low
What is true; what is a lie?
What is real; what needs to die?
To solve the mysteries on my road
To lighten the burden of my load
I must have faith in all of me
I must allow my eyes to see
All that is painful and dark inside
It's really the most important ride
I'm attached to sorrow and my pain
Hope and joy, they distract my brain
I must accept all of me
I must surrender and be free

Question Nine

About Your Parents: How much did your father rely on his inner wisdom and personal experience? Did he change what he could and accept what he couldn't? Or, did he follow the rules and try to escape through idealism, rationalization, anger, drugs, or drink?

About Yourself: How much of what you do comes from yourself? Do you copy others or do you find your own way? Are you able to accept in life what you can't change and find the courage to try to change what you believe you can? Or, do you always follow the rules and therefore find yourself looking for an escape?

The wonder of life is calling the soul. You have tasted your divinity and the power that comes with wisdom and *knowing,* and the rewards of the world have lost their luster: You want something more than glitter and gold; you want something eternal—a reward fit for a god. You're looking for the magic and miracles of life, and since they are not around you, they must lie in distant lands and in ideas and places not known. You've learned that there is always a better idea, a greater reward, so you set out to find it, believing that it is a thing to possess, rather than an awakening of the heart and spirit to its potential. To seek is to repeat unless you look upward and try to discover the right question that will get you a greater answer. The wise ones know that answers are traps; they are prisons that fool less driven souls to believe that what they have discovered explains it all. How lazy and ignorant to think that there is a limit to consciousness. As long as you're asking questions, you're still humane and playing the game. Yes, the world has become a game, and each soul a player. The road before you is a maze and a puzzle, and those who have caught on to the universe and its love of play have entered into the arena armed with an open mind, a wit that cuts much cleaner than a sword, judgments that remove those still attached to images and egos, and yes, with the courage to play with fear. This is what will divide the winners and losers now. Not the spoils of being the smartest, not the ability to find an answer, do the impossible, or change the world into a better place, but the ability to face the darkness of your soul. Who is willing to enter the tar pit of their own being and dredge up the unworthiness that holds it all together in sticky hot glue? If you're not ready to go to the bowels of your existence, you are not ready for greatness.

The Sagittarian has the consciousness to see the mystery in the moment, and now it desires to separate it and understand it so that it can be called forth when desired. It has seen the eternal in the morning dew, on the petals of a flower, in the fleeting beauty and wonder of a sunset, in the magic of a birth, and in the tragedy of death. Within each of these moments is a truth and a meaning that can't be spoken, shared, or totally understood. This is what the wise ones are seeking to grasp, to call forth on demand, to live in so that this one fleeting moment of bliss can be extended into eternity.

The mind is the vehicle to which most humans turn over this mysterious and wondrous moment to be explained. We call these *mystery explainers* philosophers because they have managed to fool us into believing that their words have defined the miracles. We are happy to have reduced something so profound and magical to a treatise that confuses and brings up more questions than one initially asked. Beauty and magic are turned into conflict and now everyone is happy. We all understand conflict, or at least we accept it without an explanation. The fact that most of us don't understand what is being said by the wise ones makes it easier to believe—shouldn't truth be beyond your knowledge? Shouldn't most of you just follow and stop trying to find your own way?

There is no answer to love; there is no question—you are love. You came down to earth as a soul to experience love your way. If love your way does not agree with my way, we could be in conflict (if I'm stuck in level one). In fact, I may gather an army together and try to prove to you that my version of love is superior to yours. The world tends to measure importance by quantity and strength. Something is great when the experts tell us it is. Ask any artist who is trying to sell a painting. Persuade someone who is supposed to know what genius is to buy your painting and everyone else will follow. It has nothing to do with what each person believes; most believe in what the authority tells them. The same concept is true with designer clothes. You are "in," if you are wearing items with labels that mean you have enough money or lack of individual style to put something together on your own. Not enough of you have the confidence to know how to pull your own personal look together. It takes courage to be different and unique. It takes strength of conviction and faith in you.

Wisdom is the voice of your uniqueness. How much strength do you have to stand up for what you believe in? When you have a strong voice, you will naturally graduate into helping others have a strong voice. Your path will be to reach out to those who can't speak up. Your dream will be to bring out strength and love in others through your unique talents. If you are a writer, an athlete, or a mother, you will seek to strengthen the ability to be free by validating the talents and differences of those you know. Your path will be to be an example of living your truth your way.

Sagittarians have mastered perseverance because they know how to bring the future into the now. They see themselves in their vision and now they bring that vision into the moment, by choosing for the vision and acting as if it were already real. Yes, they believe in themselves so much they act as if they were standing in their greatness instead of their most painful wound. They glean strength from any moment that inspires them, and they hold on to that moment and enlarge it by taking it into their heart. Many know the secret of belief and the power of passion. If you express passion everyone pays attention; it doesn't even matter if they believe what you love, they will want it because it is now associated with love. Have passion for yourself and your creations, and the world will pay attention to you.

If you have not learned to believe in yourself, you will be attracted to strong, manipulating souls who take over your life. Within you is the need to surrender to a truth and a purpose, and if you don't have one of your own, you'll seek to support the unique path of someone else. This is not a tragedy, but it does have some drawbacks. The more you have your own truth, the better it is. If you are supporting someone because they share your beliefs, your support will only increase your own power. If you are supporting someone because you have no idea who you are, that's not bad either—if you are there to learn and not to get lost in their life. Nothing is wrong if you are using it for the right purpose. The more selfish you can be, the more selfless you will be. Only someone who is whole and true to oneself really knows how to give. You can't go beyond the ego until you have one. The ego won't bend until it has been acknowledged. Pay attention to yourself and what makes you happy, and your life will be about giving to others. Ignore your spirit and your true self and you will feel deprived, and everything you give will be a sacrifice, not a gift.

Love or the Role of Hero

Love of truth and the ability to solve the mysteries of the world—this has seduced you and taken you above your desires for an earthly playmate. It's not that you don't want love or a soul mate; it's just not the highest thing on your list. You are seeking the magic of a new idea, the ability to change your perception of yourself and the world through understanding. It's a powerful feeling to turn on the light for yourself and others. This brings loyalty that's not forgotten, it brings praise and adulation, and it brings love and devotion—not the intimate kind—the kind that cheers at a distance. You are a natural leader and others tend to look up to you for answers. You have the ability to detach from the particulars and see life in greater symbols. What is missing is your connection to the shadow. Without it, you can easily be seduced into becoming someone's hero, and when you allow yourself to be raised up and adored, you are asking that you also be attacked and condemned. There is no other way.

The Shadow Has the Power

Nothing is more powerful than not caring about what others think. This does not mean that you ignore their opinions, but it does mean that you are able to pluck the truth from them and dismiss the rest. You know that the world is seeking control, that everyone wants to have power, and the Sagittarius appears as if it doesn't matter. Of course it does! It is not enough to have power, however, they need to inspire or be inspired, too. Those who inspire can do so because they have learned to put their heart and soul into what they are doing. When a Sagittarius has found its passion, the world stands up and takes notice.

When you are not afraid of pain and sadness, when you can reach into the depths of your soul, you will be able to call forth your anger when someone is trying to push you around. You'll be able to call forth your wisdom when someone is trying to fool you or take advantage of you. You will recognize true pain and not someone soliciting your help out of laziness, and you will see their behavior and not believe it unless it is backed by truth, or a commitment from their heart. You like those who have come up the hard way and admire anyone who can fight when they are down. You know that life will always knock you down, but if you're not afraid of fear, you'll get back up and try again.

Sagittarians are either very positive or very depressed, sometimes a bit of both. The positive ones are more often than not balancing a depressed parent or partner. They have learned to see the good and be happy out of necessity— someone in their life was so down that they felt they would lose themselves in darkness if they didn't hold on to the light. The gift of positive thinking, even when it is developed for the wrong reasons, helps you find solutions and new opportunity. You are able to reach out to the world for a new answer and because of that you find one. A new path is always there if you look for it. Sooner or later you will have to look inside and face your fear. Sagittarians will never reach their true potential until they've fallen into the shadow that they are hiding from. Don't be positive to keep the shadow away; be positive because you have faith in yourself and your destiny.

If you are the Sagittarius who is depressed, you will be surrounded by positive thinkers. You stay in your depression because it gives you the attention you are seeking. Afraid that your truth is not enough, you have taken victimhood to new dimensions. You hide love and the good things in your life and show others only what's wrong. This makes them want to save you. The goodness in their soul is being manipulated to feed your ego. You get attention by consciously choosing not to be happy. What you are doing is using love. Those who love you are willing to put themselves on the line over and over again to bring you a moment of light. Shame on you. You are greater than your behavior or your beliefs.

One heart is what the Sagittarius wants and its heart is committed to its higher purpose. It is not invested in its own vision or the vision of another; it's invested in unity and finding a solution. Sagittarians are great problem solvers because they don't give up; they keep twisting and turning things around until they find a way to make them fit. More often than not, they succeed out of mere perseverance. Most others give up after one or two mistakes, but not the Sagittarius. Opposition just makes you dig in and try harder. It gets your heart, mind, and spirit to work together in the struggle to find an answer.

The challenge of the Sagittarius will be to not surrender to your heroes or have others surrender themselves to you, but to choose what part you want to merge with. You can be an equal to anyone because you can take a piece of them and connect to that piece, creating unity of spirit that overcomes outer differences.

The Wisdom of Nonsense

True wisdom is the ability to act with or without reason because you are connected to your inner knowing. You know what is right for you, even if you can't explain it. The test then for true wisdom comes when you can act because you know you should, even when you can't explain it. You are basing your truth on your inner voice, and you have faith that the reason will be revealed when the time is right. Those who can transcend reason are the true geniuses of the world. All new ideas and discoveries take the thinker beyond logic and into the unknown. If you are going to be truly imaginative, you've got to venture where no one else ever has. When you're in the unknown you're in a place that is uncharted, and reason doesn't work in these waters—instinct does.

When you can play with the mind, that is, give it a poem that makes no sense—a list of numbers that leads nowhere—when you engage it to make sense out of nonsense, you have got its attention and you can go beyond it to the heart. Meditation and mantras try to still the mind by letting it have its thoughts. And when you don't pay attention to them—when you practice not being attached to your thoughts—they come and go and you can choose which ones you wish to pursue and which ones are there to distract you. The mind has power only if you listen to it.

The Father Leads You to Wisdom

It is your father who should give you the security of wisdom. It is how he dealt with the problems and crises in life that will teach you to be afraid, to confront, or to persevere. If he had faith in his instincts and his heart, he will pass that on to you. If he avoided responsibility because he either had too much as a child, or he was spoiled or afraid, you will either be over-responsible in an attempt to compensate, or you will follow his irresponsible path. It is much easier to solve life's dilemmas with faith and the ability to use your imagination. If solutions must come only from rules and knowledge, your life will be filled with problems and they will hold you down. Learn to take the weight off your shoulders by sharing your woes with faith. (See Figure 13.1 for the Sagittarius Star.)

The First Level of Consciousness

The first level of consciousness divides the eleventh house and first step, and the third house and fifth step. It asks the soul to let go of being the hero and to seek instead freedom and reward through purpose. The quest is to find meaning in life and understand why you are here and where you are going. To do this you must go beyond your need for adulation and commit to your quest with your total mind, body, and soul. Anything you give with passion will be yours.

Step One: The Eleventh House

Libra: My Truth Must Set Me Free

I thought that I had conquered my ego because I put my truth above it, but when my truth was recognized, and everyone began to praise me, I realized that my ego had not been tamed. It had only been waiting for its chance to take back center stage. My desire to be the hero was now possible, and I gave in to it because it was

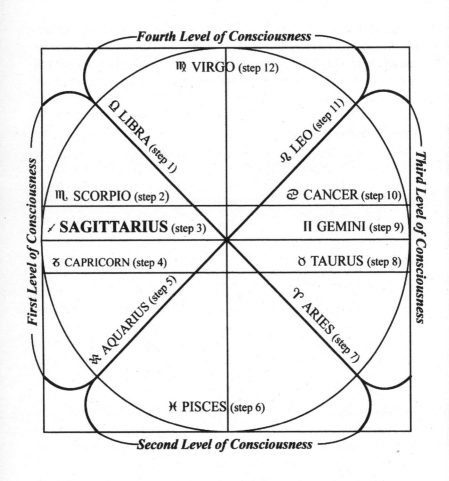

Figure 13.1. The Sagittarius Star

everything I dreamed it would be. What I didn't know was that along with adulation comes the loss of freedom. No one wants you to change if they fell in love with you a certain way. Exactly what got me my success—risk and new ideas—others are asking me to give up. I'm torn between knowing I need to let go and wanting to hold on to the dream.

You have deceived yourself, believing that you were strong, but your hidden desires were still waiting to emerge. It's important to know that whenever you give in to your ego, it will bring you down. The people who adore you will turn on you in a minute—as soon as you don't fit their image, or as soon as you do something against their wishes. This is no eternal reward. It is not the reward for greatness; it is the reward for an ego that has managed to survive the struggle untamed.

> You are in level one if truth is the solution to your problems.
> You are in level two when you challenge the vision and truth of others.
> (Levels three and four are listed at the end of step one in the fourth level of consciousness.)

Step Two: The Twelfth House

Scorpio: I Express My Negativity with Humor

I used to try to protect others from my negative feelings. Now I express them, but with humor. I have learned that others will hear what I have to say, if I don't say it too harshly. You've got to have style, that is, you need to know how to sugarcoat what you say by saying something nice first. If you just come out and attack others, they will defend themselves and not listen. The goal is to be heard.

You've learned to say what needs to be said and now you're working on presentation. There's the right moment to shoot straight and direct, there's the right moment to be kind and gentle, and there's the right moment to surround the negativity with a little positive input. If you want to be heard, you've got to begin to concentrate on who is listening and fashion your style according to the challenge. Humor, if you have it, is a way to please everyone and get your message out there.

You are in level one when you believe you are either good or bad.
You are in level two when you can hide your truth from those who are
negative.
You are in level three when you know that you are both good and bad.
You are in level four when you know that it is your intention that
makes you good.

Step Three: The First House

Sagittarius: My Choices Make Me Wise

I realize that wisdom is important and that it lies with choices, but what I must conquer is my need to be praised for my wisdom. I realize that praise is praise; it makes me dependent on others, even though the subject matter is wisdom and truth. It doesn't make me less of a child because I'm playing with bigger toys.

It is so easy to get lost in the subject matter and feel that because you have solved some of the mysteries of life or at least understood them, others look up to you. Knowledge is power, because it can separate you from others or it can also bring you close to them and unite differences. It's all in how you use it. Use knowledge to enhance your ego and you will be on the path of separateness; use knowledge to bring others a greater, more unifying point of view and you are a peacemaker.

You are in level one if you believe everything you are told.
You are in level two if you confront what others tell you.
You are in level three if you listen to your inner voice.
You are in level four if you turn your questions over to a higher power.

Step Four: The Second House

Capricorn: Fear Has a Value

I know that when I face my fears I feel stronger; when I let them go I feel worse. The path to strength is not just wisdom, it's the ability to face one's fears. If you can't look your pain in the eye, your wisdom will lack feeling and depth.

You will not be able to reach the truth and wisdom you desire without adding your knowledge of pain and sorrow. If you have never delved into your pain and sorrow and keep looking at life as a pretty picture, you will use so much of your energy trying to keep smiling. Give in to your feelings and emotions and let them have their say—you'll be able to go beyond them and you'll be able to deal with others who are in pain, instead of running from them.

When you hold on to your feelings you can't receive, and then giving is seen as a sacrifice because you get so little back. If it is a sacrifice, you will have to hold on to *things*. You will value your possessions and you will base your self-worth on what you have and how much others desire what you have. This does not support your strength or purpose; it supports your ego's need for attention through fear. To change this you've got to start making yourself a priority and take a stand even if it means you are rejected or turned away. Those who really love you will be back and those who stay away should not be close to you anyway. If someone can't tolerate your truth or your position, they don't belong in your life. If you keep them in your life, you become a slave to their truth, not yours, and you'll wonder why you feel so bad and unhappy.

You are in level one if your goals are to escape the moment or to find pleasure.
You are in level two if your goals are to follow your dream.
You are in level three when you let go of reward.
You are in level four when your reward is your life.

Step Five: The Third House

Aquarius: I Need to Be Free of the Hero in Me

I am only as free as I am free of my ego. I used to believe that it didn't really get in the way, that the pursuit of higher knowledge automatically rendered it innocuous, but that's not true. The ego that is not watched and honored as a driving force or formidable foe will find its way into your mind and work against your purpose and your desire for peace.

You have reached the point of choice and before you is your dream, the dream to be the hero, to receive praise and adulation and the new dream, the dream that has a purpose. Which do you choose? Which are you ready to embrace?

You are in level one when freedom isolates you.
You are in level two when freedom is found in the pursuit of justice.
(Levels three and four are listed at the end of step five in the second
    level of consciousness.)

The Second Level of Consciousness

The second level of consciousness divides the third house and fifth step,
and the fifth house and seventh step. It challenges you to look at the conflict
within you instead of the problems of the world. The choice is now between
your intentions. Which is more important to you—success or success and a
higher purpose? Are you willing to keep going and striving, or do you want to
stop at the top of the mountain and rest?

Step Five: The Third House (Second Level)

*Aquarius: I Am Free When My Vision to Be a Hero Merges with My
Dream*

*I now know that I want to be free more than I want to be adulated and adored.
My love of truth and wisdom has won and I choose to move on and try to make a
difference in the world.*

When you achieve your goals, it is both rewarding and terrifying because
there is nothing harder to handle than success. If success comes before self-
worth, you're in trouble. You've got to feel worthy in order to handle the pressure and demands of others. It's hard enough to manage one's own emotions
and if you haven't learned how to say no, or stand up for what you believe in,
success will bring you down and make you feel unhappy. When your ego
merges with the dream you are united and your spirit will guide you.

You are in level three when freedom comes from facing your fears.
You are in level four when freedom is in every moment.

Step Six: The Fourth House

Pisces: My Dream Does Not Need Protection

I used to hold my dream close to me and protect it from the judgments of others. It was my escape. My dream is strong, however; it is what has sustained me. I have faith in it because I know that it won't leave me as long as I believe in it. So it doesn't need my protection anymore; it needs faith. We've got an understanding.

You are now able to rely on your dream. It sits in the fourth house, creating your foundation. You know you can rely on it if you keep the faith. In fact, whatever you believe in no one can take away.

> You are in level one when your dream is what others tell you it is.
> You are in level two when you use your dream to escape.
> You are in level three when you have faith in your dream.
> You are in level four when you live your dream.

Step Seven: The Fifth House

Aries: The Desire for Perfection Haunts Me

I used to dream of being the hero, someone others looked up to. Now they do and I don't want to give it up even if it means giving up my dream—isn't that ridiculous? I've come this far and given up so much, and it is the hero in me that doesn't want to die—or is it the ego in me?

You have a right to feel stuck for a moment. It's hard to let the first dream die. It's like a first kiss or a first love; it has the strongest hold on us. However, wisdom and experience should eventually win out—you know your destiny is greater than a little praise and a feeling of being adored. You have things to accomplish in the world. Get busy and do the work.

> You are in level one if you want to save the lives of those you love.
> You are in level two when you challenge the authority that is stopping you from moving forward.
> (Levels three and four are listed at the end of step seven in the third level of consciousness.)

The Third Level of Consciousness

The third level of consciousness divides the fifth house and seventh step, and the ninth house and eleventh step. The Sagittarius is asked to see greatness in the little things, now that it has a grasp of the big picture. Can you see the hero in the little man—the beauty in the moment and not the parade? It's time to integrate what you know and weave them together. To do this you have to believe that they are one.

Step Seven: The Fifth House (Third Level)

Aries: The Hero Takes a Bow

I have let my ego have its moment of glory and now I'm going to ask it to move on. It can take a bow and feel proud that it has managed to survive all the attacks and judgments that have come its way. My ego is truly strong and I am totally grateful for its presence in my life.

When you give your own ego the recognition it needs, it no longer needs it from others. It has only been doing all those crazy things to get your attention and to win your love. Be kind to your ego; give it praise for what it has done, but don't allow it to linger in the limelight. That makes the ego weak and makes it want more.

You are in level three when you have faith in your vision and your mission.
You are in level four when your vision includes everyone.

Step Eight: The Sixth House

Taurus: I See Love in Everyone

Rewards have always been difficult to let go of. Of course, the most important one was always the pursuit of unconditional love. The more I wanted it the less I received it. It wasn't until I learned how to love myself that things changed. Now I'm being asked to give others that love by seeing in them what I now see in myself.

Love, the love of self, unites with the love of others. That's pretty powerful stuff. When you love yourself enough all you will see in others is love or the lack of love, and you will fill those gaps with a glance, a validation, and an open heart. When you do you become the healer.

> You are in level one when you expect unconditional love.
> You are in level two when you seek power.
> You are in level three when you have faith in yourself.
> You are in level four when you give unconditional love to yourself and others.

Step Nine: The Seventh House

Gemini: The Truth About Choice

Since I have gone beyond the hero in me I realize that it is not just the wise who know about life, but it is the little person—the street person, the worker—who has the answers. I open myself up to discover the knowledge I left behind.

You have learned from the great teachers, from great thoughts and great minds, and now that you have stopped associating greatness with heroes you can see the simple person as a hero and as wise. When you can learn from everyone then you are truly wise.

> You are in level one when choice means inner conflict.
> You are in level two when choice means opposition.
> You are in level three when choice means freedom.
> You are in level four when you turn your choices over to your higher self.

Step Ten: The Eighth House

Cancer: I Protect My Intention to Learn

I have learned that if you want to eliminate criticism and battles, it is sometimes best not to show the world what you are doing. I have divided the world between those I can tell almost anything to and those I seldom tell anything to. It works very well.

You have learned how to contain and reveal and so it is now done by choice. You have also learned to make your path easier where you have no investment and save your strength for the real fights, the ones that you have to make. When you learn to do this your world becomes a pleasant and safe place.

> You are in level one when you seek protection or to protect.
> You are in level two when you want freedom from protection.
> You are in level three when you want the faith to love and be intimate.
> You are in level four when you want the strength to live your truth your way.

Step Eleven: The Ninth House

Leo: I Accept the Path to My Purpose

I know that true strength comes when I let go and can see what I want in others. However, it is hard for me to let go of my truth and I know I must. It is getting in the way. It has its limitations, too. I realize that everything must eventually go, even my concept of faith.

Wisdom is not always comforting when it challenges the things you hold dear. But think about it, the truth you have formed has come from your worldly journey and it has revealed to you your spiritual purpose. Doesn't it make sense that when it's time to move into your purpose, your truth would have to surrender to a greater truth. You know how it works: You let go and something better will arrive. You're just moving up the ladder.

> You are in level one if you believe strength is physical.
> You are in level two if you think strength is control.
> (Levels three and four are listed at the end of step eleven in the fourth level of consciousness.)

The Fourth Level of Consciousness

The fourth level of consciousness divides the ninth house and eleventh step. It challenges you to merge your truth with your success and let go of the dream because there is something beyond it—your higher purpose. When you can use your dream and success to help others, you feed your ego and your spirit and achieve wholeness.

Step Eleven: The Ninth House (Fourth Level)

Leo: My Ego Is Free

My lack of freedom was connected completely to my inability to commit to my dream. Once I stopped trying to make everyone else's dream happen first, I felt free. Now my ego can use its energy to create and do for what lies in my heart. Heart and mind are united, and I feel strong.

When the ego is freed because it no longer has to please, real freedom is felt. There is nothing more rewarding than a spirit without guilt. This is when passion arises, truth is heard, and the superfluous is let go, allowing one's purpose and destiny to be seen. Follow your heart; it will lead you to your dream and your destiny.

> You are in level one when you live for recognition and praise.
> You are in level two when it is freedom that will make you happy.
> You are in level three when it is love that will set you free.
> You are in level four when it is your heart's desire and your passion that lead you.

Step Twelve: The Tenth House

Virgo: My Success Is Determined by How Much I Can Help Others

I have let go of the need to prove that I am successful, and when I do I recognize the strength in others to achieve. I want to help bring that strength out in them. I must find a way to use what I have to enlighten others. This is the true measure of my success.

You are at the point in your journey where results are no longer enough unless you can give something back. You don't stop at praise, money, or reward because it all has to have meaning to bring you inner satisfaction. If it doesn't it's all for naught. Life is not just about meeting the next challenge; it's about sharing how you tackle that challenge with others who are on their way up.

You are in level one when you dream, but lack faith.
You are in level two when all you see is the reward.
You are in level three when you see faith as strength.
You are in level four when strength is love.

Step One: The Eleventh House (Fourth Level)

Libra: You Are a Leader with a Vision

Truth is personal and it is universal—if you try to decide whose truth is best you end up in a battle. Truth, I believe, is based around a vision. If you have a vision of the world the way you would like it to be, you will create a truth to support that vision. That's the way it should be. When you can lead others because of your vision, you are giving a gift to the world.

You have accepted the individualization of truth, and if the soul is coming from love it will be coming from universal truths also. The large is in the small, the small in the large—you can't separate them. Learn the bigger picture and it will improve your daily life; it will filter down and bring new choices into your life if you are not afraid of change. Let your truth change with you and it will be a valued companion. Let your vision lead you and the world will be a better place.

You are in level three when you see truth as choice and the wisdom to
   listen to yourself.
You are in level four when you see your truth in all truths.

The Cross

The cross is composed of the eleventh, fifth, ninth, and third houses and is where change must occur. (See Figure 13.1 on page 294.) The two fixed houses represented by Libra and Aries challenge each other to see a greater truth:

Libra (eleventh house): *Truth is no help here for it will be whatever I choose it to be, and what I choose is for it to support my new vision of me and the world.*

Aries (fifth house): *I accept my reward as hero. I am successful and have achieved my dream, and now my real mission is before me. If I cannot go beyond my success, it will keep me stagnant and bring me down. I must go beyond my ego to reach real wisdom and see my true path. I accept the wisdom that my purpose leads me to, and in so doing I see the wisdom in each moment and in the greatest simplicity. How silly I was to seek grandness—whatever I needed was with me all along.*

The two mutable houses represented by Leo and Aquarius must anchor themselves in this new truth by taking a stand:

Leo (ninth house): *I give up my ego and desire to be the hero by saving others in grand ways, in order to pursue my purpose. In so doing, I feel free.*

Aquarius (third house): *My desire to remain free and spontaneous made me rebel against the need to make such a deep commitment to others and myself. Now I know it is only through commitment to my heart that I find both freedom and greatness.*

CAPRICORN: Reward
(December 22 through January 20)

Capricorn brings the winter struggle
It bursts the illusions of your bubble
To survive the cold and the frost
To realize that you can't be lost
You must be tested, face your fear
You must let go of what is dear.
Then you'll have this thing called faith
And you will rise above your fate
You will be a shining star
That all can see from near and far
They will know that love is true
And all because you are you.

Question Ten

About Your Parents: What rewards did your mother expect from life?
Did she achieve her goals? What did she fear?

About Yourself: What do you expect from life? What are you afraid of?
Do you know why you have this fear?

You are passion in a box, desire in a suit, and an idealist in disguise. You
hide behind an overcivilized appearance: worried on one hand about what
everyone else thinks, and on another, not at all. Your own duality confuses
you, because it often tears you apart. You are the sign at the top of the chart;

306

you represent the reward: the acclaim, the money, and the satisfaction that one gets from taking their journey. What a shame to discover at the end something so important—that what you wanted to receive determined your choices, path, and the amount of joy you had along the way.

The Capricorn is torn between the desire of its spirit to return to the instinctual and more primitive side of life, and the ego's need to hold on to everything it has worked so hard to achieve: a civilized attitude, a good job, security, and acceptance from its environment. It is possible to fulfill both your spiritual and egoistic needs only when you have a purpose and you're willing to compromise for that purpose. I know you want things perfect and your way, but your spirit has been compromising all along. For you to maintain such a degree of stubbornness, she had to hold herself back from her desire to express, create, and be free; now she's ready to rebel. Most Capricorns find themselves caught between hanging on to the status quo, that is, living a life that was paved by prior generations, or taking a risk in some business on the edge, or a relationship out of control. You have reached the point of no return; you can't go back and stay in that box—a 9-to-5 job is not for you if there's no place for your spirit to be creative. With too many rules you feel smothered and your spirit rebels. Whatever happened to playing, taking risks, soaring above the clouds with your imagination, scaling the fence barefoot, and dreaming about adventure? Life is not over unless you say it's over. Many of you have been more concerned with gaining approval and rewards instead of setting your spirit free, and now it's going to get your attention one way or another.

Success is only the first stop for the Capricorn. To be truly happy, a Capricorn needs to be doing something for humanity. Within the heart is the need to share, to use one's knowledge and success to make a difference in the lives of others. If this is never achieved what good is success? Sure it will buy you comfort and praise, all things of the ego. To fulfill the spirit and its needs, to keep her from rising up and shaking up your world, you need to give her something she wants, too. She needs to be of service; she needs to make a difference. Do not ignore this inner need for it is the most powerful force within you.

You have a skill that takes you beyond most of your competition—you can deny yourself the luxuries and pleasures of life, if you have a goal. You know how to glean joy from the simple things, not the big moments. When you enjoy something you hold on and don't let go. When you love, you love with all your heart, and you can't understand how anyone could put restrictions on love. The loved one should have their every whim taken care of. You are tough on the outside, and soft within. Others see you as determined and strong because punishment has no effect on a psyche that realizes how meaningless it is. Endure it and no one can control you. Live through the judgment and abuse and you are still your own person. When others can't punish you, you take away their means of control and now they have to face you with their truth. Truth to truth, you'll win every time.

Your ability to see subtleties and know what's missing, no matter how small or minute the quantity, gives you a unique and critical eye. Gifted with a palette that can tell the difference between a port wine aged to perfection and one slightly less nurtured, you can distinguish nuances in flavors, personalities, and objects. This critical eye can carry over into your personal relationships, causing it to seem like you're being judgmental—don't they know you just know better? Doesn't anyone else see these blatant inaccuracies, the missing pieces, and what about the wrinkles? If you are a Capricorn who doesn't believe in pleasure, you have cut yourself off from your main source of power. You are the highest form of Taurus, the leader of desire. You know quality, and if you can't have the right wine, the best jam, the fresh orange juice, you'd rather not have it at all. Quality has conquered quantity, choice has been refined, and only the best will do. Less is better when that less is exquisite. For example, a Capricorn might believe it is better to have one great suit than five that are so-so. Better to have one fabulous glass of wine than three mediocre ones. If you prefer not to have anything, you're still trying to control your life through controlling your pleasures and your instincts.

Within you are unfinished dreams, desires, and visions that you couldn't complete because of circumstances. Life interfered with your ability to take your desires to their apex and you are angry. Your inner world is filled with broken images, unfulfilled yearnings, and pleasures that were cut short. Yes, nothing got to go the distance, or at least it feels that way. You want control so you and only you can determine when enough is enough—not God, not fate, not even nature. You're not interested in letting go. What you will learn, however, is that pleasure decreases if it stays constant. Your body's ability to adapt diffuses the joy until it is a part of you, and if you're still looking for a high, you'll have to keep pushing the boundaries or breaking the rules. Like the tide that comes in and goes out, to have the ultimate satisfaction you must have it missing so you can long for it and build up the expectation. When it returns, the taste is oh so much better. Yes, lack, absence, and deprivation increase joy, so you let things build in your life. Then you can project this pleasure onto that one bite, that one kiss, that one moment when life stands still and you are in bliss.

Bliss exists between the comings and goings, between the pain of losing and the joy of reconnecting—it is the blend of joy and sadness that has you hooked. One is just not as good without the other. When they come together they enhance each other, highlighting the best and worst of all that they are. The danger is that you will get hooked either on a relationship that pulls you in and pushes you away, or perhaps a job that will take you on a roller coaster ride. When you accept the ups and downs within you and don't rely on either one, but steer a steady course because you're connected to your heart, your instincts, and your destiny, it won't matter which way the tide turns—you are safe.

Letting Go of Protection

Letting go is the key component to your peace and happiness. You are afraid that if you let go what you are holding will be lost (check out the chapter on Virgo). If you don't let go clutter will build up and overwhelm you. If your spirit is strong, it will snatch you out of your hell by breaking you free. She won't care if she destroys relationships, or creates pain and scars, she wants you free, she wants to be free, and she'll work on healing you later. No matter how many times she pulls you out of your prison, your fear of letting go puts you back in. When you find your passion, when you stumble on to your dream, you get a new vision of yourself and now you can let go because you have something greater to hold on to—you have your destiny.

Self-Denial

You want control because you are controlled by what you want to see. You are a master at denial. You can shut out negativity, or anything else for that matter, and refuse to see what doesn't fit. Please add the negative, look at it, then let go. Be aware of its presence; it's the only way to steer a correct course. When you just shut things out or cut them off, they come back and bite you. The all-or-nothing syndrome is at the source of most of your problems. You haven't learned how to have just one bite, a taste of the cake, or one kiss. You want it all. When you have it all your life becomes dominated by desire, and nothing makes you feel more out of control than a runaway desire. Without a purpose or a goal, desires will make you obsessive and crazy. Self-discipline is essential to the Capricorn: without it your environment has the power. Of course, there are Capricorns that control their desires and pleasures, but to do this you must cut it out of your life. Without feelings you can do what you want without a conscience. It sounds like bliss, but it's not. Life without warmth, spirit, and love is a life not worth living. You can have it all, if you don't take it all. You must take only what you need, not everything you want. Not everything is meant to go the distance. Choice is now essential if you're going to fulfill your destiny. All of you has to cooperate; if one part of you won't, you will not achieve the greatness in your heart.

Balance

Balance is what the mountain goat, the symbol of Capricorn, does best, and you will automatically choose what you need to balance your life. Because you're at the top you have no choice—balance is a dire necessity. No more extremes: both sides of the polarity must have equal importance. If you are leaning one way, you will attract the other for balance. The only way to peace is through acceptance of all that God created. When you accept you can choose; when you resist you create opposition. There is no escape. You must learn how to cooperate with your environment without losing yourself or your individuality. This is done by expressing your uniqueness. If you have not been paying attention to this very important part of you, you feel swallowed up by life. Stop hiding behind pleasing others, or representing their ideal images. Own your power and use it to achieve your goals.

You Play with Fear

You face your fears, and when you get good at it, you start playing with the fears of others. You realize that if you know what someone is afraid of, you have power over them. Yes, threaten them with their greatest fear and they remain your servant. The problem with misusing this talent is that your day will come. If others build up resentment, the smallest person can bring you down; all they need is the right moment and the right piece of information. All great gifts come with a responsibility and the need for *good intention*. If your intentions do not come from your heart, they will backfire and bring you down. The higher up you go, the more you see that it is not life that defeats you, but it is yourself. You've chosen your way to this moment and only you can choose your way out.

As the Capricorn you live in a synchronistic world of miracles. Yes, you have been saved more times than you have fingers and toes, and it's not because of anything you did or didn't do. God wants you to know that He's out there looking after you and that no matter how much you screw up, there's always another chance, a way to redemption. Your love of complexity often keeps you from turning problems over to your higher self. You love to unravel intrigue and follow the single thread to the secret passage. You know that the great ideas lie in mystery and that what you don't understand holds the answers. So you are a devotee of puzzles, an inventor, a detective, and a leader who brings in new policies and better ways.

You Create Yourself

Everything comes together in Capricorn—all your strengths and weaknesses—and they are out in the open for you and everyone else to see. This makes you a bit self-conscious because you can't hide from yourself any longer. Don't use your critical eye to beat yourself up or to tell yourself that you don't measure up—that you're useless, hopeless, or a fool. Life will gladly do that for you. What you need to do is go inside and decide what comes to the surface. How do you want to be perceived by the world? What talents do you want to express or experience? It's time to re-create yourself and let go of what others told you you were. What you need to get the job done is faith. The challenge of the Capricorn is to see within you everything you want to be. If you can see and love it, God will bring it forth. If you have faith in you, God will have faith in you. It's as simple as that. Where you lack faith He can't help you. He needs an invitation and if you want a quick response, offer faith.

Paradise

Most Capricorns are looking for paradise. They're on their way home to Eden. Paradise, they believe, is any place where there are no rules. You're looking to live without law, authority, and limitations. You want a world within a world, a safe place for you to go where no one enters. Sacred space is the one thing you're serious about. You don't want your things touched, but you don't mind inviting others in to share. If you are not strong enough to cut out a space for yourself, you try living in remote areas where you feel you are outside of life and its demands. Of course, there is no place where you can hide from worries and fears—you take them with you no matter where you go. So stop searching the world for the perfect spot. Paradise lies within you, all you have to do is see it with your own eyes.

The Lure of Surprise

You want life to be a series of surprises that free your spirit and force you to discover something new about yourself. To bring forth the surprise you hover near the edge, the danger zone of life, seeking meaning and certainty in what others have cast aside. You feel alive and close to your own power when you feel the power of nature, of the unexpected, of being supported by the unknown. You seem to know where you are going and who you are, but inside you're just as confused as everyone else. The difference is you have the courage to take the plunge, to step forward and play with the magic, and persevere until something new comes up for you to hold on to. When you perfect perseverance and faith, you will know how to hold on and let go. Yes, the magic wand is finally yours.

Master Manipulator

You are attracted to the super-salesman—the man or woman who can weave a reality out of nothing right before your eyes. To do this takes confidence and a do-or-die attitude, but it's what you love the best. It's the man or woman who can talk anyone into anything without having a penny in their pocket who gets your attention and sometimes your heart. The danger here is that this super-salesman will sell *you* a false bill of goods. Your desire to get away with things is how others get you. There is no one easier fooled than the person trying to fool. You are in love with the game, the process, the struggle, and the ability to get others to respond to your needs. You've learned the magic lesson of reward. Find out what's important and give it. This does not have to be a big request; it can be a little thought. If you're the only person who brings your client's secretary a bottle of perfume when you come to the office, you will become special to her. If you know someone likes mangoes and you arrive with a bag of good ones, you have just made a connection to their heart (pleasure goes right to the heart). You know that everyone wants a reward, and if you give them their reward, they'll give you what you want and maybe a bit more.

Love

Love is what you are seeking, and it is also what you don't trust. You must learn the difference between seeking love and loving yourself. When you learn to love you, you become the magic. You have the ability to inspire others when you love yourself, and that is no small gift. You are better without money and without certainty; that's when you find yourself flying by the seat of your pants. When you are holding on to nothing but faith to create a solution, you come alive. When you have money you try to make everyone else happy, and you lose your identity. Don't let your loving heart keep you from the success that is your reward.

The Reward

The reward you choose to have at the end of your journey will determine your journey. The end point that you hold on to creates the path you take. If you choose for fame, money, and recognition, your path will steer that course; if you choose for spiritual happiness, your path will lead you wherever that can be found. If you can choose a worldly goal and leave your path and purpose up to God, you will have a journey that fulfills all of you—your ego and your spirit. To put your path in the hands of your higher self means you'll have to give up your feelings of isolation, your worthlessness and sense of lack. Yes, you will become love because love is what you will be doing for a living.

Capricorns can see the path they took once they get to the top of the mountain. Looking back you now know how important every thought, action, and deed was. They all interlinked to bring you to this moment. With understanding comes compassion for those who don't understand, and from this compassion comes your purpose. In addition, you see the importance of choosing the right environment for your dreams. For example, if you are looking for trout and you cast your fishing hook in waters where they don't exist, you will not come up with trout. It doesn't matter that you like the river better, or that the view is nice. If what you are doing will not produce results, you are taking a vacation from your destiny, not pursuing it. Is the environment you are in conducive to the results you want? Is the man you are pursuing capable of marrying you or being in love? If he is so damaged, and you know it, why do you lose faith in love when he can't say yes? It was an impossible situation to start with. If you want something to work, give it the proper environment. If you want your spirit to soar, give it an adventure; if you want to save money, put some in the bank and don't buy everything your heart desires. You are responsible for the environment you place your dream in. Give it love and nourishment and it will manifest. You were your parents' dream and if you didn't get the proper love and nourishment it was hard for you to grow and reach your potential. Learn from your past, don't repeat it. Know what you want, then support that desire until it can walk on its own.

The Mother Teaches You to Face Fear

It is your mother who teaches you how to overcome fear. Her fears, if she couldn't deal with them, eroded your inner sense of safety, for it is the mother who must provide the faith and the ability to spiritually persevere. If your mother didn't let her fear stop or paralyze her, you will be able to face fear and take a risk for your dreams. If your mother faced her fear but controlled you, you may be afraid to risk yourself because someone else may control you. Mothers who are debilitated by fear pass their wounds on to their children. If this is you, then facing her fear is your first mission. As a child, you interpreted your mother's situation and came up with a solution to the problem. This solution was made by a child, not an adult with knowledge and wisdom. Go back and look at why you believed your mother was afraid and what you thought would fix it. Does it make sense to you now? So many women avoid marriage because their mother's dream was given up for a husband who didn't appreciate her and children who were demanding and a burden. You are not your parents, unless you choose to be. If their fate was death at an early age, it doesn't mean you will die early too. Change the patterns of their lives, create your own, and you will find your own limitations through your own life's adventure. (See Figure 14.1 for the Capricorn Star.)

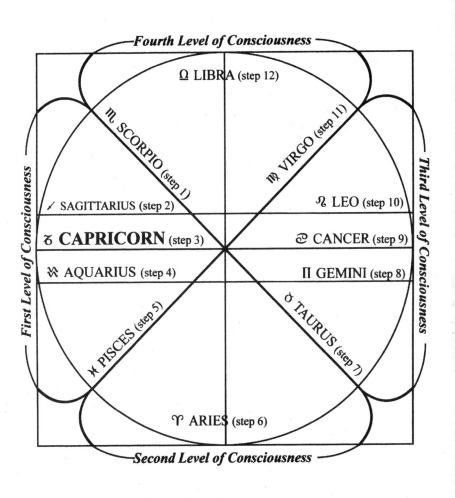

Figure 14.1. The Capricorn Star

The First Level of Consciousness

The first level of consciousness divides the eleventh house and first step, and the third house and fifth step. It challenges the soul to feel the pull of opposites once again. The ego wants the dream with all its rewards, and the spirit wants total freedom, the kind that's found in the wilderness. You can have it all if you are willing to go beyond success and seek your higher self. The first level places you in situations where the road to success means following the rules. What you need to learn from limitation is self-discipline, not spiritual imprisonment. You need to connect with your passion and go for it; otherwise you die inside. Once you have self-discipline, your journey begins.

Step One: The Eleventh House

Scorpio: I Accept Deception When It Comes to Love

I know that it is not right to let someone treat me badly or for me to treat someone badly, but when you give so much to love you accept what others don't accept, because you know the reward. I will do anything to be in the presence of love, and that kind of surrender gets me into trouble.

You are a soul of extremes and you have learned how to give your all, which creates other problems. When you want love so badly, you will endure more than you should. You know you are being manipulated, but you don't seem to care; you want love in your life and you're willing to pay the price. However, it's the anger that gets in the way. If you don't set up limits and boundaries, you will find that love becomes abusive. The passion you desire will come with too great a price.

> You are in level one when you are afraid of knowing what others think of you.
> You are in level two when you challenge how others see you.
> (Levels three and four are listed at the end of step one in the fourth level of consciousness.)

Step Two: The Twelfth House

Sagittarius: Wisdom Is Unique to Each Moment

I used to think that truth was something permanent and obvious, but rules can only poorly impersonate wisdom; each moment has its own truth. I have learned to deal with life moment by moment and to step out of knowledge when it interferes with truth—the spirit of what I want to express. Without a connection to my instincts, truth would not be possible.

The Capricorn does not even have wisdom to rely upon; it must trust its instincts and the needs of the moment. If you are not connected to your inner voice, rules will rule you, expectations will drive you, and your world will not be about you or your truth. Instead, it will be about control and finding a way to hold on to something that brings security. Change is inevitable in life, and the only way to adjust to change is through belief and faith.

> You are in level one when wisdom is what others tell you it is.
> You are in level two when wisdom is what you cannot grasp or know.
> You are in level three when wisdom is love.
> You are in level four when wisdom is faith.

Step Three: The First House

Capricorn: What I Protect Keeps Me from My Truth

I know that to be great I must be able to face my fears, and I do, but what I realized is that I'm a protector—I protect the things I love. What I've protected holds me back and keeps me from getting stronger and wiser. I need to be able to let those I love find their own way and trust that the things I love won't be destroyed by judgments and negativity. When I don't protect others, I understand my own truth better.

The Capricorn environment is a strange one: there is love with too much protection and love without protection, and both are lacking in providing a sense of security. What the Capricorn must now let go of is its need to be taken care of through love. It's time to love yourself and have faith that you can create love around you no matter where you go. Your ability to reach out to the hearts and souls of others is a great gift. People respond to your charm, humor, and ability to enjoy life with a passion. You must go beyond protection to accomplish your dreams and your mission, so you must see it as the fraud it is. No one can protect you from life; your only protection is your faith and your God.

> You are in level one when the reward you want is physical pleasure or possessions.
> You are in level two when the reward is your ability to find someone you love.
> You are in level three when your reward is faith in yourself.
> You are in level four when your reward is whatever the moment brings you.

Step Four: The Second House

Aquarius: My Values Are Surprise and Magic

I hold on so tight in my past that I love anyone or anything that is free, or makes me feel free. That's why I love nature and the wilderness. It is not yet tamed by man. It's wild, and in me is a wild spirit that is yearning to be free.

You may not be totally aware of this, but you value whatever gets you out of the box. You may seem to cling to the past, to rules or limitations, but what turns you on, what you attract and reach for, is the element of surprise or the unexpected. In the unknown you come alive. You love the primitive, the uncivilized, the primal force of life that surges through your veins when you're not sitting at a desk doing something you hate. If you're creating new ideas at your desk, if your mind is challenged to invent, probe, or go beyond what everyone knows, you will feel alive. Know that your heart and your soul desire to imagine and dream what no one else has. Know that you will never be happy if your spirit is not free to soar and to explore. Know that you need to choose these things over security, safety, and a big paycheck. If you don't, you will put yourself in a box and slowly die.

> You are at level one when freedom is isolation.
> You are at level two if freedom is your ability to go against the authority.
> You are at level three if freedom is facing your fears.
> You are at level four if freedom is your middle name.

Step Five: The Third House

Pisces: I Choose My Dream

Part of me wants to take the tried and true route: work hard, make money, and feel safe. The other part of me wants to throw it all to the wind and be free. I'm not sure what my dream is—the CEO of a company, or a canoe instructor on the Colorado River.

The dream is where your heart is. Choose with your heart every day, and this and this alone will keep you from building a box around your spirit. Do not surrender to the limitations of your life; surrender to your dreams and let go of everything that stands in its way. You must learn to play with life—to be the magic—by your ability to toss what's important to you to the wind. When you can you will find that there is always something greater waiting to come in.

> You are in level one when your dream is an escape.
> You are in level two when your dream is your goal.
> (Levels three and four are listed at the end of step five in the second level of consciousness.)

The Second Level of Consciousness

The second level of consciousness divides the third house and fifth step, and the fifth house and seventh step. It demands that you go beyond your need for love and begin to give it to yourself. So long as you need love from others, you will be controlled by them. When you have love in your heart, because you have learned to love and accept yourself, you will never have to look for love—you will be a magnet for it. In the second level you give up trying to please for love and choose instead the selfish path. From this position you will begin to see that either choice brings you to the same results—dissatisfaction. Love is not in desires or things, but rather it lies within you.

Step Five: The Third House (Second Level)

Pisces: My Dream Chooses Me

Once I believe in my dream it is always there making sure I don't put someone or something else first. I don't have to worry about whether or not it's going to be there. Its presence is always there.

When you believe the work is done, when you have faith in your dream, it is always around doing the work for you, reminding you, and supporting you. There is no better friend than faith that is acted upon through choice.

> You are in level three when you have faith in your dream.
> You are in level four when the world is one.

Step Six: The Fourth House

Aries: I Protect My Vision

My vision of a perfect world used to be made up of broken images and dreams. I needed a new vision, and it came to me once I started to take care of my own needs and began to love myself more.

So long as what you are seeking depends on others you will feel out of control and unable to see your true path. As soon as you choose for your own dream and think of you, you are able to see your vision and succeed at it, which allows you to do and give to those you love.

> You are in level one if you need to be the hero for someone.
> You are in level two if someone else is your hero.
> You are in level three when you have faith in your vision.
> You are in level four when you are living your vision and seeing a greater one.

Step Seven: The Fifth House

Taurus: Love Is My Authority

I used to put love on a pedestal and the people I loved had to stay there, too. What it did was prevent me from actually experiencing real love and intimacy. I still believe in love but no one has to be perfect for me to love them, because I don't have to be perfect for me to love myself.

Love is one of those emotions that change as we get wiser. The child wants unconditional love and the child in the Capricorn is still looking for it. Until you learn how to love yourself and make yourself happy, love will be your authority and it will interfere in everything you do.

> You are in level one if you are seeking and giving unconditional love.
> You are in level two if you are confronting the rules of love.
> (Levels three and four are listed at the end of step seven in the third level of consciousness.)

The Third Level of Consciousness

The third level of consciousness divides the fifth house and seventh step, and the ninth house and eleventh step. It demands that you not use your ability to see into the wounds and fears of others for the right reasons, and not just for control or to get your needs met. When you have enough self-discipline not to give in to temptation, you won't misuse your knowledge, and this is the path to love. If you misuse your powers, others will wait for the right moment to bring you down. Share your bounty and others will not be jealous.

Step Seven: The Fifth House (Third Level)

Taurus: Loving All of Myself Gives Me Power

I was always seeking perfect love and I actually expected to find it. What I didn't know was that the longing in me was for me to love me. The parts of me that I had judged as bad, weak, or boring were the parts that had the longing. My relationships represented anything but perfect love. I kept picking up lost souls that I nurtured or tried to save. It wasn't until I turned inward and started seeing myself as loving and great that life turned around and I began to see the power of self-love.

You have reached an important turning point. You must love yourself to be able to maintain success in life. If you hate yourself you won't be able to handle the adulation of others—the praise or everything you thought you wanted.

If you don't feel good about you, your ego will take over and instead of love and satisfaction you will feel needy and lacking, the more you have the worse you will feel.

> You are in level three if you have faith in your dream.
> You are in level four if you give yourself unconditional love.

Step Eight: The Sixth House

Gemini: I Choose for Others

I don't understand choice at all. When I try to be helpful, others want to butt in and they don't let me do it my way. So I let them do it their way. Is it possible that there should be an exchange of ways and choices?

Your problem once again is all or nothing. Either you have to do it all without interference or you don't want to do it at all. Life doesn't work without interference. That's no way to learn. If you're always telling others, you'll never learn from others. Let go and go with the flow. Turn your choices over to your higher self and you'll get the best solution and an answer you could never have thought of on your own.

> You are in level one when choice is made to please others.
> You are in level two when you oppose the choices of others in order to
>   be free.
> You are in level three when choice is made for a new and better idea.
> You are in level four when choice is made for truth.

Step Nine: The Seventh House

Cancer: I Protect What I Love

I used to protect what I loved, but I felt paralyzed and overwhelmed by responsibility because everything depended on me. When I realized that too much protection makes one weak, I began to let go and I saw that things worked out even when I didn't do them—my way.

You need to know that you can help those you love by making them strong, not invalids. Your need to appear perfect in the eyes of others makes you want to do everything for everyone else. Let go of being perfect, accept yourself, and you will teach those you love to accept themselves, too. Real strength comes from making mistakes and learning from them.

> You are in level one if protection is something you are seeking for yourself and others.
> You are in level two if protection is something you are opposing.
> You are in level three if you are risking yourself for your dreams.
> You are in level four when you realize that life always has a better way if you can persevere with an open mind.

Step Ten: The Eighth House

Leo: My Ego and My Spirit Have the Same Intention

I used to see myself as strong because I could stand up to others and back them down, or take their punishment without flinching. However, now I know that real strength comes when I can remove my ego or add it to the moment. My flexibility is my strength.

You now know that life is not an all or nothing journey. The ones who succeed are the ones who can adapt, and the faster you can adapt and use your wisdom or whatever you have available, the greater are your options for success. You must learn how to switch your position without losing a connection to your truth or your vision. Change the appearance of the presentation, but kept the essence the same.

> You are in level one if you feel strength is found in approval or dominance.
> You are in level two if you feel strength is challenging the authority.
> You are in level three if you feel strength is faith.
> You are in level four if you feel strength is turning your problems over to a higher power.

Step Eleven: The Ninth House

Virgo: I Can Hold On and Let Go

I used to hold on to everything I loved and now I know when to let go. It's a constant learning process. The more I have faith that I will have what I want the more I can let go and listen to my instincts.

When you can hold on and let go because the moment tells you to and not because your needs or desires are in the way, you will always make the right choice because you have listened to your instincts and your inner wisdom. Inner wisdom cannot kick in until you can go within and stop running away from yourself.

> You are in level one when letting go is seen as a sacrifice.
> You are in level two when holding on is your source of strength.
> (Levels three and four are listed at the end of step eleven in the fourth level of consciousness.)

The Fourth Level of Consciousness

The fourth level of consciousness divides the ninth house and eleventh step. It asks the soul to take as its reward the inspiration to go higher and achieve even more than it thought was possible. To achieve more requires you to use the faith you have earned from your journey and let it inspire you and others. When you share what inspires you, you invite God to inspire you and you feel His presence and you don't need to know anything more.

Step Eleven: The Ninth House (Fourth Level)

Virgo: I Accept Myself Because Others Have Faith in Me

I can finally see the faith that others have in me and that makes me have faith in them. Seeing that others believe in me helps me believe in me.

Once again the soul sees itself through the eyes of others. You are strong and reliable and others come to you for advice and help. You solve their problems or make them feel better. If they believe in you, you must have something to offer. Once you accept yourself and let go you begin to see all the love and support that was always around you. When you see it you honor and return it. Life becomes an act of love through giving and receiving, and this is the greatest wisdom of all.

> You are in level three when you rely on miracles to set you free.
> You are in level four when you can hold on and let go depending on the needs of the moment.

Step Twelve: The Tenth House

Libra: My Reward Is My Ability to Inspire

I used to want pleasure or possessions as my reward. Now I know that the greatest gift I can have is the ability to inspire others. When I can inspire others I can motivate them to either help me or help themselves.

You have just plugged into a great gift and reward: The gift of inspiration is what can change you and the world. You become an inspiration when you allow yourself to be inspired and when you love what you believe in. The more you can be inspired by the little things in life—the small miracles—the more powerful a voice you will have.

> You are in the first level when truth is what you are seeking.
> You are in the second level when truth is what you oppose in others.
> You are in the third level when truth is what you have faith in.
> You are in the fourth level when truth is whatever it is.

Step One: The Eleventh House (Fourth Level)

Scorpio: The Intention That Drives Me Is Love

I used to believe that I had to give someone everything in order to make them happy. Now I know that if my intentions are good and pure I don't have to be perfect; the person knows that I want to do the right thing even when I can't.

Love has now freed you; you do not have to do every little thing to make someone happy. If you can communicate your intention, and if someone is strong enough to value that intention over results, you've got yourself a great love.

> You are in level three when your intention is to discover the truth.
> You are in level four when your intention is more important than love.

The Cross

The cross is composed of the eleventh, fifth, ninth, and third houses and is where change must occur. (See Figure 14.1 on page 315.) The two fixed houses represented by Scorpio and Taurus challenge each other to see a greater truth:

Scorpio (eleventh house): *I have lived through criticism, abuse, and anger for love, believing that I had to take it all in order to make someone happy. But that's not true. When I reveal my love and I am true to my intention to be a loving person, I am free to love more than one thing.*

Taurus (fifth house): When I learn to love myself enough because I can limit myself and not wait for others to do it, I am able to love someone without losing myself and my dreams. The more love I can give the easier it is for me to achieve my goals and the less I have to protect others, because I know that it is only through experience and risk that persons learn about themselves and life.

The two mutable houses represented by Virgo and Pisces must anchor themselves in this new truth by taking a stand:

Virgo (ninth house): *I can both accept and let go, so all of life is a dream.*

Pisces (third house): *In the past, I could not have my dream and love, too. I gave everything to the people I loved, and there was nothing left for my dream. When I have the strength to choose for the dreams of my heart, I have it all.*

Conclusion

The first level of consciousness is back. You're about to return to the beginning of life with all its magnificence and wonder. Within you is the knowledge of all that you've learned and done. You know that the images of life are there for you to play with, so you dress yourself up in pageantry or you let go of it all and experience your nakedness. Your friends are spirits and souls you admire, and they come from all walks of life. They have faith in themselves and what they wish to create, so you admire their art and value their opinion. Your world is divided by those who understand that they are unique and express it, and those who are struggling for consciousness. You have great compassion for those who have lost their faith because you once did. You see their self-judgments because you judged yourself, too. If only they would just have gone a little further and passed beyond their desires and fears to the greater truth that is always there—if you have faith that it exists.

Whichever direction you take leads you home. If you go far enough anywhere you come back to the beginning. And now you realize it's almost time to choose again. You have done what you set out to do, you have created your dream, and you have played with fate and felt the magic. Now the next dream is calling you, and you resist. You want to share your wisdom and experiences with others. You want a little more time to see if what you have to offer can make a difference. After all, isn't that what the journey is all about anyway?

INDEX

Also available from Rider . . .

INTUITION AND BEYOND
A Step-by-Step Approach to Discovering
Your Inner Voice

Sharon A Klingler

Would you like to create more abundance in your life and experience greater financial freedom? Have better success in choosing the right business and personal relationships? Reach a higher expression of your creativity and ingenuity? And live a healthier, more fulfilling life?

In this immensely practical and insightful book, Sharon Klingler helps you to open the door of possibility by learning to listen to a voice that doesn't even make a sound – the voice of your intuition. In four clear sections, you can discover:

- what intuition is and how to identify your intuitive voice
- how notable people past and present have used intuition to inform their most important decisions
- your current I.Q. or 'Intuition Quotient' by answering a simple questionnaire
- the A, B, Cs of Applied Intuition and how to create the intuitive experience at will

INTUITION
The Key to Divination

Gina Giacomini

Among the countless methods of divination used in all corners of the world, the common thread that unites them all is intuition. To gain insight you need only cultivate a conscious connection to your intuition and a working knowledge of an age-old system of 'seeing' much needed in a world that seems to have forgotten its roots.

Intuition: The Key to Divination is filled with easy-to-use techniques that give immediate results and explains simple strategies to:

- develop your intuition and apply it to six tried and true systems of divination that are popular today: astrology, dreams, tarot, I Ching, runes, and numerology
- learn how to interpret and transform your daily life
- become you own divination consultant, seeking inner guidance on such matters as health, relationships, finances, career, and home life

THE ULTIMATE ASTROLOGER

Nicholas Campion

In this comprehensive and immensely practical book Nicholas Campion, well-known for his astrological columns in national newspapers such as the *Daily Mail*, applies his wealth of experience and substantial expertise as a teacher to take the reader through the steps involved in the calculation and interpretation of birth charts. In straightforward language, he then explains the predictive techniques and methods used for comparing two charts.

The Ultimate Astrologer will teach you to become your own astologer and work out horoscopes for your family, friends and colleagues. However, the fascinating information in this book extends way beyond the study of birth charts; it includes both Eastern and Western systems of astrology as well as the application of astrology to:

- The answering of specific questions (horary astrology)
- The selection of auspicious moments to begin new enterprises
- Health and healing, love and relationships
- Gardening and agriculture, business and finance

Buy Rider Books

Order further Rider titles from your local bookshop, or have them delivered direct to your door by Bookpost

- [ ] **Intuition and Beyond** by Sharon A Klingler   0712634428   £7.99
- [ ] **Intuition: The Key to Divination**
  by Gina Giacomini   0712629343   £8.99
- [ ] **The Ultimate Astrologer** by Nicholas Campion   0712610200   £10.99
- [ ] **Aspects in Astrology** by Sue Tompkins   0712611045   £14.99
- [ ] **Freeing the Spirit** by Steve Nobel   0712615830   £8.99
- [ ] **Discover Yourself** by Lillian Too   0091879485   £14.99
- [ ] **Beyond Fear – The Teachings of Don Miguel Ruiz**   0712661816   £10.99
- [ ] **The Complete Guide to the Kabbalah**
  by Will Parfitt   0712614184   £12.99

FREE POST AND PACKING
Overseas customers allow £2.00 per paperback

ORDER:

By phone: 01624 677237

By post: Random House Books, c/o Bookpost, PO Box 29
Douglas, Isle of Man, IM99 1BQ

By fax: 01624 670923

By email: bookshop@enterprise.net

Cheques (payable to Bookpost) and credit cards accepted

Prices and availability subject to change without notice. Allow 28 days for delivery.
When placing your order, please mention if you do not wish to receive any additional information.

www.randomhouse.co.uk

Most Rider books are available at special quantity discounts for bulk purchases for sales promotions, premiums, fund-raising, or educational use. Special books or book excerpts also can be created to fit specific needs.

Bulk copies can be purchased from Special Sales. For a quote please call 020 7840 8468.
Or write to Rider Special Sales, Random House, 20 Vauxhall Bridge Road, London SW1V 2SA.